ON BLONDES

ON BLONDES

Joanna Pitman

BLOOMSBURY

Published by Bloomsbury, New York and London
Distributed to the trade by Holtzbrinck Publishers

ISBN 1-58234-120-6

First U.S. Edition 2003

1 3 5 7 9 10 8 6 4 2

Typeset by Palimpsest Book Production Limited,
Polmont, Stirlingshire, Scotland

Printed in Great Britain by Clays Ltd, St Ives plc

For Giles

CONTENTS

AUTHOR NOTE

The etymological origins of the word 'blonde' are unclear, although it could be linked to 'blandus', the Latin for charming, and later to the Medieval Latin word 'blundus' meaning yellow. The word entered French in the twelfth century and appeared in English in the fourteenth century, used by Chaucer in the form 'blounde'. References to hair that was 'fair', which in the Middle Ages also meant beautiful or pleasing, and to yellow hair, were found in English until the word 'blonde' re-emerged in the seventeenth century from French, and was treated as a French adjective, requiring an 'e' for the feminine version. It was not until the 1930s that the word was ushered into our vocabulary as a noun by the vampish sirens of Hollywood.

Much heated discussion has gone into the question of how to spell the key word in this book. In the end, I have decided to use 'blonde' throughout, unless referring exclusively to men.

ACKNOWLEDGEMENTS

There is something about 'The Blonde' which excites interest and provokes opinion, and there have been few people consulted who have not kindly contributed something to this book. Given the extent of material covered, I have relied gratefully on the knowledge of a wide selection of experts, ranging from geneticists to hairdressers, cinematographers, costume historians and even a pomologist. My particular thanks go to Michele Thomas of the Bibliothèque Nationale de France, Susan Reed of the British Library, Carrie Tovar of the J. Paul Getty Museum, Professor Jonathan Kuntz of UCLA, Richard Jewell of the University of Southern California, Christopher Horak of the Hollywood Entertainment Museum, Professor Steve Jones of UCL and Professor Jonathan Rees of the University of Edinburgh.

Professor Aileen Ribeiro and Dr Margaret Scott of the Courtauld Institute, Dr Jane Bridgeman, David Ekserdjian, Lesley Downer, Geraldine Sharpe-Newton and Olivia Stewart all kindly read through parts or all of the text. Virginia Darcy, Grace Kelly's hairdresser, and Brian Carter, Baroness Thatcher's, both shared their expertise on the subject of hair colour. Cally Blackman was heroic in her research efforts, and the staff of the London Library never hesitated in the face of obscure and peculiar requests. A huge debt is owed to Matthew Butson and Kate Berry for providing many of the pictures. I would also like to thank Bethan Davies, Barbara Girardet, Charlotte Hoyle, Gill Morgan, Peter Pitman, Jenny Pitman, James Pitman, Matt Ridley, Ben Macintyre, Terence Pepper, Jamie Fergusson, Emma Bassett and Nicky Hirsch.

This book would have been impossible without the generous support and skills of Alexandra Pringle and Marian McCarthy at Bloomsbury and of my agent Bill Hamilton at A.M. Heath. And finally thanks and love to Giles for his endless supply of ideas, encouragement and fine judgement.

INTRODUCTION

ABOUT FIFTEEN years ago I was briefly mistaken for a saint, on account of my blonde hair. I had been working for a medical aid charity called SAIDIA in the Samburu district of northern Kenya and was probably the only white person in this baking hot semi-desert for several hundred miles around. At any rate, I was certainly the only white woman. Labouring out in the sun every day, making mud bricks to build our small clinic, my short hair had become bleached a bright golden yellow. I vividly remember cutting it without a mirror, using the scissors of a Swiss Army penknife, and being astounded to discover its colour.

Talk of a blonde woman had spread around the surrounding valleys, and so when a local warrior ran wide-eyed and terrified into our camp one evening, a spear in one hand and a large knife tied at his waist, my Samburu friends and co-workers were not surprised that he was looking for me. He had sprinted eight miles to tell us that his brother had been bitten by a highly venomous snake. I was to come and save him. 'The blonde! The blonde!' he jabbered. 'She must come!' He shouted again, pointing at me with his spear, and then came over and touched my head, turning to the others and gesturing frantically at my hair as if this was all that was needed to patch up his brother. Plenty of Samburus had already mistaken me for a missionary or a nurse, but I now realised that some

1

bizarre association of blonde hair, white woman and medical charity had created this incongruous picture of a heaven-sent saviour.

Feeling more like the interloper doomed to failure than the saviour, I sped off in a clanking four-wheel-drive Toyota and found the victim, Isaac, lying on the ground with a swelling ankle where the snake had bitten him. His wife had cut around the bite and put salt and tobacco in the wound. I suggested a tourniquet on his leg. Then Isaac's brother reappeared with pleading eyes and handed me an ancient-looking medical kit containing two rusty syringes and a serum of some sort. I had no medical training. If I tried to use this I would almost certainly kill him. As it was, he had at most two hours to live, I was told. The nearest doctor was a good two hours' drive away. Two dozen pairs of eyes swivelled in the gathering darkness to fix on me and my hair. 'We'll drive,' I said.

I can safely say that this was the worst car journey of my life. Isaac moaned and writhed in agony in the back, his foot blown up to the size of a football, as we bounced and crashed along dirt tracks. By the time we had reached Wamba and located the doctor in the town's only bar, he was out cold. The doctor administered an injection and carried him off. Our job was done.

A week later I went to see Isaac. He was on his feet again, wandering up Wamba's main track. Spotting me from a distance, he waved and hobbled over, his bandages stained a reddish brown from the dust. He grinned broadly, displaying a single tooth. He wanted to give me his goats – all twenty-eight of them. His wife appeared and announced that she wanted to give me one of her babies, as I had none of my own.

An exquisite miniature of herself lay snuggled to the breast. Fumbling for an appropriate response, I got away with just giving it a name. And then they both lavishly admired my hair, shyly reaching out to touch it. This rumpled crop of bleached hair had become fixed in their minds as the symbol of my ludicrous imagined sainthood.

In the isolated and dusty communities of East Africa blonde hair may still, for all I know, bestow sainthood on other unsuspecting and rather grubby foreign aid workers. Missionaries have been spreading religious material there for many years and Isaac and his family had perhaps seen pictures of angels, saints or the Virgin Mary with blonde hair. Blondeness seemed to have been translated into a kind of mystical asset, a potent symbol of magical powers that set its owners apart.

When I began the research for this book, I realised that throughout history people have been in awe of blonde hair. In Medieval Europe, for example, men were intoxicated with its sexual allure and supposed supernatural powers. In 1930s Germany, on the other hand, the blond Nazi stormtrooper became a symbol of Aryan superiority. Blondness was projected as the epitome of male beauty even as, paradoxically, it became associated with some of the most grotesque racially motivated barbarism ever perpetrated.

Blondeness has become so rich in its own language of symbolism that it has developed far beyond a mere colour. It has become a blazing signal in code, part of a value system laden with moral, social and historical connotations that has rooted itself in the human subconscious of the West and increasingly across the rest of the world.

Its story begins in Ancient Greece where Aphrodite, the

goddess of love and fertility, had golden-blonde hair of such legendary sexual potency that she inspired ambitious imitations among the dark-haired courtesans of Ancient Greece, and set the tone for a certain type of blonde who has stirred the fantasies of men and fed the aspirations of women ever since. But the history of the blonde is not as simple as that. Its bounty is inexhaustible. Every age has restyled blonde hair in its own image and invested it with its own preoccupations. Blondeness became a prejudice in the Dark Ages, an obsession in the Renaissance, a mystique in Elizabethan England, a mythical fear in the nineteenth century, an ideology in the 1930s, a sexual invitation in the 1950s and a doctrine of faith by the end of the twentieth century. Its distinctive imagery of youth, vitality and wealth, built up over thousands of years, has woven itself into the most popular materials of the imagination. We see it and absorb its messages every day. Blonde hair is attractive and sexy, and often worn as a trophy. In every popular forum of our age – in film, television, fashion, pop music and politics – many of the most powerful players are blonde.

But there is something strange about all these blondes. Very few of them are genuine. Only one in twenty white American adults is naturally blonde, and roughly the same ratio applies to white northern Europeans. But you would never think it, walking down a crowded street in the urban West. Here, virtually one in three white adult female heads is dyed a shade of blonde, be it honey, platinum, ash, 'dirty pillow slip' or any other colour from our rich lexicon of blonde shades. To achieve it, women have gone to extraordinary lengths. In Ancient Rome, the most ruthless beauties used pigeon dung; in Renaissance Venice they resorted to horse urine. Today women spend hundreds of pounds sitting for hours in hairdressing salons having their hair lightened.

Why do we do it? One of the key reasons is youth. At its most basic, people associate blonde hair with youth. The rationale is perfectly logical: babies tend to have paler and more delicate hair and skin than their parents. Some children retain the blondeness of their infancy, but most lose it once puberty sets in. And to emphasise the equation with youth, women find that after their first pregnancy their hair and skin darken permanently. The result is that the paler the hair and the paler the skin, the younger a person appears to be. Blonde hair in women might originally have evolved, along with other childish traits such as a high-pitched voice and fine body hair, as part of a package of sexual attraction, an evolutionary adaptation for attracting a mate. Just as adults find babies attractive, men were attracted to women with such signs of youth. Blonde hair, although not intrinsically more beautiful than dark, became associated, through these long evolved mechanisms in the male brain, with youthful fertility. It was a kind of visual certificate of reproductive success.

These biological processes of sexual selection have gradually been transformed over thousands of years into aesthetic and cultural preferences. Blonde hair, with its genetic allure, has become linked to femininity and beauty. This is why Marilyn Monroe dyed her mousy hair blonde. It also softens facial lines and is flattering to mature faces, which is why Baroness Thatcher has for years dyed her hair blonde.

In spite of its intriguing cultural story, and its sociological and biological significance, we still know very little about the origins of blonde hair. Recent excavations in China's

Taklamakan desert have found mummies, thought to date back as far as 1800 BC, with strikingly blonde hair. Early twentienth-century ethnologies report blonde hair recorded in southern Russia in the eighth century BC and around 200 BC in the part of China which today falls within the borders of Turkestan, where contemporary writings note local curiosity about 'green-eyed yellow devils'. But such studies dried up after World War Two, partly because of the association of blonde hair with the Nazis and the Aryan race and partly because of a perceived triviality.

Blonde hair is only now becoming an acceptable subject of serious scientific study. A team at the University of Utah has begun research into the origins of the so-called Aryan race, using DNA testing. And a group of researchers at the University of Edinburgh is half-way through the first large-scale study of the genetics of blonde hair.

A few months ago, I decided to carry out a small study of my own. After my year labouring under the Kenyan sun, I had returned to the dim-lit climes of northern Europe and my hair had reverted to a shade of brown. I decided – purely for the sake of research, of course – to bleach it blonde again and see what, if anything, might change in my life. It was not an experiment to be taken on lightly. I was well aware that women who try on masks and radically change their appearance often do so in response to a crisis. I spent an entire afternoon having my hair bleached at colossal expense, and emerged blinking into the street. People seemed to stare. The way they looked, it felt as if my head was radiating some kind of spectral glow. I drove home in crouched position. A police car dawdled past and two policemen smiled patronisingly. I could just see written all over their faces the words 'Ah yes . . . a blonde.'

Safely inside the front door, I found that my two young daughters mercifully hadn't noticed the change. My husband, on the other hand, thought I looked like Andy Warhol. The bleach had turned my hair a shocking whitish shade and its new brittleness made it stand up in thrilled defiance of gravity. My hairdresser had assured me that it would soon calm down into a glossy platinum curtain. Should I hang around all day in a silky kimono playing with a poodle? Should I firm up the cliché with a Wonderbra? At home I shrank from mirrors, but in the street I became a zealous investigator, scrutinising faces, hunting for reactions from passers-by. Some people ignored me, others fled my gaze. I got wolfish looks from men and complicit smiles from blonde women, who seemed to acknowledge my beacon-like hair as if I was now a member of an elite club. At the London Library, where the male staff tend to bury themselves in books while the women deal with enquiries, I had male librarians almost vaulting over the counter to help me. I got preferential treatment jostling for attention at the market. Friends thought I looked younger; some considered it such a deliciously sleazy experiment they rushed off to do the same. Strangers smiled at me, unbidden. Soon I began to smile back. After a while I wondered whether I could afford not to be blonde.

In the end I lasted four expensive months. It had certainly brought me more attention, a sort of instant decadent glamour. It had also redefined my mood in some way, making me feel younger and, strangely, more positive, in the abstract way that one does when it is sunny. Throughout history, millions of women have been inspired to become blonde; and millions of men have been intoxicated with the results. This book will, I hope, go some way to explaining the many reasons why.

APHRODITE RISING

S HE WAS tall, voluptuous and magnificent, with translu-
cent skin as smooth as the surface of oil, and the graceful,
ample nakedness of pure pleasure. Her features were soft: exquisite eyes, a lush, full-blown mouth and hair so abundant in its
heavenly blondeness that it rippled in snaky profusion as it coiled
back over her ears into a loosely knotted chignon. She stood
relaxed and easy, leaning slightly forward, a smile playing like
a faint blush on her lips. One hand hovered over her genitals
in a gesture of provocative timidity. Of course, connoisseurs and
especially ardent worshippers leaned forward to peer behind the
hand, thrilling to the irresistible glimpse of what one contemporary enthusiast described as 'those parts pressed inwards by
either thigh – what an incredibly sweet smile they have'.

Aphrodite to the Greeks, Venus to the Romans, this
divine figure, the life-size statue known as the Aphrodite
of Knidos, was the first universal blonde, the world's original model of sexual fantasy and power. The statue itself
has not survived, but it was lovingly fashioned by the
sculptor Praxiteles in about 360 BC, carved from Parian
marble and coloured with gold and other tints, a divine
goddess whose image was to fill the erotic imaginings of
men and women for centuries to come, from Homer to
Ovid, to Chaucer, Botticelli, Rossetti, Hitchcock, Monroe

and Madonna. In later years, according to the prevailing lusts of the moment, her breasts would swell or shrink, rise heavenwards in whalebone corsets or squeeze themselves into the pointed satin cones of a late-twentieth-century bra. Her hips would balloon heroically or slim down into bony androgyny. And her hair would transform itself into glossy curtains of golden silk, spring into tight ringlets or bounce into fantastic haloes of spun candy-floss curls. But whatever the fashion details of her latterday showpiece incarnations, Aphrodite would always be blonde and always vibrant with erotic allure.

In the Greece of two and a half thousand years ago, Aphrodite represented love in all its forms. With a certain elasticity of approach, she encouraged love between men and women, love between women and girls, and love between men and boys. As the most beautiful of all the great mythical gods of the Mediterranean, she was the crucible of all erotic energy.

Fortunately for the ordinary citizens of Ancient Greece, the divine and the living were divided by the most diaphanous of veils. Aphrodite, ever-generous with her favours, performed fairly dependable miracles every day, allowing herself to descend to mortal status. Turning heads as she went, she walked the streets of Corinth and Athens, her body tantalisingly visible beneath layers of filmy gauze, her hair dyed a radiant golden blonde. She appeared at religious festivals and social events, manifesting herself thousands of times over in the bodies of those in the business of the sensual arts. It was a good match. The prostitutes of Greece openly borrowed the ideological and aesthetic vocabulary of this goddess. They rendered her human and at the same time made her one of the most popular deities of the Olympian pantheon.

Naturally, the prostitutes nibbled at Aphrodite's style, imitating her best attributes, her silky nakedness and her hair. They smoothed their bodies, singeing and then plucking their pubic hair and rubbing their skin with pumice stone until it glowed and shone, and probably stung, too. Then as now, pain was no barrier to personal beautification and the working girls of Greece constantly pushed themselves to their thresholds to achieve their aims. But above all else it was the golden-blonde hair that became the signal of a dedicated follower of Aphrodite.

Struggling to subdue their strong, dark Mediterranean locks, they developed a new line in cosmetically inventive genius. They rubbed handfuls of dye containing saffron into their scalps and then painted their hair with coloured powders to achieve blonde highlights. Some oiled their hair and set their curls with yellow muds, a range of gooey unguents that were plastered on wet and then lightly brushed out later when dry. The elbow grease and the expense were both considerable; and the stench, too, must have been impressive. But concepts of personal hygiene were rather less dainty in those days, and the interesting odours that trailed behind them were probably barely noticed. Nor were the humiliations of the comic poets and playwrights of the era, scornful men such as Menander, who mocked that 'no chaste woman ought to make her hair yellow'. Menander damned blondes as downright dangerous: 'What can we women do wise or brilliant, who sit with hair dyed yellow, outraging the character of gentlewomen, causing the overthrow of houses, the ruin of nuptials, and accusations on the part of children?'

Such contempt fell on deaf ears. Men continued to fantasise about blondes, and prostitutes continued to slap on the dye. For especially erotic or remunerative assignations, they wore full blonde wigs, acquired at great expense from distant northern lands. Thus smoothed, daubed, coloured and powdered, they ventured out into the streets like flocks of brightly coloured exotic birds, flashing and scintillating in the sun, flaunting their iridescent bodies beneath silky diaphanous dresses and tossing their blonde heads as if they carried the desires of all men in those great glowing curtains of gold.

In many ways they did. The men of Greece were bewitched by blonde hair. It was exquisite. It represented a piece of fantasy and wealth. Above all, it was sexy. Luminous and bright, it shimmered and glowed, producing, in a country of few natural blondes, a rare and exciting contrast to the mass of Mediterranean dark hair all around. And it was also symbolically charged with fertility and the powers of cre-ation. Men flocked to gaze at blondes. Men worshipped and adored blondes, singling them out and celebrating them in verse. The poet Alcman conformed to the prevailing colour code in his seventh-century-BC songs, praising golden hair as one of the most desired characteristics of female beauty. 'The girl with the lovely yellow hair' and the girl with the 'hair like purest gold' are raised as the most beautiful in Alcman's practical experience. Alcman came from Sparta, where physical fitness and beauty were particularly cultivated by women, so his aesthetic ideals would have influenced the views of many.

With Aphrodite's seal of approval, blonde hair had become a tangible sign not only of great beauty but more explicitly of sexual attraction. For the Greeks, golden blondeness was already associated with some powerful imagery. Homer lingered obsessively over his gorgeous Aphrodite, raising her fully formed from the foaming sea wearing nothing but her rippling blonde hair. 'Golden' was the master epithet for Aphrodite in all of Homer's work. To him she was intrinsically golden. She also, Homer tells us, had flashing eyes, soft skin, a charming smile and golden ornaments. And the beauty of her breasts was such that Menelaus dropped his sword on catching sight of them during the sack of Troy, narrowly missing his toes. Sappho, too, made Aphrodite golden in homage to her physical beauty. Since gold is pure of rust, she wrote, golden hair symbolised Aphrodite's freedom from pollution, ageing and death.

The colour gold had long been established in the classical canons of beauty and power. Almost two thousand years before Homer, in the time of the Proto-Indo-Europeans, the colour was connected to the worship of sun and fire, and to the adoration of a yellow dawn goddess. For the Phoenicians and the Mycenaeans, both ardent trading civilisations, possession of gold metal had been a sign of the utmost superiority. The Persians had plaited their beards with gold threads, wearing their riches on their chins. The Assyrians had gone one step further, displaying and disposing of their wealth in one stroke by powdering their hair with extravagant clouds of gold dust.

The Greek sense of beauty was therefore saturated with ancient allusion and example, and in the pantheon of popular feminine imagery the golden-haired woman was among the most mighty. Everywhere she was reflected and celebrated in images of Aphrodite, in the statues that peppered the public spaces of Ancient Greece. More were made in worship of her than of any other ancient divinity. In marble, stone and terracotta, her flesh painted in natural colours, her hair coloured blonde, this beautiful woman infiltrated the gardens and public and private spaces of Greek society in an entirely natural and provocative way.

The most famous by far was the statue by Praxiteles of Aphrodite, enshrined and worshipped at Knidos, a harbour on the Asiatic shore of Greece. The sculpture was originally commissioned by the people of Kos, but when they inspected the completed work they were so shocked by its nudity and untrammelled eroticism that they immediately cancelled their order. Instead they opted to buy for the same price another statue of the goddess. This one, also by Praxiteles, was more soberly draped. In the meantime the people of Knidos had got wind of the sensation and they hurried to view it. Being more daring and – as history proves – more artistically discerning, they snapped it up on the spot. Theirs, as it turned out, was the superior deal. The Knidos Aphrodite became for several centuries an obligatory stop on any tourist itinerary of eastern Greece, and an unfailing source of revenue for the city. So valuable did it become, as Pliny the Elder put it, that King Nikomedes tried to buy it from the Knidians, 'promising that he would cancel the city's whole debt, which was enormous. They preferred, however, to bear everything, and not without reason. For with that statue Praxiteles made Knidos famous.'

Given the marked aptitude of the Greeks for regular and ingenious forms of sexual gratification, it is no surprise that the tall, naked blonde attracted such attention. Some visitors even recorded the intimate erotic fantasies they had experienced upon gazing at it. Pliny was not impervious to the pleasures of the statue himself: 'Superior to any other statue,' he wrote in his

Natural History, 'not only to others made by Praxiteles himself, but throughout the whole world, is the Venus [Aphrodite] which many people have sailed to Cnidus [Knidos] to see.' He described it placed in a shrine, visible from all sides, and told the delicate story of a young man who, overcome with passion for the statue, managed one evening to conceal himself inside the locked enclosure. He 'embraced it intimately; a stain bears witness to his lust.' Another traveller describes, in a play attributed to the Roman philosopher Lucian, how the crowds used to visit the Aphrodite of Knidos, set in fragrant gardens of myrtle, bay trees, cypresses and vines. In the deepest shade of this sylvan retreat there were 'pleasure booths' to cater for those particularly inspired by this most exquisite goddess.

The Knidos Aphrodite was so thoroughly celebrated – and vicariously enjoyed – that before long thousands of copies began to appear in temples, gardens and villas all over Greece. At the same time more explicit images of the goddess, an *Aphrodite the Whore*, an *Aphrodite of the Beautiful Backside*, and an *Aphrodite who Rode Astride*, sprang on to plinths in public places in splendid evocation of the inspiration of love and beauty. More than two thousand marble Aphrodites survive today, as well as many more in bronze and in terracotta, from temples, tombs and gardens. So two thousand years ago her image must have been seen by everyone, a universal and utterly democratic blonde goddess inspiring Greeks of all classes, ages and inclinations.

The Knidos Aphrodite remains one of the most celebrated statues ever made of the goddess, but the woman who is thought to have modelled for it has won her share of fame too. She was Phryne, the voluptuous mistress of Praxiteles. As a powerful courtesan, Phryne naturally plundered much of her sexual imagery from Aphrodite, and one of the key weapons in her arsenal was her abundant hair, probably dyed blonde, with which she attracted many powerful and wealthy clients. Fact and fable are difficult to distinguish in her story, but enough biographical anecdotes have collected around the name of Phryne to put together a picture of this beautiful and manipulative woman. Her power and reputation in her lifetime were considerable, and her sexuality was described on a correspondingly vast scale. She was born in about 370 BC in Thespiae, north-west of Athens, the daughter of Epikles. As a young girl, she moved to Athens, where she lived for a while in the sort of Cinderella-like poverty necessary to her spectacular story. Her outstanding beauty, however, soon allowed her to make a living by taking lovers and she was quickly elevated to the status of hetaira, which classed her as a superior 'companion' to men. Within only a few years of arriving in Athens she had become a top-class courtesan and had learned to play men like puppets.

Phryne clearly had a talent for personal image-making and she soon turned herself into a striking impersonator of Aphrodite. She employed a household of slaves to attend to her appearance, styling herself as the sensuously smooth goddess whom Homer had so lovingly described. Phryne's beauty and her carefully nurtured powers of sexual appeal were to inspire poets, painters and writers for many hundreds of years to come. A nineteenth-century engraving of her, presumably shaped by the personal fantasies of its anonymous maker, shows a tall, voluptuous and naked beauty, her slender arms spreading open a length of wispily transparent chiffon to expose a long mane of hair streaming down around her breasts. Her face is slim, her nose is of tiny, nineteenth-century proportions and her expression is open and proud. She advances delicately on tiptoe towards an appreciative crowd of men. It is the face, body and posture of a shameless seductress, an uncanny preview of a twentieth-century movie star.

Phryne's talents for mimicry brought her notoriety. Given her special fondness for exhibitionism, she became very popular with the Athenians in religious rituals, appearing frequently at the festival of Poseidon in her favourite role. Many years later, in AD 200, the poet and essayist Athenaeus described the scene, during the festival, of Phryne entering the sea naked, with her hair flowing provocatively loose. It is an enduringly sexy yarn, which William Sanger recreated in 1859, with the help of a little fanciful embroidery: 'she appeared on the steps of the temple at the seaside in her usual dress, and slowly disrobed herself in the presence of the crowd. She next advanced to the waterside, plunged into the waves, and offered sacrifice . . . returning like a sea-nymph, drying her hair from which the water dripped over her exquisite limbs, she paused for a moment before the crowd which shouted in a phrensy of enthusiasm as the fair priestess vanished into a cell of the temple.'

It is possible that Phryne first met Praxiteles at Eleusis when she was the star attraction of the festival of Poseidon. Athenaeus tells us that she also caught the eye of Apelles, who painted his *Aphrodite Anadyomene* rising from the sea with Phryne in mind. The painting has not survived, but a number of sculptures of Aphrodite rising from the sea and wringing out her hair have been found and are believed to have been based on it. Phryne was known as the most beautiful woman in Athens and her love affair with Praxiteles was evidently passionate, celebrating both his fame as a sculptor and the exoticism of her profession as a courtesan. But as her powers of attraction grew Phryne took many more lovers besides Praxiteles, and she became fabulously wealthy. She dedicated a beautiful figure of Eros to her hometown, Thespiai, and she is said to have been rich enough to rebuild the walls of Thebes, which had been destroyed by Alexander the Great in 335 BC. She was also acquisitive, and cunning with it. Pausanias tells the story of how she pestered Praxiteles to tell her which masterpieces he considered his favourites. When repeatedly he refused to say, she sent a message claiming that his studio was on fire. As he hurried over, Praxiteles revealed that he hoped his statues of Eros and a satyr had survived. Phryne was delighted, admitted it was all a trick and asked if she could have the Eros. Praxiteles bowed cravenly to her demand and offered it to her. Greedily, she accepted.

Phryne was proud, ambitious, uninhibited, vulgar and vain, the third century BC's equivalent of Marilyn Monroe. And she was seemingly incapable of living without the addictive *frisson* of scandal. Her growing number of conquests and the trail of ruined men left in her wake soon brought her up against legislation and she was charged with profaning religious occasions. Dragged into the all-male court, which was no doubt packed for the occasion, she found that her case nicely highlighted the ambivalent attitudes of educated Greek men towards the glamorous and seductive hetaira class. The orator Hyperides, who happened to be one of her lovers, took up her defence, but the case began badly for Phryne. She was an independent courtesan, educated, opinionated and with a taste for self-publicity – precisely the opposite of the model Athenian woman, whose sole job it was, according to many historians, to conceive and bring up heirs, unobserved and in silence. There were some sticky moments as Phryne's critics slung down well-argued and convincing accusations. The case seemed lost until – as the story related by Athenaeus goes – Hyperides, in a last-ditch attempt to save his lover, ripped open her dress to reveal her naked breasts. This proved to be the knock-out argument. How, he argued, no doubt gesturing approvingly at the bared breasts, could such god-given attributes possibly profane any religious festival? To press charges on Phryne would be to bring charges against Aphrodite herself, and that would be inviting divine retribution. The judges, no doubt electrified by the show, agreed, and all charges were dropped. But the story survived and hundreds of years later it was still being appreciatively chewed over by the blonde-obsessed Venetian poets of the Renaissance and again later by nineteenth century painters. In 1861 Jean-Léon Gérôme painted the sensational scene showing Phryne standing in court stripped entirely naked, smooth as a classical statue and golden-blonde, her face hidden behind her arm in supposed shame. The ageing judges have abandoned all pretence of composure and are seen lurching forward for a closer view, their faces charged with leering approval.

Phryne was perhaps an unusually influential hetaira in her link with one of the most famous works of art of all time. She was dangerously alluring, it is true, but society (governed by appreciative males) never regarded her as immoral. In the context of her times, she was one of the foremost champions of her class. 'In one sense,' according to the historian Elaine Fantham, 'the hetaira was the only woman in Greek society who enjoyed a freedom comparable to men, running her own household and finances, with the right to choose the company she admitted to her home, and to attend the symposia and dinner-parties of the men-folk.'

While an entirely *déclassé* and miscellaneous riff-raff of other prostitutes scraped a living on the fringes of society, it was the hetairai who were the most elevated both in the hierarchy of whores and in female society as a whole. Only they visited the studios of the greatests artists of the Greek world. They alone listened to Socrates reasoning and discussed politics with Pericles. They were the only women participating in the intellectual fray of Greece. As a result, many of them were well-connected and well-informed and some established their own salons where men would gather to listen to conversation, poetry and philosophy. No wonder Athenian men soon became addicted to the glittering company of hetairai, relegating their wives to the status of domestic drudge.

This was not a sexual democracy, much less a utopia for women. While hetairai, given the privilege of immodesty, were free to drive through the streets with their blonde heads brazenly uncovered and displaying their gorgeous clothes, most scholars believe that respectable Athenian married women led stunted indoor lives of obedience, patience and dependence. On the rare occasions when they were free to venture out in public, for funerals or special festivals, they were expected to swathe their bodies and heads in copious thick veils. Inside the home, the women were restricted to their own quarters and kept strictly out of sight of visitors. Had they been allowed to socialise with the highly educated men of their class, they would have had nothing to say, for education and intellectual knowledge were forbidden, as the mark of the whore. The contrast between these mute married ladies, all shrouded and hidden, and the striking golden-haired high-class courtesans with their fine clothes, their confidence and their wealth could not have been greater. Aphrodite was the inspiration behind these powerful blondes, and her influence was to extend down the centuries in a variety of different but equally compelling guises.

2

THE EMPRESS AND THE WIG

R UMOUR HAS it that Cleopatra was a blonde. A great queen of fabulous wealth, exceptional power, unlimited ambition and flamboyant sexual charisma, she has always represented a bounty of inexhaustible speculation. Every age has restyled her in the image of its own preoccupations. Pliny claimed that she challenged Mark Antony to outspend her and then, to win the bet, dissolved the world's largest pearl in a jug of vinegar and drank it. It is a popular but improbable tale. Equally improbable is that she arranged to meet Caesar for the first time by having herself delivered to his quarters rolled in a carpet, as another early chronicler wrote. Sextus Propertius alleged that 'she fornicated even with her slaves'; and another ancient fantasy had her copulating with crocodiles. Whatever the reality of this bewitching character, her reputation as a voracious and fatal temptress was firmly established within her own lifetime. It is no wonder that admirers imagined her as a blonde. Tiepolo painted Cleopatra as a blue-eyed golden-blonde, her curls vital with erotic energy. Vasari also painted her as a blonde, as did Cagnacci and several other Renaissance painters. Cleopatra lived fast and died young just as the power of her empire was beginning to ebb, and her fascination endures precisely because she has always been the source of wonderful, timeless myth.

By the late second century BC, the Ancient Greek civilisation had blazed its way to astonishing achievements in
almost every field of human endeavour. In religion, philosophy, literature, music, art, architecture and science Greece
had experienced great awakenings and consolidated a culture
which was to form the core of later European history. But its
political and military strength was exhausted. The advance of
the Roman legions was relentless and Rome was beginning
gradually to unite the Mediterranean world under its own
banner. Within three years of the death of Cleopatra in 30
BC, Augustus controlled an empire which extended from
Spain to Syria, and the absolute supremacy of Rome was an
established fact.

Rome's cultural debt to Greece was enormous. In their
literature, philosophy and science, the Romans consciously
used Greece as their model. In the case of religion they
embraced the Olympian gods, changing only their names.
Zeus became Jupiter, Aries became Mars, and Aphrodite was
seamlessly converted into the exalted Venus, who became as
important a deity for the Romans as she had been for the
Greeks. Venus retained all the finest aspects of her Greek
forebear: the epiphany from the waters who became the
goddess of love, beauty and sexual desire, and a divine body
which was permanently youthful, naked and prodigiously
pleasurable. Cult images of Venus, painted with pale-coloured
flesh and golden-blonde hair, soon adorned theatres, baths,
fountains and palaces and were commonly seen inside private
houses. Roman writers took up her cause, too, and the body of
their work has been bequeathed to us in a rich legacy of poems,
eulogies and colourfully erotic epigrams to the goddess.

Sadly, all the historians, poets and satirists of the Roman

Empire were men – few women wrote books, and of those written none has survived. But romantic men such as Catullus and Propertius composed reams of passionate prose to their women. Ovid and Horace, highly cultivated philanderers, also produced volumes of satirical and poetic erotica. These writers, whose works were crammed with erudite literary allusions, were naturally drawn to write for and about women who would appreciate their work. Not for them the chaste and dull wives, veiled and wilfully ignorant. These poets wrote for their witty and extrovert mistresses; and it is these elegant and cultured women of Rome, the elaborately blonded imitators of Venus, whom we have to thank for so much that is charming and exceptionally obscene in Roman poetry. Catullus referred to his mistress by the pseudonym Lesbia, and Ovid's poems are often addressed to his mistress Corinna, a monumentally beautiful – if we are to believe him – blonde dame. It is clear that Ovid was obsessed with her physical beauty, and glorified with uncontrolled relish every possible pleasure of the flesh. He was fascinated, in particular, by hair, its uses and abuses.

> I told you to stop using rinses – and now just look at you!
> No hair worth mentioning left to dye.
> Why couldn't you let it well alone? . . .
> No rival's incantations
> Or tisanes have harmed you, no witch
> Has hexed your rinse, you haven't – touch wood – had an illness;
> If your hair's fallen out, it's not
> Any envious tongue that's to blame. You applied that concoction

Yourself. It was you that did it. All your fault.
Still, after our German conquests a wig is easily come
   by –
A captive Mädchen's tresses will see you through.
You'll blush, it's true, when your borrowed plumage
   elicits
Admiration galore. You'll feel that the praise (like the
   hair)
Has been bought. Once you really deserved it. Now each
   compliment
Belongs to some Rhine maiden, not to you.

There must have been thousands of German blondes taken captive only to find their hair being cut off to be made into wigs for the fashionable ladies of Rome. Successful wars were one source of supply of northern slaves because whole nations were often sold after a victory. But the piecemeal kidnapping of able-bodied men and women – particularly blonde ones – throughout the Empire went on for hundreds of years, the eagle-eyed dealers ever on the watch to seize a handsome boy or maiden for the Roman marketplace.

One of the most notorious beneficiaries of the fruits of these kidnappings was the eccentric Empress Messalina, wife of the Emperor Claudius. She was a legendary lady of fantastically debauched pleasures and infamous public vices who enjoyed wearing blonde wigs. Juvenal, the satirical poet who gloried in the ugly little adulterous conflicts that breached class and convention, wrote his famous Sixth Satire warning men against women's insatiable appetites for sexual gratification.

Postumus, are you really
Taking a wife? You used to be sane enough – what

Fury's got into you, what snake has stung you up?

And as for your insistence on a wife with old-fashioned
Moral virtues – man, you need your blood-pressure
    checked, you're
Crazy, you're aiming over the moon.

He goes on to recount the tale of Messalina's astonishing sexual
drive. Bored by the traditional frolics on offer within the palace
walls, she made regular nocturnal visits to a brothel, her black hair
hidden beneath an ash-blonde wig. There she would strip off in
a reserved whore's cell and take in all visitors, for cash, until the
brothel keeper finally closed his doors at dawn. Always the last to
leave, she would trail away sadly, 'retiring exhausted, yet still far
from satisfied, cheeks begrimed with lamp smoke, filthy, carrying
home to her imperial couch the stink of the whorehouse.'

It is clear that Messalina's choice of a blonde wig was designed
to attract attention rather than to disguise herself. She often came
home, so the story goes, having forgotten it, and the next day
publicly reclaimed the tousled mass when it was returned from
the brothel. As Martial, who longed for such untoward behaviour
to use in his verses, later wrote of this lethal woman, 'Her toilet
table contained a hundred lies; and while she was in Rome, her
hair was blushing by the Rhine. A man was in no condition to
say he loved her, for what he loved in her was not herself, and
that which was herself was impossible to love.'

From this is shaped the grand opera of Messalinian mythology. Jacques Roergas de Serviez, a seventeenth-century historian of Roman imperial life, gives a brief character sketch of
the Empress Messalina: 'It is hard to conceive the miserable
conditions of an Empire that is governed by a woman, who

has nothing at heart but the gratification of her appetites, whose violence, meeting with no resistance, spreads their indiscriminately fatal influence upon all those whom her caprice inclines her to persecute.'

When not busy flaunting her blonde wig in brothels, Messalina was conjuring up monstrous Borgia-like plots to have her rivals murdered. She was an imaginative woman, particularly in the ways of false accusation. Any foolish man who spurned her or refused to meet her demands was promptly accused of treason, sent to jail and then quietly put to death. Powerful men such as Vitellius, one of Claudius' more corrupt courtiers, who had attracted Messalina's roving eye, resorted to base flattery to stay alive. He always carried with him one of Messalina's old shoes, which he kissed continuously and unashamedly in public as if it were a kind of sacred relic. This bizarre insurance policy worked and he survived her, but others were not so lucky.

Messalina finally met her end, according to some accounts, after flouting convention unforgivably by publicly taking the handsome, wealthy and noble Silius as a second husband. This act startled even Emperor Claudius, accustomed as he was to her depravity and ruthlessness in the affairs of state. Soon afterwards, in AD 48, the imperial orders were issued which resulted in her death.

Messalina was not alone in her imperial obsession with the dangerous sexual powers of blonde hair. Her rival in vice, extravagance and power-crazed lust was Poppaea, another infamous blonde. Poppaea was brutal, beautiful and ripe with the promise of intrigue. She used her beauty, her wit and her charms to persuade Emperor Nero to remove all barriers to her own ascendancy of the throne. The emperor, no stranger himself to gluttony, cruelty, murder and spectacular sexual abominations, was lured by Poppaea first into murdering his own mother, Agrippina, in AD 59, and then into killing his young wife, Octavia, as a punishment for her supposed adultery. Octavia died, according to Tacitus, in an overheated bath, smothered by the steam, leaving Poppaea triumphantly free of rivals as empress.

Nero was captivated by Poppaea and, according to de Serviez, 'admired her beauty as much as she valued it herself, and never omitted an opportunity of extolling it, which he did by the most delicate and studied praises. He went so far as to compose verses upon the delightful brilliancy of her hair, which he compared to amber.' Amber when new is bright yellow: Poppaea clearly went for the brassiest shade available, taking no chances in the business of captivating and keeping her emperor. She was a sensationally vain woman, her jealous rivals noted, who was observed peering into her looking-glass at every available moment. The haughty empress looked in her mirror one day and, according to de Serviez, found herself somewhat less handsome than usual. 'Foreseeing with sorrowful heart the sad but inevitable decline of her charms, she wept bitterly and prayed to the gods that she might die before she grew old.'

It is clear that Poppaea was an accomplished beauty, but few spent such immoderate time, money and effort on preserving and heightening their charms and tricking time's ravaging fingers. Lavish sums disappeared on washes and pomatums for Poppaea's complexion as well as saffron tints for her hair. She had a herd of five hundred lactating she-asses kept at vast expense to provide the milk to fill her daily baths. Nothing, she believed, was comparable to this special product for preserving the skin. Intoxicated with her own beauty and power, she wore magnificent gowns, precious jewels and gold chains, and had the mules attached to her litter shod with solid gold and their reins threaded with gold wires. Naturally, no good was to come of such unseemly displays. The citizens of Rome, far from blind to their empress's malicious cunning, fed their anxieties on her blatant vanity and extravagance, and loudly ridiculed Nero for his stupidity. Poppaea met her particularly unpleasant end in about AD 65. Having berated Nero for his music and chariot-driving pleasures, she angered him to the extent that he turned and, so the story goes, gave her such a kick in her pregnant belly that she died immediately. The Romans were delighted. But when Nero recovered from his fury he was inconsolable. According to Pliny, Poppaea's body was stuffed with Arabian spices, beautified and embalmed, oriental fashion, in clouds of incense. More perfumes were consumed on her funeral pile than Arabia was then able to produce in a year. In the end, the gods had answered Poppaea's prayer to vanity.

Poppaea's story gives us some indication of the lengths to which Roman women — both members of the aristocracy and top-ranking courtesans — went to make themselves beautiful. We can safely assume that it was the goddess of beauty and love, Venus, whom these women had in mind when they put the elegant verses of Martial, Ovid and Lucian to practical effect. Martial, writing in the first century AD, advised those wishing to colour their hair blonde to use a dye known as 'sapo', made of goat's fat mixed with beechwood ashes and rolled into balls. For those more squeamish than vain, he suggested the 'spuma Batava' or Batavian pomade, a form of dyeing soap which had been discovered in use in the Rhine district. Pliny, in his *Natural History*, advised the most ruthless bleachers to use

the 'lees' or sediment of vinegar, an altogether more caustic –
and malodorous – method of achieving the blonde look. The
outstandingly brave incorporated pigeon dung in the mix, for
the bleaching powers of its ammonia.

Martial reserved his most mordant wit for savaging the
women who succumbed to such vanities.

Although, yourself at home, you are arrayed in the middle
of the Subura, and your tresses, Galla, are manufactured
far away, and you lay aside your teeth at night, just as you
do your silk dresses, and you lie stored away in a hundred
caskets, and your face does not sleep with you – yet you
wink with that eyebrow which has been brought out for
you in the morning, and no respect moves you for your
outworn carcass – which you may now count as one of
your ancestors. Nevertheless you offer me an infinity of
delights.

Merciless with their pens, these poets were at the same time
entirely susceptible to the attractions of their blonde mistresses.
Any shade of blonde, from ash to amber, would do, as long as it
put them in mind of Venus and fed their fantasies. Some singled
out particular shades as being reserved for particular purposes.
The colour known as 'carrot yellow', for example, was said to be
favoured by high-ranking courtesans and was probably achieved
using saffron. This was the world's costliest spice, at one time
measured in carats and said to be worth more even than its
weight in gold. It was derived from the stigma of the crocus
flower and, used as a hair dye, it produced a rich yellow shade.
Meanwhile, those described as having a 'white head', meaning
heavily bleached blonde, marked themselves as women of 'not

31

very serious intentions'. Could these have been the world's first recorded blonde bimbos? Propertius attacked all such female vanities in his elegies. 'Do you still in your madness imitate the painted Britons and play the wanton with foreign dyes upon your cheeks? All beauty is best as nature made it . . . In hell below may many an ill befall that girl who stupidly dyes her hair with a false colour!'

Ovid's gracefully erotic poetry was rather more flattering, and got its delicate little hooks into the soft flesh of society women. Soon they were lapping up long treatises on appearance and beauty in his *Art of Love*. 'What attracts us is elegance,' wrote the ever-attentive Ovid:

> so don't neglect your hairstyle. Looks can be made or marred by a skilful touch . . . But a woman can use imported rinses to touch up those white streaks, produce a better than natural tint. A woman goes out in a built-up purchased postiche, replaces her own hair with a wig, cash down – and unblushingly boutiques display them under Hercules' nose, right beside the Muses' shrine . . . I was about to warn you against rank goatish armpits and bristling hair on your legs . . .

Nothing was left to chance by these men, who imposed every detail of a Roman woman's most intimate beauty routine.*

* They even suggested contraception methods. Pliny recommended an amulet made by opening the head of a hairy spider, removing the two little worms believed to be inside and tying them in a deer skin. Aetius suggested wearing the liver of a cat in a tube on the left foot.

Dyed blonde hair or a blonde wig might have given away the profession of the prostitute in the early years of the Roman Republic. But by the late Republic and Empire periods, it was becoming more difficult, despite the carrot-yellow code, to distinguish the professional, beautifully coiffed courtesan from the increasingly liberated society lady. No doubt egged on by the provocative poems of Ovid, the austerely moral married matrons of former days, whose virtues had included frugality, modesty and simplicity of life, were beginning to transform themselves into frivolous and extravagant butterflies. No longer afraid to be seen publicly with their heads uncovered, they became ruthless beauties, desperate to compete – as did their men – in the daily contest for image and the social position that it brought.

Elaborate hairstyles and clothes were the most effective way of demonstrating leisured wealth. During the first century AD, a period of sheer fantasy in feminine coiffure was ushered in by Julia, the beautiful daughter of the Emperor Titus, which easily competes with the eighteenth-century passion for wedding-cake hairstyles. Professional hairdressers were employed, devoted teams on whom powerful beauties depended utterly for their reputations. Touching epitaphs still survive, composed by ladies mourning the deaths of their most able and loyal hairdressers. These women, highly skilled in their intricate art, mixed the thick hair dye, slapped it on to the hair in a slick of shining slime, rubbed it vigorously into the scalp and then scraped it all off hours later when dry. They washed the hair, dried it, applied further colouring powders and then embarked on the tricky business of styling. This was a task in which success brought rich rewards, while failure sometimes resulted in stabbings with bone hairpins or worse by disgruntled mistresses. Piling the hair up wave upon wave, they arranged each layer on crescent-shaped wire frames until the whole concoction eventually soared up in frantic profusion to tower over the forehead. These splendidly coloured and curled edifices were designed to be viewed from the front only. Society ladies solemnly competed to manoeuvre themselves at important occasions so as to keep their polished façades in view and the complex scaffolding at the backs of their heads out of sight. Juvenal gleefully mocked the fashion in his Sixth Satire:

See the tall edifice
Rise up on her head in serried tiers and storeys!
See her heroic stature – at least, that is, from the front:
Her back view's less impressive, you'd think it belonged
To a different person.

Some women reached a joyful compromise by having a selection of wigs constructed for use on different days. Faustina the Elder, wife of Emperor Antoninus Pius, who reigned from about AD 138 to 161, is said to have got through three hundred wigs in nineteen years. The evidence, as seen from the fragment of a Roman statue now in the Getty Museum in Los Angeles, is that portrait busts of women were made with detachable marble wigs, revealing the practical realities of life.

Men, too, indulged in wig-wearing. Caligula wore a full wig to disguise himself while prowling around the brothels at night. For parties and special occasions he fixed a false gold beard on his chin, his choice of colour presumably designed to display his wealth as well as his sense of style. Nero, a finicky connoisseur of fashion who never appeared in public without his hair artfully styled, wore gold dust and coloured powders in his hair. Emperor Commodus wore an oiled wig auspiciously powdered with scrapings of gold to give the impression of a glowing halo – all the better to persuade the public of his divinity. Caracalla wore a blond wig to ingratiate himself during a visit to a settlement of German tribesmen. Hadrian had his hair curled and dyed, as did his adopted heirs, Lucius Caesar and Lucius Verus. Hadrian latterly wore a wig to conceal his baldness and had his beard dyed to match.

The growing appeal of blonde hair, on both men and women, may have been linked to the rise in numbers and social status of Germans, some of whom had gained considerable power in the last few hundred years of the Roman Empire. Ever since the first century AD, blonde German prisoners had been pouring into the Empire, following successful northern military campaigns, to work on agricultural estates all over Italy. Each successive victory admitted more northerners into the households of Rome as slaves. During the reigns of the last Roman emperors, Germans rose to hold military command, becoming consuls and chiefs, and some of them were admitted into the inner circle of the Roman aristocracy. Many of these German officers, such as the consul Richomer, were men of brilliant talents and noble bearing. As polished men of the world, they may have had considerable social influence. Three edicts of Honorius, for example, issued between 397 and 416, banned the wearing of trousers, long hair and fur coats in the 'barbarian' (German) style within the precincts of the city. Clearly, the rage for radical German fashions had become widespread. And as more and more Roman ladies discovered that their husbands were attracted to the exoticism of blonde slave girls, they, too, turned themselves blonde. Then they trumped the slave girls with their extravagant hairstyles, dress and jewellery.

The swagger and glitter of these lifestyles, the common riot of gluttony, the vanity, effeminacy and advanced moral laxity, quite apart from the political decadence, were of course exactly the kinds of profligate behaviour most deplored by the early moralists and preachers of Christianity, which was in due course to gain universal appeal and become the official religion of the Roman Empire. This addiction to opulence was a contagion, the preachers raged, an outrageous degeneracy which could lead only to the material and moral wasting of the Empire.

By the second century AD, some Christian preachers were beginning to attack Venus and the effects she had on women. Clement of Alexandria, a ferocious name-caller and propagandist, jeered at the goddess as a 'dirty-minded little waitress' and reprimanded all the women of Rome, not just prostitutes, for bowing to her influence and dyeing their hair blonde or wearing blonde wigs. Hair-colouring by women and its effects on men he regarded as a moral menace of frightening proportions. While he was at it, he likened women to 'painted apes'.

> Additions of other people's hair are entirely to be rejected, and it is a most sacrilegious thing for spurious hair to shade the head, covering the skull with dead locks . . . Unawares, the poor wretches destroy their own beauty by the introduction of what is spurious . . . So they dishonour the Creator of men, as if the beauty given by Him were nothing worth.

In succeeding centuries, the howls of outrage were to be repeated again and again by the mouth-foaming fanatics, but never with the slightest effect.

Tertullian, another early Christian proselytiser, took up the puritan cause in his *De cultu feminarum*, written in the early third century. One of his targets of special loathing was dyed blonde hair. 'I see some women dye their hair blonde by using saffron. They are even ashamed of their country, sorry that they were not born in Germany or in Gaul! Thus, as far as their hair is concerned, they give up their country.' And as for such monstrosities as wigs, Tertullian thundered, 'you may be putting on a holy and Christian head the cast-offs of hair of some stranger who was perhaps unclean, perhaps guilty and destined for hell. In fact, why do you not banish all this slavery to beauty from your own free head?'

Constantine the Great, the first Christian emperor, who reigned from about 306 to 337, was alert to the changing mood and made a concerted attack on the old pagan mythology of Rome. His soldiers dragged statues of the gods and goddesses out of the darkness of the temples and into the light. People shouted and jeered as they broke off their decorations and, as a Constantine sympathiser tells us, 'exhibited to the gaze of all the unsightly reality which had been hidden under a painted exterior'. Coloured images were desecrated, stripped down to their bare marble. Arms, legs and noses were lopped off and bodies mutilated, reducing many of these smooth elegant beauties to the fragmented torsos that we see today in museums.

To the Christian Fathers, the blonde and naked Venus was the ultimate demon, the most shameful of the company of Olympian demons, plucked as an example of the odious immorality of her times. Thousands of images of her must have been destroyed as symbols of Rome's decadent past. Yet it was exactly this sensationally erotic goddess, more than any other of the demonised deities, who was to survive her attacks for many centuries to come. Venus was to find a new and lasting guise in the medieval world of Christianity, where her abhorred blonde hair would become an essential element of her power.

3

THE DEVIL'S SOAP

W HATEVER THE turbid mix of brigandage, superstition and plague that ruled Europe in the Middle Ages, it is clear that by the thirteenth century the medieval Church was in crisis. The people could see that the ideals of Christianity bore no relation to reality. Their lives swung between joy and despair, pious fervour and calamity. Grand contrasts of pageantry and perfume, of lepers with rattles and public executions, lent a flavour of excitement and passion to everyday medieval life. The men of the Church despaired at their failing ability to exercise leadership in this rising spiritual quagmire. One of their problems was women.

Medieval clerics were afraid of women. They were afraid above all of their sexuality; and one emblem of these feared female powers was the mane of flowing blonde hair. Women were all sorceresses to a degree, it was claimed. Many of them were in league with the Devil, their bodies a bundle of animal instincts, their minds unquenchable infernos. Burdened as they inevitably were with all the sins of the world, they were fornicators, deliberately bewitching and inflaming men with their base trickeries.

The Middle Ages was a time when most mature and married women were expected to live beneath the veils in which male authority enveloped them. The slightest glimpse of a lock of golden hair, a curl by the ear, a glint of blonde at the brow, was imagined to be enough to kindle the fever of desire. These powers of attraction were closely entwined with the excitement of temptation and denial. Just as in the Victorian age, when the glimpse of a finely turned ankle beneath weighty layers of petticoats could send men into a frenzy of sexual excitement, in the Middle Ages the near-total concealment of hair further enhanced its seductive powers. Fear and fascination existed as one in the licentiously flowing blonde hair that haunted men's dreams.

All across England and across Europe, too, preachers, parsons, monks and friars were drumming the hellfire message of woman's devilry into their congregations. They condemned women as creatures of evil, dangerous beings to be kept at a distance and controlled. Nobody was left in any doubt as to why. It was woman's powers of seduction that had become the reason for her vicious denunciation. Every Sunday, catalogues of womanly sins were dragged out and scathingly picked over from the pulpit. Her scandalous love of evil fashions and cosmetics, her habit of looking in the mirror, her use of dyes to blonde her hair and the habit of wearing blonde wigs made of false hair – all these were thrown up as evidence of woman's deceptive wiles and her carnal provocation of good men. Bishop Brunton of Rochester, the Yorkshire friar John Waldeby, John of Mirfield from St Bartholemew's in Smithfield and many other great virtuosi of fire and brimstone delivered fine bravura performances from the pulpit. They castigated all those who made a habit of tampering with the handiwork of God by putting unnatural colours in their hair and using 'the Devil's soap' (cosmetics) on their faces. 'Everyone knows', ranted the Benedictine monk Robert Rypon, warming to his subject with a most pungent simile, 'how a sow rolls its nostrils in the foulest dirt. Thus do such foolish women roll their beauty in the foulest dirt of lust . . . With them it is as with the worms that glow resplendent at night, but in the daytime appear most vile.' And the Dominican John Bromyard of Hereford, not to be outdone, condemned women's fancy hairstyles, their blonde dyes and wigs, comparing them to devilish fires, 'each a spark breathing out hell-fire . . . so that in a single day, by her dancing and perambulation through the town, she inflames with the fire of lust – it may be – twenty of those who behold her . . .'

Saint Bernardino, a radical Franciscan preacher who toured Italy in the early fifteenth century, often concentrated his electrifying sermons on the fashion-conscious work of the Devil whose influence persuaded women to go to mass wearing false blonde hair. 'Oh the vanity of thee, woman, who deckest thy head with such a multitude of vanities. Remember that divine Head at which angels tremble . . . that Head is crowned with thorns while thine is adorned with jewels. His hair is stained with blood, but thy hair, or rather that which is not thine own, is bleached artificially.' Saint Bernadino was a famous clerical star of ferocious energy who often preached in the form of running dialogues with his audience. News of his imminent arrival caused a stir in any city, attracting additional crowds from the surrounding countryside. Impatiently awaited, his sermons shook people up, triggering sudden outbursts of collective penance. His words whipped up such fervour that they were often followed by huge public bonfires on which were piled masses of false bleached blonde hair, feeding the raging infernos of the Church's disapproval.

This traditionally misogynistic pulpit theme was based on the convenient premise that Eve was the source of all evil in women. By the early Middle Ages, Eve's malign character had been fully developed in Christian literature. She had become an important tool of the Church in its efforts to discredit and stifle female sexuality. Eve was disobedient, subversive, lascivious and – perhaps most dangerous of all – beautiful. She was also the 'foremother' of all women. Naturally, growled the bullying preachers, her female descendants had all inherited her maddening combination of sexual allure and adulterous villainy. By now, the dreadful fear of effeminacy and luxury which had occupied the earliest Christians in Ancient Rome, more than a thousand years earlier, had built itself up into a fear of women's powers to seduce. As the ultimate source of beauty and sexual temptation, Aphrodite and Venus had been transmogrified into Eve. And again she wore the sign of the seductress: blonde hair.

Eve is the subject of a story told everywhere, in words and in pictures, throughout the Middle Ages. The story first appears at the beginning of the book of Genesis, describing the origins of the human race and the foundation of the world's moral and social order. The fathers of the Church, in monasteries and cathedrals around Europe, were much exercised by the text and scrutinised its every word to clarify further its meaning. They logically concluded that Eve, as temptress, was the party most to blame. She was responsible for the sexuality of the human race, for its guilt and for its disenchantment. The libidinous Eve had succumbed to temptation; her appetite for pleasure had caused the Fall of mankind from God's grace.

By the mid-fourteenth century, descriptions and images of Eve were consistently giving her the free-flowing cascades of golden blonde hair that marked her as the devilish temptress. An image of 1356 by Bartolo di Fredi in San Gimignano depicts the creation of Eve, a pale and sensuous blonde emerging from the ribcage of a sleeping Adam. Masolino's 1420s painting of the handsome couple shows Eve poised on the brink of sin, voluptuous and enticing beneath a head of delicately waved blonde hair. Artists of this subject were of course not necessarily concerned with realism; they depicted symbols and images. But it was through their work and the supporting words from the pulpits that perceptions were created and accepted by society at large. Their message was clear: blonde was both beautiful and dangerous, both eternally desirable and for ever forbidden.

Literacy did not trickle far down the social scale; but for those Christian women who could read, and for the majority who instead heard the stories in church, the Old Testament was the source of carefully coded narratives designed to put them in their place. If Eve was held up as the first archetypal blonde bad girl, in her wake trailed Mary Magdalene, one of her most promiscuous descendants. Mary Magdalene, too, was depicted as a blonde, a classic combination of feminine beauty, sexuality and sin.

As the favourite penitent of the medieval Church and an important saint, Mary Magdalene appears in countless devotional images of Christ's life. She can be seen at the Crucifixion and Resurrection, cloaked usually in red. Her blonde hair flows loose as she sits gazing up at Christ's face, or sprawls shamelessly as the beautiful prostitute at his feet. She is a brazen presence in Masaccio's Crucifixion of 1426, kneeling with arms raised at the foot of the cross, her long blonde hair spread luxuriantly over her scarlet cloak. Her symbolic elevation from lechery to sainthood so fascinated medieval churchgoers that she emerged in her own right, depicted as the heroine of her own story in stained-glass windows, frescos and altarpieces, in paintings, miniatures and sculpture.

And of course her hair flowed loose, freed from the veil, in an exuberant exhibition of what Eudes of Châteauroux called 'women's most precious possession'. Again, men were both attracted to Mary Magdalene and frightened by her. Hair let down on a mature woman was closely associated in their minds with the pleasures of the bed. Mary Magdalene's flesh half-glimpsed beneath flowing hair was the ambiguous and disturbing picture they absorbed of her. And this is the image that has been passed down in the sensual portraits by Titian and other artists to form the impression we still have of her.

Her story was all about Luxury, a concept linked with Lust and Lechery. Eve was already known as a figure of Lust and Lechery, unable to tame her desire for pleasure. And Mary Magdalene soon joined the ranks of libidinous desire made manifest. In the frantically misogynistic climate of the Middle Ages, the literary images of Luxury, Lust and Lechery were all inevitably personified as blonde women. Taddeo di Bartolo's 1396 fresco of *Hell* at San Gimignano depicts 'Lussuria' in a state of abandon. Her golden hair is entwined in the serpent tail of the Devil, while another devil blows flames over her, and yet another tickles her suggestively with its serpent-headed tail.

Bromyard, the Dominican preacher from Hereford, was a regular denouncer of the dangerously attractive Mary Magdalene. She appears in his preaching anthology as Luxuria, the personification of all filth relating to sensual desire and forbidden pleasures. Fornication was the typical feminine crime, he believed, and the weapon of temptation was her beauty. 'A beautiful woman is a temple built over a sewer,' he declared, warning the men in his congregation that to look at a woman was unsafe and that to overcome thoughts of them he should close his eyes and occupy his mind with holy thoughts. Beauty, the Devil's instrument, he said, attacks through the female glories, primarily her hair; and those who dye their hair blonde do so with sexual motives in mind. The Dominican friar Thomas Cantimpre ranted against the vanities of women spending hours tending their hair in imitation of the seductive Mary Magdalene. They washed, combed and coloured it, he claimed, in order to 'consume and madden with their manes'. For good measure, he added the revolting reflection that these coiffures and complex headdresses of bought hair were a haven for worms and lice and their eggs. His words echoed the warnings of Gilles d'Orléans, a contemporary of Bromyard's preaching in Paris, who regularly reminded his parishioners that the fashionable blonde wigs they wore were likely to be made from the hair of those now enduring hell or purgatory. It is not known how much hair was pillaged from the graves of female corpses for the purpose of wigmaking, but for many hundreds of years such accusations formed the ammunition of moralists.

It is not altogether surprising that women were attempting to imitate Mary Magdalene's hair, because they certainly had ample evidence of its powers. It was the very glories of that magnificent head of hair, so feared by the men of the Church, that she used alternately to seduce and then to repent her sinful past. That golden curtain which she had tended and dressed to lure young men, she then gathered up and humbly used to dry

Christ's feet. In the late fourteenth-century *Livre de la Passion*, now in the Vatican Library, Mary Magdalene is depicted cutting off her offending hair beneath the caption '*Marie Magdaleine coppe ses cheveux et offrit contrition*'.

So blonde hair offered the unemancipated woman of the Middle Ages an unexpectedly powerful tool of influence. Many clearly did indulge in dyeing their hair. Had they not, the regular thunder-claps of clerical exhortations would not have been necessary. The tide of rhetoric ebbed and flowed and, over the course of hundreds of years, generations of churchmen made spirited and imaginative attempts to frighten women away from the practice. The blonde Whore of Babylon was a favourite example repeatedly cited as a demon of exceptional malignancy. She appears in one of her early and most lavish representations in *Hortus deliciarum*, a magnificent illuminated manuscript of the late twelfth century, dressed in her finery, her long blonde hair hanging loose down her back. As the embodiment of luxury, vice, tyranny and all abominations and filthiness, she meets her fate in the colourfully licking flames of purgatory. She is an example to all women of what lies in wait for those who dress themselves in finery and incite with the treacheries of golden hair. Many books of manners for ladies were written, circulated and read out for the instruction of illiterate women, condemning such vain and evil behaviour and threatening divine punishment.

But the wrath of God proved to be a poor deterrent. Wealthy and leisured women stashed away elaborate collections of cosmetics and beauty aids with which they committed their vain and evil crimes. The privileged visitor to a lady's private room would have picked her way through semi-darkness into a small private pleasure dome scattered with little tables and chests overflowing with a glinting treasury of the tools of beautification. Through the gloom, she might have seen a chaos of curling irons and small hand-mirrors, smoky with age, stacked against boxes full of delicate tweezers, crusty toothbrushes and evil-looking razors. An ear-picker made of ivory or bone might have been visible, as well as wooden toothpicks and even tongue-scrapers for the most fastidious in their personal hygiene. That was the hardware. Then came the software: perhaps a maze of little boxes of billowing white powders for the forehead and nose, rouge for the cheeks and wheat powder for night-time use on the face and neck. Stacked in rows at the back were bottles filled with various preparations for the hair which were mixed weekly in a large copper bowl. The medieval lady washed her hair in 'lye', a mixture of wood ash and water. Soap compounds of beechwood ash and goat tallow could be mixed in to give the hair a 'saffron' blonde colour. And sometimes they added – more in the spirit of hope than of science – a dash of wine to strengthen the dyes and add shine. *L'Ornement des dames* of the thirteenth century gives a range of recipes for curing falling hair and five for dyeing it blonde. One requires 'henbane and orpiment [yellow arsenic]'. Another popular hair-bleaching recipe, which must have been effective as it was passed down through the generations into the Elizabethan period, required the creation of a kind of voodoo salad: 'a quart of lye prepared from the ashes of vine-twigs, briony, celandine-roots, and turmeric, of each half an ounce; saffron and lily-roots, of each two drachms; flowers of mullein, yellow stechas, broom and St John's Wort, of each a drachm'.

Given the struggle to obtain the ingredients, mix the cocktails, and then soak the hair for hours in the putrid results, it seems unlikely that all married and mature women would then have smothered their newly coloured hair with veils. In church, women always covered their heads as the norm: monks from mute orders used to pass a hand over the head in imitation of a veil to indicate the word for 'woman'. But only the most pious and most God-fearing women would actually have veiled themselves at all times. Fewer still followed clerical instructions to carry tweezers around with them to pluck offensive hairs detected sprouting at the edge of the veil or the back of the neck.

Women who did go to the considerable extent of blonding their hair must have been delighted to discover that their lives were enriched by an unexpected range of powers. Supernatural fantasies, the medieval equivalent of our urban myths, were frequently linked to the blonde. These fantasies, which were of course energetically condemned by the Church, took a specific form in which the female 'victim' was visited in the night by a highly charged sexual supernatural being, known as an 'incubus'. Chaucer wrote about the phenomenon, noting mischievously that incubi had been much less heard of since bands of wandering friars had appeared on the scene. Like travelling salesmen in the 1960s, these happily nomadic friars had the reputation for leaping in most ungodly fashion into bed with married women when their husbands were away. The Church could not of course recognise such behaviour among its own and was forced to accept the reality of these supernatural beings, claiming that they were devils in human shape. By the time Saint Thomas Aquinas picked up on the issue, ranting at length against these demons, it was considered heresy not to believe in their reality.

The belief began to circulate that women with blonde hair were more frequently visited by incubi. In *Discoverie of Witch-craft*, a history of witchcraft written in the sixteenth century, the medieval period is characterised by the view that blondes, while perhaps more wicked, definitely had a great deal more fun. Under the heading 'Bishop Sylvanus, his lecherie opened and covered again, how maides having yellow hair are most combred with Incubus', the story is told of how an incubus once came to a lady's bedside and made 'hot loove unto hir'. The blonde lady cried out loudly during this exchange and the company came and found the incubus hiding under her bed in the likeness of Bishop Sylvanus. The belief in the supernatural attractions of blonde hair was still alive in 1650, when John Bulwer, in his book *The Artificial Changeling*, quoted a saying of St Paul: 'A woman ought to have her head covered because of the Angels.' 'This some have understood of the evil Angels,' Bulwer explained, 'whose lust they thought was vehemently provoked and inflam'd by the beauty of womens hairs: and hence your incubi are more troublesome and prone to vex women who have a fair head of hair.' The myth of the incubi is likely to have both fuelled demand for hair dyes and spurred the Church to even greater hysteria in its condemnation of the outrageous sexiness of blonde hair. Ironically, the Church itself was developing an entirely different symbolism and vocabulary for blonde hair which would cast a new and lasting spell over mankind.

4

IS SHE NOT PURE GOLD?

B LONDE HAIR and sexual attraction were unmistakably entwined. Aphrodite and then Venus had set the parameters of beauty and sexuality in the ancient world. Eve and then Mary Magdalene had added a new and intoxicating flavour of wickedness to the brew, playing the role of iconic bad girls whose behaviour sparked cults of defiant imitation and worship. Yet in spite of the apparent runaway power of blonde hair as a sexual signal, the medieval Church did eventually find itself in possession of one supremely powerful blonde paragon, an opposing examplar whose hair signalled exquisite purity and whose presence and behaviour were beyond suspicion. If Eve and Mary Magdalene were archetypes of blonde vice, the Blessed Virgin Mary, Mother of God and Queen of Heaven, once unveiled in the late fourteenth century, was a pillar of blonde virtue.

Unlike wanton women and all their daughters on earth who invoked damnation and death, Mary was an agent of redemption who blessed mankind with salvation and eternal life. Mary was in all ways perfect. One of her many distinguishing characteristics was her freedom from carnal desire. Not only had she been conceived immaculately by divine intervention, but her purity had been preserved by the miraculous birth of Jesus Christ. The Virgin Mary was everything that Mary

Magdalene was not. She was sacred and sinless. She was modest and humble. She did not seek to inflame men with fripperies and fashions. In contrast to Eve and Mary Magdalene who had brazenly flowing blonde locks, the Virgin Mary wore a modest veil in most of her early devotional images. Gilles d'Orléans, fulminating from the pulpit in 1350s Paris, had already made it clear that the Virgin Mary, a woman of chastity, would never have considered wearing silk belts and jewellery and dyeing or displaying her hair in the way that fashionable women did in his parish. To emphasise her admirable innocence of the sins of fashion, some painters depicted her with brown hair.

But the Blessed Virgin Mary was eventually to succumb to the powers of blonde hair and emerge in dazzling capillary raiment of an entirely new sort. The change came at the end of the fourteenth century, when the graphic revelations of the Swedish visionary Saint Bridget swept medieval Europe and began to influence visual portrayals of the Virgin. Saint Bridget, born in Sweden in 1303, was the founder of the Bridgettine order and spent most of her adult life in Italy, touring shrines, looking after the poor and working among them the sort of inexplicable cures essential for posthumous canonisation. During her lifetime she was already widely known for her visions, which were written down in Swedish and translated into Latin. But as the Bridgettine cult grew, copies of her revelations were translated into most European languages (about 150 Latin manuscripts still exist in libraries around the world and there are numerous records of translations of the book in fifteenth-century wills). Within a few decades of her death in 1373, the revelations had became a standard part of works of devotion. Saint Bridget was canonised in 1391 for her virtues, for her work as a foundress, her services to the poor and the sick and her devotion to helping pilgrims. But it was her visions that had caught the public imagination. Of these the most pictorially vivid were those of the Virgin Mary, long hymns in praise of her beauty, specifying long blonde hair, bright like sunshine, falling freely over her shoulders.

Her vision of the Nativity in Bethlehem is recognised as her most important because of its striking departure from mainstream representations of the scene. The Latin original gives a long and detailed description:

> I beheld a virgin of extreme beauty . . . well wrapped in a white mantle and a delicate tunic, through which I clearly perceived her virgin body . . . With her was an old man of great honesty, and they brought with them an ox and an ass . . . Then the virgin pulled off the shoes from her feet, drew off the white mantle that enveloped her, removed the veil from her head, laying it by her side, thus remaining in her tunic alone with her beautiful golden hair falling loosely down her shoulders . . .

The vision continues with a description of Mary kneeling down as if praying at the moment of the birth, rather than in the traditional lying posture shown in portrayals up to then. Art historians have argued that Saint Bridget's visions revolutionised depictions of the Nativity in Christian iconography. From this point on, beginning in Italian art and spreading to all European art, the stable scene with the Virgin lying on a bed was often replaced by the scene outside the stable door, with the Virgin kneeling and worshipping the newborn baby. Saint Bridget's striking vision of flowing blonde hair was also adopted by artists and influenced some of the most transcendently beautiful fifteenth- and sixteenth-century paintings of the Virgin.

It was owing to the newly blonde Virgin Mary of the late fourteenth century and her accompanying pantheons of sinless angels that blonde hair began to acquire a powerful new symbolism. On the Virgin it became the ultimate manifestation of pure, superior beauty. The exquisite blonde virgin and her blonde angels were the celestial messengers of God. As such they stood high above the ranks of ordinary mortals. They were there for legitimate worship.

Few perhaps made the comparison at the time, but the symbolic purity of the Virgin Mary's colouring provided the first evidence of the dichotomy in blondeness that was to plague and intrigue men and women for hundreds of years to come. With the unveiling of the Virgin, blonde hair was shown to possess a dangerous ambivalence. It could signify immaculate, innocent and uncorruptible beauty – no one could better the Virgin Mary in divine beauty, or it could signal the greedily manipulative desire to seduce, manifest in such wily operators as Eve and Mary Magdalene. Context was essential for judgment and the clues were generally pretty clear. Both types of blonde are shown in the 1410 image *Virgin and Child Enthroned with Angels and Saints*, painted by the Master of the Straus Madonna. Eve, dressed in a diaphanous shawl, lies at the feet of the enthroned and magnificently aloof Virgin. Eve's blonde hair tumbles luxuriantly over her shoulders, pointing suggestively down towards her breasts. The Virgin Mary's is more modest and partially veiled, though no less splendidly blonde. The differing symbolism of the two blondes is abundantly clear in this picture, but it has not always been so. In the centuries to come, blondes of all sorts were to learn to manipulate this ambivalence to their advantage.

The aesthetic passion for blonde hair at this time, whether honey- or amber-coloured, golden or saffron, was linked to the contemporary love of light and colour. This was a spontaneous response to beauty, pure and simple, which was expressed in the paintings, miniatures, frescos, literature and poetry of the period. The fifteenth-century poet Olivier de la Marche wallowed in erotic fantasy as he marvelled at the beauty of sunlight on golden hair. And Baldwin of Canterbury wrote at length on the aesthetic appeal, the exceptional succulence, of gleaming plaits. The delight in bright colours as an expression of beauty was linked with the brilliance of light, and both were seen at their most dazzling in the stained glasswork of Gothic cathedrals. Ordinary people of the period were enthralled by brightness and luminosity, by the brilliance of daylight, sunshine and fire. They often formed a conception of God in terms of ecstasies of beauty which appeared as shining golden light. Church illumination and imagery were designed to lift humble spirits, to leaven the dull lives of ordinary people and make them bearable with the dream of another world. The effect was much like that of the movies. The medieval Church's gleaming blondes were an early incarnation of the iconic blonde goddesses waiting to slink out on to the movie screens of 1930s Hollywood.

For medieval artists, therefore, the colour gold, according to the standard iconography of the day, came to signify a sacred realm.* They painted religious figures against gold backdrops

---

* Being the most expensive colour available, it was the obvious choice to honour God and other heavenly figures.

and with a variant of the same colour for the often luxuriant hair wreathed around their faces. Contemporary artistic thought held that faces would radiate light when set against the intense gold of the hair and background. Competing theories of optics were raging at the time, and many artists were convinced that an abstract gold frame would also sharpen the contours of a form and make it appear almost tangible. It was recognised that the power of the painted golden aura and its effects on the common people were considerable. To those churchmen in the business of inspiring awe, they were clearly worth analysing and harnessing.

Highlighting the Virgin Mary's symbolically immaculate blondeness were hosts of angels, the spiritual messengers of God, who were always blonde. Angels were sexless and therefore sinless, and were depicted as innocent young beauties. Hundreds of thousands of blonde angels emerged from the brushes of medieval painters. Some of them, such as those painted by Fra Angelico, were creatures of exquisite grace. The eleven angels in the famous Wilton Diptych, painted by an unknown artist around 1395, are celestial beings of sublime beauty, blessed with curling pale gold ringlets of hair held in place beneath crowns of blue and white flowers.

The concept of the angel was hugely popular in the Middle Ages. Sometime during the thirteenth century, the heavenly host had been totted up, after a fashion. It was found to number over three hundred million, prompting the eruption of a kind of angel fever. Angels were believed to govern not only the seven planets, the four seasons, the months of the year and the days of the week, but also the hours of the day and night. The fact also, according to biblical lore, that every blade of grass had its own personal guardian angel urging it to grow meant there was a teeming proliferation of blondes up in heaven.

The Archangel Gabriel was almost universally depicted as a dazzling blond. Stefan Lochner's Annunciation, on the closed panels of his *Adoration of the Magi* of 1445, shows a glistening blond Angel Gabriel bringing news to an equally radiant Mary, their long waving golden hair symbolic of their purity and divinity.

In many cases the hair and haloes of these celestial beings were actually gilded. The gold was pounded and beaten into delicate wafer-thin leaves so fine that they would fly away and crumple to virtually nothing in the slightest breeze. The leaves were applied to an image with great difficulty and smoothed on millimetre by millimetre, finally held in place with a fixative. The fascination with the lustre of blonde hair derived some of its power at this time from the contemporary obsession with gold, the metal of ultimate desire. The similarities were considerable. Gold, like hair, is supremely malleable. It can be heated and stretched, hammered, baked, sizzled and crimped, and still it never dulls. Resisting corrosion and oxidation, gold never loses its luminous glow. One gram of gold can be drawn into wire almost three kilometres long; and according to Pliny, an ounce of gold can be pounded into 750 fine leaves, each four inches square. Gold's fiery power lay, it was believed, in its purity, just as the Virgin Mary's power lay in her purity and, in ancient times, Aphrodite's power lay in her golden purity, which was free, as Sappho tells us, from pollution.

Abbess Hildegard of Bingen, the Benedictine nun, mystic and preacher, had written at length in the twelfth century about the powers and curative properties of gold. She raised its spiritual and aesthetic appeal for the many ordinary men and women who knew of her visions and teachings through anthologised snippets. Gold, she wrote in her medical treatise *Physica*, is hot and its nature is like the sun's. Anyone suffering from 'virgichtiget' (arthritis?) should reduce a piece of gold to a powder, knead it with flour and water into a cake and cook it for eating before breakfast. Even the deaf, she claimed, could be cured with gold: 'prepare a paste with gold dust and fine flour, and stick a little of it in the ears. The heat will pass into the ear and if he does this often he will recover his hearing' – either that or his ears will be fatally and expensively blocked.

As a celebrated prophet, famed for her denunciations of bishops and emperors, Hildegard was one of history's great autodidacts. She hoovered up everything she could lay her hands on, from biblical commentaries to translations of Arabic medical writers borrowed from her monastic friends. She made forays into medicine, poetry, music and astronomy, but was probably most famous for her visions in which she witnessed golden light as the original metaphor for spiritual reality. Images painted to spread the news of her visions often showed figures associated with the Church as golden blondes.

Hildegard's own hair colour has been obscured by the passage of time and by the ecclesiastical wimple. But one of the earliest surviving images of her unveiled is in a copy of an 1175 book of her visions. A figure thought to be Hildegard herself is seen dressed in dark red with long flowing blonde hair, surrounded by eight blonde virgins. A hand-coloured lithograph of Hildegard made in 1493 in Nuremberg (admittedly three hundred years after her death) shows a young figure dressed in the robes of the convent holding a reed, with her long and abundant golden yellow hair tumbling down over her shoulders.

Whatever its true colour, Hildegard's hair had its own special curative properties. As a mystic to whom crowds flocked from all over France and Germany for blessings, Hildegard gained a reputation as something of a miracle worker. The monk Theodoric of Echternach, the final editor of Hildegard's memoir, *Vita*, explained in the text that when a small lock of her hair was applied to any of the sick, they were restored to their former health. The wife of the mayor of Bingen, for example, suffering in childbirth, was given a plait of Hildegard's hair to gird round her naked waist. 'When this was done, she happily went forward with the birth, and was freed from death'. And he reports that Henry, a canon of Bingen, said on oath that when he applied hairs of the blessed Hildegard to two sick women, they were immediately set free from the demons. During the years that she was touring the country as a celebrated mystic, much miracle-working and many sudden healings and unexplained feats were performed with the help of Hildegard's hair.

There were, then, ample reasons why the people of medieval northern Europe should have been particularly aware of blonde hair. It denoted, they were frequently told, lust and lechery, weakness and sloth, and was associated with all the sins of the world. It was also considered to be something special, powerful, sacred and almost supernatural, and in the case of women, the crowning evidence of pure beauty. In addition, it had created a currency for itself as a desirable property, particularly in the East Mediterranean and Arab world, where its rarity guaranteed its demand. The Crusades had played a part in the commercialisation of blonde hair, generating a brisk trade in the Middle East for European women of loose morals and keen business noses. Thousands of them travelled out to Muslim countries to follow and sustain the fighting men of Europe. A colourful account survives from Imad ad-Din, a twelfth-century Arab historian, of a shipload of western European prostitutes arriving to service the Crusaders:

> There arrived by ship three hundred lovely Frankish women, full of youth and beauty, assembled from beyond the sea and offering themselves for sin. They were expatriates come to help expatriates, ready to cheer the fallen and sustained in turn to give support and assistance, and they glowed with ardour for carnal inter-course. They were all licentious harlots, proud and scorn-ful, who took and gave, foul-fleshed and sinful, singers and coquettes, appearing proudly in public, ardent and inflamed, tinted and painted . . . selling themselves for gold, bold and ardent, loving and passionate, pink-faced and unblushing . . . blue-eyed and grey-eyed, broken-down little fools.

These pale-skinned and probably tinted blonde north-ern European women, known generically to the Arabs and Byzantines as Franks, stood out dramatically among the dark-skinned and black-headed crowds of the Arab world, height-ening their appeal and no doubt raising their prices.

Europe had not been free of trafficking in women either. Horse-dealers and other rough nomadic traders who lived on the fringes of organised society had long pursued a sideline during the early Middle Ages, arranging for the sale of young blonde women to eastern Europe and beyond. The blonder the hair the higher the prices paid. A Spanish Jew, Ibrahim ibn Jaqub, who had converted to Islam, left a report of his late-tenth-century travels through Bohemia, central Europe and the Baltic region, demonstrating that one of the objects of his journey was to purchase blonde prisoners who had been captured by the Baltic tribes in battle with the Germans. Such reports are difficult to verify, as non-believers were often accused by the Christian fathers of trafficking in women, and the finger was typically pointed at Arab merchants as the buyers at the end of the line.

The power and appeal of the blonde, both as spiritually immaculate beauty and as sexually attractive demon, had not merely survived throughout the Middle Ages. It had been positively augmented, on the one hand by the divine magnetism of the Virgin Mary and on the other by several hundred years of misogynistic ranting from the men of the Christian Church.

But one more monumental fantasy blonde emerged in the Middle Ages that would have a profound effect on the sensibilities of the educated, vividly and enduringly colouring the arts, literature and poetry of centuries to come. The cult of chivalry, which developed in the late twelfth century, celebrated, among other things, the worship of the aristocratic lady after generations of female suppression. Chivalry and courtly love made use of romance to cover up women's assumed inferiority, and, for the first time in centuries, great ladies became the beneficiaries of romantic literature and art. Women were placed on a pedestal and celebrated for their beauty. The chivalric ideal codified the worship of a beautiful lady as being close to that of God, and upper-class ladies became the source of all romance and the object of all worship. For them all deeds of valour were performed. They had but to command to be obeyed.

Blonde hair became part of a standardised code for earthly feminine beauty and romance in literature. Gallant knights, poets and troubadours began celebrating their love of blondes with much eager serenading. Felicitious poems and romantic tales bursting with golden-haired heroines poured from the pens of passionate lovers. Blonde hair was soon, to the enduring fury of the Church, officially adored on temporal beauties.*

Meanwhile, bands of wandering troubadours roamed the countryside in quest of amorous adventures, initially in Provence and later, as the tradition spread, all across Europe. They worked in the households of powerful lords, whose wives and daughters they professed to love. Gallantly they served these ladies' every wish. The troubadours were often the younger sons of aristocratic families who had been denied arranged marriages in order to avoid the carving-up of family landholdings. They pledged themselves to the beautiful ladies of their lords' households, playing elaborate games of flirtation and coquetry and often indulging in semi-sanctioned affairs. And many of them set down their longings in sensual lyrical poetry, elaborately praising the objects of their passion, but usually gallantly obscuring their identities. Arnaud Daniel, a poet from Périgord, writing in the twelfth century, pined somewhat mournfully for the object of his idealised blonde passion.

* Some historians believe that the Church, unable to suppress this flourishing courtly love movement, eventually appropriated its imagery, including its worship of blonde hair, and incorporated it into the cult of the Virgin as a way of attracting and sustaining allegiance.

> Thousand masses I've attended
> Lights of wax and oil I'm burning,
> That God may to pity move
> Her 'gainst whom I can't protect me,
> When I see her golden tresses
> And her figure fair and slim,
> Nought on earth so much I treasure.

And this German love song of the thirteenth century eulogises long pale-gold hair as an essential element of feminine beauty.

> Where did ever mortal eye
> See two lovelier cheeks displayed?
> Lily-white, without a lie,
> Sweetly, featly are they made.
> Long and pale and gold's her hair.
> If hers and mine the whole realm were,
> I would give no one else a share!

Romance novels and long lyric poems of courtly love offered escapist fantasy to the upper classes (those noblemen and ladies who could not read heard public narrations) and often wove the seductively beautiful blonde into their pages as heroine. She appeared as Iseult in the twelfth-century tale of Tristan and Iseult, a blonde 'Queen of the Hair of Gold' whose appeal was so enduring that she reappeared centuries later as Isolde in Wagner's opera. Iseult was an exemplary figure of femininity, the most beautiful woman 'from here to the Spanish marches'. Her face was radiant, she had clear eyes and above all she was crowned with that key romantic asset, tumbling golden hair. Sewn into his jacket as a talisman, a lock of her hair inspired Tristan to undertake perilous voyages and do battle with terrible fiery dragons in order to reach her.

Chrétien de Troyes, one of the acknowledged masters of courtly love and romance tales, made regular use of blonde hair as an essential element in his Arthurian romances of the late twelfth century: *Erec and Enide*, *Cligés*, *Yvain and Lancelot* and *Perceval*. Naturally, Guinevere was a blonde whose hair was kept in lockets close to the hearts of her many admirers. In one of the stories, Lancelot on his travels comes across a comb of gilded ivory forgotten by the road. In it is tangled a handful of golden hair. When told that the comb and the hair belong to Queen Guinevere, Lancelot falls into a swoon. The text of de Troyes' story descends likewise into a state of blonde dementia:

> Never will the eye of man see anything (sic) receive such honour as when he begins to adore these tresses. A hundred thousand times he raises them to his eyes and mouth, to his forehead and face: he manifests his joy in every way, considering himself rich and happy now. He lays them in his bosom near his heart, between the shirt and the flesh. He would not exchange them for a cartload of emeralds and carbuncles, nor does he think that any sore or illness can afflict him now; he holds in contempt essence of pearl, treacle and the cure for pleurisy; even for St Martin and St James he has no need; for he has such confidence in this hair that he requires no other aid. But what was this hair like? If I tell the truth about it, you will think I am a mad teller of

lies. When the mart is full at the yearly fair of St Denis, and when the goods are most abundantly displayed, even then the knight would not take all this wealth, unless he had found these tresses, too. And if you wish to know the truth, gold a hundred thousand times refined, and melted down as many times, would be darker than is night compared with the brightest summer day we have had this year, if one were to see the gold and set it beside this hair.

Another of Chrétien's Arthurian romances, *Cligés*, also glorifies the blonde hair of a sumptuously beautiful damsel by the name of Soredamors. She sews a few strands of her hair into the white silk shirt given to her manly hero, Alexander. When the queen reveals the truth about Soredamors and the shirt, he

can hardly restrain himself for joy from worshipping and adoring the golden hair. His companions and the Queen, who were with him, annoy him and embarrass him; for their presence prevents him from raising the hair to his eyes and mouth, as he would fain have done, had he not thought that it would be remarked. He is glad to have so much of his lady, but he does not hope or expect ever to receive more from her: his very desire makes him dubious. Yet, when he has left the Queen and is by himself, he kisses it more than a hundred thousand times, feeling how fortunate he is. All night long he makes much of it, but is careful that no one shall see him. As he lies upon his bed, he finds a vain delight and solace in what can give him no satisfaction. All night he presses the shirt in his arms, and when he looks at the golden hair, he feels like the lord of the whole wide world. Thus Love makes a fool of this sensible man, who finds his delight in a single hair and is in ecstasy over its possession.

The most famous romance of the Middle Ages was probably the *Roman de la Rose*, a long allegorical love poem written in the thirteenth century by two poets, Guillaume de Lorris and Jean de Meun. For nearly three hundred years after its composition it was one of the most widely read works of the French language. As French was the language of the English court, it became important in England, too. The blondes in the *Roman de la Rose* were fantasy images of love and seduction, linked in carefully crafted symbolism to Venus or to Eve. In their day they were the last word in raw blonde power.

Early in the story, the hero meets a beautiful girl who guards a charming but inaccessible garden. She has 'hair as blonde as a copper basin, flesh more tender than that of a baby chick, a gleaming forehead and arched eyebrows'. In more reams of ecstatic praise he attempts to do justice to her large grey-blue eyes, her straight nose, her sweet breath, dimpled chin, snowy bosom and so on. On her head she wears a chaplet of roses, an emblem of a follower of Venus. In her hand she holds a mirror and comb, the traditional attributes of 'luxuria'. 'By the time she has combed her hair carefully and prepared and adorned herself well, she has finished her day's work . . . 'I am called Idleness,' she said, 'by people who know me. I am a rich and powerful lady, and I have a very good time, for I have no other purpose than to enjoy myself and make myself comfortable, to comb and braid my hair.' Soon Idleness lets him into the garden. 'Believe me, I thought that I was truly in the earthly paradise,' he says. Later he meets Joy, another paragon of beauty. 'Her forehead, white and gleaming, was free of wrinkles, her eyebrows brown and arched, her gay eyes so joyful that they always laughed regularly before her little mouth did . . . Her head was blonde and shining. Why should I go on telling you? She was beautiful and beautifully adorned.'

By the end of the story, the hero is regretting his infatuation with blondes. 'He who acquaints himself with Idleness is a fool; acquaintance with her is very dangerous, for she has betrayed and deceived you. Love would never have seen you if Idleness had not led you into the fair garden of Diversion.' The end of this long poem poses the familiar theory that women use their beauty to trap men. If she does not possess seductive blonde hair, it says, she finds some false hair, either of blonde silk or '*cheveus de quelque fame morte*'. And with this she weaves her spells.

These popular tales, poems and songs glorifying blondes – some of them innocent, some dangerous, all attractive – lingered on throughout the Middle Ages and became important reminders of what it meant to be human. The polished Virgin Mary and the tarnished Eve were the superstars at the two extremes of sacred myth. But the gorgeous objects of courtly love were often based on real figures of flesh and blood, worshippable – even imitable – women whose enchantment was to extend the boundaries of blonde influence into some surprising new territory.

5

THE CARDINAL AND
THE BLONDE BORGIA

I N ITS heyday in the fifteenth and sixteenth centuries, Venice was a city more splendid, more glamorous and more powerful than any other in Europe. It was the New York of its time, boiling with prosperity and immense cultural energy. By 1500 the Venetian Empire had sovereignty over Istria, most of the Dalmatian coast and its offshore islands, Cephalonia, Negroponte, the Aegean Islands, Crete and Cyprus, as well as the Italian mainland stretching from Friuli in the east to Cremona in the west. Venice's powerful fleets sailed home with exotic cargoes of treasure, gold, precious stones and sacred relics. It had the most cosmopolitan population in Europe and a prolific bounty of trade: the Venetian lagoon had become the principal emporium linking East and West. In its cornucopia of stores the dedicated shopper could buy a dazzling selection of opulent silks, spices, jewels, porcelain, ebony and glassware of startling extravagance, as well as love potions, unusual cures for unusual conditions and everything required to fit out a ship. The Venetians' passion for public pomp was indulged to the full with pageants and festivals more sumptuous than any other in Europe. They gloried in their aristocracy, rejoiced in their arts and revelled in their bargaining finesse – from source to consumer they shamelessly milked all parties. The place was electrified with gossip, vanities, peccadilloes and transactions. Naturally, this brilliant city was a magnet for visitors. Pilgrims came; traders and tourists came. Poets, painters and patrons flocked. Thomas Coryate, a seventeenth-century visitor from Somerset, went into raptures, declaring that he would deny himself four of the richest manors in his county rather than go through life without seeing the city.

Splendid as Venice was, with its foreign treasures, its gleaming domes, its staggering panache and pageantry, one of its most famous attractions, as compelling a lure as any of these, was its women. They were reputed to be the most gorgeous in all Europe, and Venetian men prided themselves on their highly developed appreciation of feminine beauty.

Handsome women were everywhere, vain birds of paradise parading beautifully in their finery and displaying their attributes as glorious inspiration for Venice's cultured men of arts and letters. And they were duly worshipped in paintings, evoked in music and caressed and adored in poetry. A feeling of confidence and hope pervaded the work of the artists of Italy and they referred constantly to the glories of art and scholarship achieved in ancient Rome as they set out to create a new art after the turmoil of the Middle Ages. Venice's women provided artists with the raw material for a heady classical ideal of physical beauty. This beauty became a manifestation of divine perfection, its contemplation a route to a greater understanding of God.

In the Middle Ages, it was largely women of aristocratic houses who might have been worshipped for their beauty and wooed by chivalrous lovers with rarefied ballads. Now sensuality joined the cult of beauty and love, embracing even those women hitherto classed as outcasts by virtue of their wanton profession. By the late Renaissance Venice's courtesans had joined high-bred pure beauties on pedestals to be openly worshipped like saints or goddesses.

Venus was the goddess in vogue and it was she, with her blonde hair and her expanses of creamy rose-tinted flesh, who most strongly influenced the canon of female perfection in paintings, in poetry – and in practice. Natural blonde hair was occasionally seen in Venice at this time, but it was rare and typically came matched with dark eyes, olive skin and dark eyebrows. Most prized was the blonde hair and pale complexion of the fantasy beauties of the mythical past. Its rarity, combined with its centuries-old erotic status, made it the most envied goal of aspiring beauties.

The Italian Renaissance poets too were well versed in a knowledge of antiquity and in the romantic writings of the troubadour poets. They developed a language and style which reinforced the standards of feminine beauty set in earlier times, constantly appraising Venetian beauties in relation to the ravishing blondes of ancient Greece and Rome. Petrarch, who lived in Padua in the fourteenth century, set a towering blonde standard in the *Rime sparse*, a series of exquisite love poems written to immortalise his adored lost Laura. Although Petrarch's work was only one step removed from that of the troubadour poets, his '*dolce stil nuovo*' – his sweet new style – was characterised as a harbinger of the Renaissance and it certainly set the tone for the period. Passionate eulogies to Laura's blonde hair fill his poetry: lines like 'Those tresses of gold, which ought to make the sun go filled with envy', and 'Amid the locks of gold Love hid the noose with which he bound me'.

Pietro Bembo, a Renaissance cardinal born in Venice in

1470 who wrote one of the earliest Italian grammars, designed the typeface used in this book, and was widely known for his poetry, also paid amorous homage to the beauties of blonde hair. *Gli Asolani*, his treatise on the torments and joys of men's love for women, was published in 1505 and dedicated to his mistress, the blonde Lucrezia Borgia, Duchess of Ferrara.

> Never such a thief of love or one so fleet
> Left her footprint in the grasses;
> Never nymph so comely lifted leafy bough
> Or spread along the wind such golden tresses;
> Never decked her gracious limbs in airy vesture
> Lady so resplendent and seductive as
> This lovely foe of mine.

Popular history has painted Lucrezia Borgia as a fantastically wicked operator, accusing her of colluding in many of the crimes and excesses of the unsavoury Borgia family. She was born in 1480, daughter of the Spanish cardinal Rodrigo Borgia, who later became Pope Alexander VI, and his mistress Vannozza Catanei. She was a beautiful girl, blonde and fair-skinned with a captivating smile and an ample share of the family's love of display.

An image of Lucrezia aged about twelve, painted by Pinturicchio in his fresco *Dispute of St Catherine*, shows a ravishingly pretty girl with milky skin, large eyes, a rosebud mouth and streams of wavy golden hair. Some years later, a painting by Bartolomeo Veneto, thought by some art historians to be of Lucrezia, shows a delicate almost ethereal creature with the face of a madonna looking suggestively towards the viewer.

Her white skin is like alabaster, her lips rosy, her eyes dark, her exposed breast as round and pert as an apple. In her slim fingers she holds a posy of daisies, anemones and ranunculi, and perched on top of her head is a white headdress crowned with a wreath of myrtle. But it is her hair that is the most striking feature of the image, tumbling down over her shoulders in tight snaky ringlets of metallic gold. To the modern viewer she looks as if she has just had a disastrous perm.

As a child, Lucrezia was the little idol of the Vatican. But not for long. She grew up in the company of two phenomenally powerful men: her father, described approvingly by Machiavelli as a man who 'never did or thought of anything but deceiving people', and Cesare Borgia, her supremely ambitious elder brother. Less an active participant in the crimes of these men than a useful pawn, Lucrezia was betrothed to five men and married to three of them in the space of ten years, all in accordance with the political and dynastic ambitions of the men who controlled her family.

Betrothal to two Spanish nobles was followed by two marriages in swift succession, first to Giovanni Sforza, Lord of Pésaro, and then to Alfonso, Duke of Bisceglie. In 1500 Lucrezia, still aged only twenty, watched her second husband strangled in their apartment despite her frantic efforts to save him. Within months another politically expedient Alfonso had been selected for her. This time it was Alfonso d'Este, eldest son of the Duke of Ferrara ruler of one of the most glittering courts in Italy. This third marriage took place in February 1502 after a spectacular month-long journey to Ferrara by way of the Borgias' newly conquered territories, carefully stage-managed by Alexander and Cesare. Lucrezia was accompanied by a thousand-strong entourage of Roman and Spanish gentlemen, ambassadors, prelates, men-at-arms, servants, craftsmen, cooks, entertainers, ladies-in-waiting and 150 mules carrying her trousseau. Amid this ant-like trail of travellers and associated hangers-on, Lucrezia would have stood out in her spectacular trailing cloak of crimson silk and ermine and a plumed hat, her long blonde hair streaming down her back.

The journey required constant stops for the cavalcade to rest and for the bride to attend to her appearance. A few days out of Ferrara, Lucrezia ordered a rest-stop in Pesaro, where she was met by local noblewomen and led into a private apartment. For the whole of the following day, while some of her ladies-in-waiting danced with the people of Pesaro, Lucrezia locked herself inside the apartment to wash her hair and renew her blonde tints. Reading between the blurred lines of history, we can imagine her maids quickly mixing potent-smelling marinades of celandine roots, cumin oil, box shavings and saffron, and the young bride shedding her rich travelling garments, washing her hair in a basin and then having it anointed with the resultant sludge. For twenty-four hours she sat quietly resting while it dried and fixed the colour. Finally it was then washed off with an evil-smelling lye of cabbage stalks and ashes of rye straw.

A few days later, for what must have been one of the great and glittering pageants of the century, the bride arrived in Ferrara on a pale grey stallion. She rode beneath a canopy of crimson satin followed by her entourage. Her gown was of mulberry velvet striped with gold, topped with a mantle of cloth of gold and lined with ermine. Over her glittering blonde hair she wore a jewelled cap. Niccolò Cagnolo of Parma described Lucrezia at this time: 'She is of medium height and slender build; her face is oval, the nose is well formed; her hair is golden, her eyes tawny; the mouth is full and large with the whitest teeth; her throat is smooth and white yet becomingly full. She is all good humour and gaiety.' The time spent in cosmetic preparation had clearly paid off. The wedding was completed successfully, and the match lasted, untampered with by her scheming male relatives.

When Alexander VI died in 1503, Lucrezia ceased to play such an overtly political role for her family. She led a more normal life at the brilliant court of Ferrara, which was a centre for the arts and letters of the time. It was here that she met Cardinal Bembo, a leading member of the Ferrara circle of classical scholars. Bembo and Lucrezia carried on a long and ardently amorous correspondence during their secret affair. A collection of the letters and sonnets composed by the two of them has survived and is preserved today in the Ambrosiana Library in Milan. Lucrezia was clearly aware of the power of her long blonde hair and in July 1503 she sent him a lock. 'I rejoice,' Bembo wrote when he received it, 'that each day to increase my fire you cunningly devise some fresh incitement, such as that which encircled your glowing brow today.' One of Bembo's surviving sonnets hints that he had long coveted such a trophy.

> The glowing hair I love despite my plight,
> Since love abounds the more I feel the smart,
> Had slipped the snood which keeps the rarest part
> Of all the gold I crave locked out of sight;
> When (alas, past recall now from his flight)

Into that silken hoard straight winged my heart,
As might a fledgling to green laurel dart
Then go from bough to bough in his delight.
Whereat two hands lovely beyond compare
Gathering the loosened tresses to her nape
Entangled him within, and bound them taut.
Cry as I would, the voice that did escape
Lacked any strength, my blood had chilled for fear:
Therewith the heart was torn from me and caught.

Bembo preserved his prize inside a folded sheet of vellum wrapped around with four pink ribbons. Today the lock of hair is still displayed in the Ambrosiana Museum, like a holy relic, lodged between two sheets of glass in an elaborate 1920s pearl and malachite reliquary. But the romance of Lucrezia's hair has one more flourishing coda. In 1816 Byron visited the Ambrosiana and read the letters, which he declared 'the prettiest love letters in the world'. He became enchanted with and then obsessed by the lock of hair, which he described in a letter to a friend as 'more blonde than can be imagined'. He committed some of the letters to memory as he was not allowed to make copies and then, when the librarian was out of the room, he stole one long golden strand from that lock of hair, 'the prettiest and fairest imaginable'.

While the poets competed in their worship of blonde hair, so the Italian painters of the Renaissance developed their own artistic standards of beauty in accordance with the irresistible classical conventions set in antiquity. Sandro Botticelli, many of whose magical paintings of the human form were done under the patronage of the Medici family, produced dozens of images of female perfection. These ethereal goddesses are now considered to be among the most powerful manifestations of the Renaissance. The *Primavera*, *The Birth of Venus*, *Pallas and the Centaur*, *Mars and Venus* – all of these works depict women conforming to the standard beauty ideals of the time. The painting by the Botticelli workshop of Venus of about 1486, now in the Berlin Staatliche Museen, is one of the most stunning evocations ever made of the goddess of love. Venus stands on a simple grey plinth against a pure black background. She is naked except for her mass of luxuriant golden-blonde hair, which cascades down below her hips and is then lifted like a loose folding curtain to cover her genitals. Her body is a lush feast of creamy flesh, her face a picture of graceful and delicate beauty. But the eye is drawn again and again to the mass of flowing hair in which the powerful sexuality of this image lies. Botticelli's working of the hair is a piece of unapologetic virtuoso work displaying his total mastery of the form. Smooth sinuous locks flow softly in the wind. Tighter curls, vital with erotic energy, quiver beneath a delicately loaded paintbrush. Snakily braided plaits hang down to her breasts and long loose tresses descend with a sensuous shimmer over her shoulders, their curling golden ends catching the light at her elbow and above her knee and sparkling against the black background like twitching fireflies. The motifs of the hair were probably influenced by the architect Alberti's famous passage on hair in *Della pittura*: 'Let it wind itself into a coil as if desiring to knot itself and let it wave in the air like unto flames: let part weave itself among the rest like a snake, part grow to one side, part to the other . . .'

Botticelli set a stupendous visual standard of feminine beauty for the late fifteenth century. As well as creating some of the most evocative blonde goddesses ever painted, he was also commissioned to paint some of northern Italy's most powerful ladies, for whom appearances were of crucial importance. One of these was Caterina Sforza, a woman of high birth who used her augmented feminine beauty to disguise her unladylike ambitions in the political sphere. Caterina was born in 1462, the illegitimate daughter of Galeazzo Maria Sforza, later Duke of Milan, and his mistress. As a child she was a beautiful tomboy – her biographers note her pearly white teeth, her creamy skin, her blonde hair and blue eyes – and she was soon parcelled off into a politically expedient marriage, at the age of fifteen, to Girolamo Riario, nephew of the then Pope Sixtus IV. Boisterous childhood adventures soon evolved into genuine martial activities on behalf of her spouse, and by 1483 Caterina was busy defending her husband's territory of Forlì – an area stretching from Ravenna through the Romagna – from the Venetian threat. A painting of the early 1480s, attributed by some to Botticelli and thought to be of Caterina, shows her in profile gazing thoughtfully out of a window at an Arcadian landscape. Her dress is simple, her hands large and capable and her neck bullishly strong. Her face has all the classic features of the unisex early Renaissance Italian aristocrat: high-bridged nose with flaring nostrils, plump chin, full lower lip and large, determined eyes. But it is the hair that strikes the viewer most forcefully. Bunched into a fat and complicated wreath at the back, it is smooth on top and curled into a pattern of wormlike waves over the ear. And it is a stunning shade of white blonde, overtly bleached in contrast with her dark eyebrows. Her complexion is pale and fine, her hair the ultimate in Italian beauty. Both would have cost Caterina dear in terms of time and expense. Both were part of a deliberate statement.

When her husband died in 1488, murdered by the Orsini family, Caterina effectively became the ruler of Forlì. For the next twelve years she defended it against attempted incursions from neighbouring territories, papal claims and finally the arrival of the French. For her role as the beautiful, invincible virago, she cultivated a dual image, using whichever mask suited her situation to greater advantage. At times she presented herself as a rare warrior woman. Cruel and unforgiving, she developed a ghastly desire for revenge against the Orsini and arranged public executions, secret murders and eventually the grotesque public killing of the eighty-year-old Orsini patriarch, Andrea.

She also occasionally affected the timidity and modesty of a delicately pretty high-born lady, imbued with the sort of 'mere womanliness' expected of ladies of her age and background. In a letter to her uncle Ludovico Sforza, predicting the threat of a Venetian invasion of Marradi, she wrote: 'nobody believes me . . . being just a lady and timid, too'. She took great pains to develop and preserve a ladylike beauty and wrote a book around 1499 on her personal cosmetic secrets. *Experimenti* showed Caterina to be obsessed with her appearance: preparations of nettleseed, cinnabar, ivy leaves, saffron and sulphur were regularly applied to maintain the colour of her famously blonde hair and to help it grow down to her ankles. Other lotions, made from boiling fruits, eggshells and other ingredients, removed unwanted hair, and teeth were polished with burned rosemary stems and pulverised marble. Her eyes were bathed in rose-water, and special creamy concoctions were slathered daily on her milky-white breasts.

Naturally, such vanities did not augur well for Caterina. Soon after her book was written, she lost her territories of Forlì and Imola to the predatory Borgia family. Characteristically hungry for vengeance, she resorted to trickery and dispatched a series of lethal letters to the Borgia pope, Alexander VI, some of them impregnated with poison, others infected with the plague. But no Borgia was ever easily disposed of, and her plans failed. Caterina died in 1509. Her life had been wild, brave and tragic, the life of both a virago and a victim as well as a celebrated beauty who had gone to great lengths to make sure she fitted the model of feminine perfection as laid down in the poetic canons of the period.

Perfection in Caterina's day required the creation and maintenance of a head of blonde hair, and this was a fantastically expensive business in fifteenth-century Italy. Exotic ingredients for blonde hair dyes were hard to come by. Some recipes required powdered silver in the mix. Most needed quantities of saffron. So in an age when power and wealth were brandished in displays of conspicuous consumption (fashionable clothes made from costly brocades and silks, enormous banquets of expensive food and drink, palace receptions, tournaments, concert parties, theatrical evenings, masked balls and lavish gifts), blonde hair was one more sure way of displaying one's means.

As in previous centuries, the ecclesiastical authorities were of course violently opposed to the Italian delight in luxuries. By the end of the fifteenth century a series of targeted backlashes had attempted, without notable success, to banish such excess. The Patriarch of Venice Lorenzo Giustinian had already tried introducing sumptuary laws in 1437 outlawing fake blonde hair in the city as well as excessively sumptuous clothes for women. He had threatened excommunication for all who disobeyed. But on the whole, in spite of a magistracy set up to deal with the problem of display, these laws were feebly enforced and energetically flouted: perhaps native acumen recognised the value of conspicuous glamour and realised that beautiful women were a commercial asset to the city.

Some years after Giustinian's attempts, however, Florentines became aware of a Dominican preacher named Girolamo Savonarola, who furiously disapproved of feminine luxuries and vanities commanded an extraordinary following for his electric sermons, much like those of Saint Bernardino, who had toured northern Italy some years earlier. Savonarola never tired of warning those who attended his sermous that they could have no blessing from God and no abiding prosperity unless they repented their sins. And their sins were apparently multiple. Savonarola sent out spies who reported back in suitably shocked tones that the Italians gambled, read lascivious classical poetry, gazed at erotic paintings, and adorned themselves with rich clothes and vanities. What is more, they went shopping on holy days. His sermons must have been truly cataclysmic, for one of the writers employed to record them omitted large portions, being unable to continue for weeping. As men and women left his sermons they reportedly tore off their ornaments and gave them as offerings to God. From the pulpit of Santa Maria del Fiore, Florence's cathedral, Savonarola hurled down his denunciations of every form of inquity, and the vanities and luxuries disappeared from the streets and the homes of Florence. A kind of wholesale reformation of manners took place. Workmen, it is said, began to devote their leisure hours to reading the Bible. Men of business were inspired to return money they had unjustly acquired. Churches became crowded and the number of candidates for admission into the priesthood rocketed.

But not everyone agreed with Savonarola. His attempts to repress every kind of immorality with moral fervour were eventually to lead to his downfall. Convinced that vice should not be tolerated, he did battle with the Florentines prohibiting the balls and festivals so beloved of them. He drilled bands of children to scour the towns, knocking on the doors of the rich and demanding that all things of luxury and vanity be given up. Carnival masks, dresses, wigs of bleached hair, musical instruments, books containing indecent or immoral tales and pictures were to be handed over. In 1496 Savonarola arranged for a huge bonfire to be built in the Piazza della Signoria in Florence. The Bonfire of the Vanities, as this came to be known, was an eight-sided pyramid, 60 feet high by 240 feet wide. Each side had fifteen steps, on which was deposited all the evidence of self-indulgence, classified according to type. On one side were indecent dresses, on the second were pictures of the beauties of Florence, many of them provocatively blonde. On the third there were chessboards, dice and packs of cards; on the fourth were music, harps and lutes. The fifth side contained women's cosmetics and beauty aids: matted clumps of false bleached hair, piles of mirrors and jewellery. The sixth side was devoted to lascivious and provocative books written by the poets, including volumes of Petrarch and an entire collected edition of Boccaccio. The seventh side contained masks, beards and other carnival ornaments; and the eighth side was piled up with erotic sculptures in ivory and marble.

The spectacle could not have been better designed to rouse the Florentine masses, notoriously greedy for excitement. The piazza was teeming with people, buzzing with the religious frenzy of the occasion. Stoking the atmosphere were

Savonarola's teams of children, who were massed to one side, chanting religious songs. The tension was electric. Finally, at a given signal Savonarola's men lowered burning stakes to four corners of the pyramid and four huge tongues of livid flame leaped up into the sky, rising quickly to engulf the whole. A team of trumpeters blew a series of furious blasts, the bells of the Palazzo rang out and the crowd raised a deafening shout.

Some of the contemporary accounts of the bonfire, which was repeated a year later, are thought to be exaggerated. But reputable writers, including Giorgio Vasari and the poet Girolamo Benivieni, recorded the burning of lewd, vain and detestable things, some of them by their own makers, including Fra Bartolommeo, who was roused to throw his paintings of nudes on to the fire. In 1498, Savonarola himself was hunted down by a mob acting on instructions from the Pope. He was arrested, tortured, hanged and burned for defiance of the pope, false prophecy, false pride and other indiscretions.

6

FOUR BLOCKS OF CAVIARE
AND A
FEATHER BED

T HE TIDE of the Italian Renaissance was reaching its gilded height. The harsh austerities of Savonarola's canon had failed to take root in a culture still steeped in the sensuous pleasures of beauty and luxury. It was in such a climate in the first half of the sixteenth century that a new and daring master of painted beauty emerged, whose work was arguably to represent the Renaissance peak of Italian cultural power and influence. Titian was a man imbued with the glories of Venice, a lover of women, a connoisseur of all the subtle little hints in a woman's appearance that signalled the presence or absence of morality, virtue, rank and relationships. He was also obsessed with the colour, texture and aura of golden hair.

A lady's hair was an essential part of Renaissance Venice's coding system. Respectable married women of this period were expected to conceal their hair under a veil or net to keep erotic imaginings under control. Uncovered, free-flowing hair cast a potent sexual spell for the Italians. Rarely seen on mature women in public, it was connected with the bewitching fantasy sirens and the sensual goddesses of antiquity.

Titian's gallery of female subjects is filled with examples of the temptress. He painted these sensual beauties as mythological creatures, revelling in their blonde locks, the sign of their eroticism. Titian's blondes appear in all guises, repeatedly as Venus (he painted at least ten of them) and as Mary Magdalene, but also as Lucrezia, Diana, Flora, Violante and as anonymous 'ladies' variously at their toilet. Each one is portrayed as a vision of passive beauty and palpitating sexual delight. Titian's 1538 *Venus of Urbino*, for example, is a sleek and seductive goddess, a blatantly sexual created object whose loose golden hair, delicate coral mouth, soft pale thighs and directly inviting gaze are all designed to provoke erotic thoughts in the beholder. One of his depictions of Flora, which hangs in the Uffizi, is a siren half-undressed, her blonde hair tumbling down over her round white shoulders and in her hand a bunch of flowers. These are not innocent girls, chaste and modest and pure. These are knowing women, dressed as goddesses or saints, who are fully aware of their own ravishing appeal.

There was one female subject whom Titian invariably depicted with brown hair – the Virgin Mary. It may be that for Titian, living in the rich and cynical display-culture of High Renaissance Venice, blonde hair was so closely associated with sexuality, with artifice and manipulation, that he wished to emphasise the Virgin's immaculate innocence with her contrasting brown hair. In Titian's paintings, the Virgin Mary is untouchable in her perfection and is guarded from base male thoughts by her hair colour.

On the whole, though, Titian favoured blondes. But he was not painting them in isolation. Carpaccio's much admired painting of around 1495, *The Two Courtesans*, shows two defiantly blonded ladies sitting on their balcony amusing themselves with peacocks and dogs in the heat of the day while waiting for their men to return from a hunting expedition. Ruskin described it as 'the best picture in the world'. One of Palma Vecchio's loveliest images of a woman is his portrait, entitled simply *Blonde Woman*, now in Milan's Museo Poldi-Pezzoli. This uninhibited and intimate painting is lavishly coloured and textured. The subject's silken gown glimmers as it falls down from her right shoulder, its brocade edging elaborately patterned and quilted, her soft white undershirt voluminous in its pleats and folds. All this rich, high texture serves to accentuate and enhance the luminous milkiness of her exposed breasts and shoulders and of course the exquisite waves of her blonde hair. Over her shoulders cascades this flood of hair, shining, loose and free, the crowning glory of this overtly sensual painting.

There is little doubt that the mythological paintings of Titian and his contemporaries were regarded as explicitly erotic images. Titian himself would have agreed. In a letter to Philip II, he wrote that after the 'Danae where one could see everything from the front', he promised to send another painting, of Venus and Adonis, in which it would be possible to view 'just to vary things . . . the other side'. Ludovico Dolce, a friend and admirer of Titian's, wrote to Alessandro Contarini about the same *Venus and Adonis*:

> the miraculous shrewdness of that divine spirit [Titian] is also revealed that in her intimate parts we recognise the creases on the flesh caused by her seated position. Why, it can in truth be said that every stroke of the brush is one of those strokes that nature executes with its own hand . . . I swear to you, sir, that there is no man so keen in sight or judgement, that seeing does not believe

her alive; nor anyone made so cold by the years, or so hardened in his being who does not feel a warming, a softening, a stirring of the blood in his veins. It is a real marvel . . .

Among the powerful circles of well-connected men who viewed these kinds of sensual painting, blonde hair was all about the titillation of dangerous pleasure.

Deliberately erotic images, then, were held in great numbers in the private networks of the élite. Leonardo da Vinci was well aware of the potent spell that his paintings could cast. 'The painter's power over men's minds,' he wrote:

is even greater [than the poet's], for he can induce them . . . to fall in love with a picture which does not portray any living woman . . . It once happened to me that I made a picture representing a sacred subject which was bought by one who loved it and who then wished to remove the symbols of divinity in order that he might kiss her without misgivings. Finally his conscience overcame his sighs of desire and he . . . was obliged to remove the painting from his house.

In an ironic twist, the very churchmen who had for generations so energetically damned such wickedness were accused themselves of harbouring paintings of blonde biblical and mythological beauties for their own erotic gratification. In a treatise published in 1552, Ambrogio Politi, a Dominican cleric, accused priests of downright idolatry and was unconvinced by the excuses of 'corrupt' men who alleged that they collected and preserved these pictures 'not for the purpose of revering them or adoring them, but for the enjoyment of the spectacles and in memory of the ancients, as a demonstration of the skill of the artist'.

Sin came in many forms in the sixteenth century, but initially avarice was the sin discussed and abhorred at greatest length in manuals for confessors, with lust following a close second. By the end of the century, however, lust had emerged in the confessionals as the number-one sin. There is no simple explanation for this, but the historian Carlo Ginzburg believes it may be that, with the spread of printing and the increased circulation of images, sight was emerging as the pre-eminent erotic sense. This, combined with the Counter-Reformation's repression of sexual life in Catholic countries and Calvin's equivalent repression in Protestant countries, perhaps turned lust into the primary sin.

In Italy, it was recognised that images possessed great power to arouse. Erotic pictures were often hung in the bedchamber as a kind of fertility talisman, 'because once seen they serve to arouse one and to make beautiful, healthy and charming children'. To conceive a child under the sign of Venus, it was believed, increased the chance of generating beauty – and blondeness. In 1587 an English translation was published of the ancient Greek story *Aethiopica* by Heliodorus about the birth of a fair-haired and fair-skinned girl, Charicleia, to royal Ethiopian parents, both dark-haired and dark-skinned. The story turns on the improbability of her belonging to this family, until her mother, Persina, admits that during conception she thought about a painting of the naked blonde Andromeda which hung in the palace bedroom. Eventually the girl's unique birthmark is found and recognised, and she is accepted. The story became very popular and its central concept must have been widely circulated and understood.

Images and their stories in this way reinforced the singularity of blondeness for contemporary Italians and, increasingly, given the growing scope of travel, for a wider European audience too. Painters and poets fed off each other for inspiration. Poetry was cast in a wide arc from Venice, the works of High Renaissance poets such as Firenzuola and Luigini vigorously promoting the Venetian ideal of feminine beauty to a broad European public. Firenzuola, in his 1548 *Dialogue of the Beauty of Women*, describes the imagined conversation at two social gatherings of leading Florentine men and women. Celso, the author's mouthpiece, fills page after page with his detailed discussions of feminine beauty. He defines it in both theoretical and empirical fashion, and lists the ideal shape, proportions, colour and ornamentation of the female body. He describes the precise details of the face, eyes, nose, eyebrows, eyelashes, teeth and gums. Even the tip of the tongue is discussed. On hair he is unwavering in his worship of blonde.

> A lady's hair is of fine gold, woven in a crown of bright and crisped gold . . . you know that the true and right colour for hair is fair yellow . . . the hair should be fine and fair, in the similitude now of gold, now of honey and now of the bright and shining rays of the sun; waving, thick, abundant and long . . .

He goes on to quote Apuleius on the same subject: 'If you should remove from the shining head of any well-favoured maiden the glory of the bright light of her fair hair, you would find her bereft of every grace and lacking all charm . . .'

Federigo Luigini's *Book of Fair Women*, published in 1554, is set in the villa where Luigini dreamed that he and four male friends, one evening after a day's hunting, had set themselves the pleasurable task of 'taking up brushes and colours' to 'paint', in words, the image of the perfect woman. The five gentlemen work their way systematically down through an elaborate catalogue of the parts of the female body from head to toe, referring to the beauties described by classical and contemporary poets known to them. Hair is tackled first:

> I desire to take first her hair, for that, methinks, is of more importance to her beauty than any other of her charms, seeing that without it she would be even as a garden without flowers or a ring without jewels . . . Tresses, therefore, must adorn our Lady, and in colour they shall be like unto clear shining gold, for that in truth affords more delight to the eye than any other whatsoever . . .

He goes on to refer to the Knidos Aphrodite, to Venus, Poppaea, Ovid's blondes, Petrarch's Laura and to the writings of Bembo and other blondophile Renaissance poets. In conclusion he says: 'our Lady's hair shall be long, thick, golden and softly curling, flowing down her back in fair loose tresses, not hidden away in any net of gold or silk, but open to the gaze, so that each favoured mortal may behold it without breathing an inward malediction on that which half hides it from his view.'

Blonde was the colour on the lips of all the poets of the time, not least Pietro Aretino, poet, dramatist and pornographer. Aretino was famed throughout Europe for his lewd sonnets and dialogues. He settled in Venice in 1527 where he became great friends with Titian, and lived in a grand and dissolute style, writing satirical attacks on the powerful, and scurrilous exposés of prostitutes and their clients. In his *Dialogues*, in which the blonde Nanna teaches her daughter Pippa the fine arts of courtesanship, he describes the difficulties that courtesans have in a city overrun with rivals. 'Why nowadays whores come in hordes, and a girl who can't perform miracles of wise living will never rub a supper against a lunch. No, it's not enough to be made of good solid flesh, have lovely eyes and blonde tresses – you need art or luck to get through the undergrowth, and all the rest is just bells to hang on a cat's neck.' Nanna advises Pippa to cultivate an intellectual image, to leave volumes of Petrarch's poetry and Boccaccio's stories open and prominently visible in her salon.

Aretino was well acquainted with the courtesans of Venice. He probably introduced several of them to Titian, who may have employed them as the models for his mythological and biblical subjects. As the art historian Rona Goffen notes, 'The actual identities of these models have been lost to history, although they may well have been prostitutes, given that such women often combined modelling with the oldest profession; and for all we know, they may indeed have been employed by Titian also in this sense.'

So who were these courtesans who made Venice famous throughout Europe as the 'terra da donne'? Thomas Coryate, an English traveller who walked from Somerset to Venice and back in the early seventeenth century, wrote in his *Coryat's Crudities*, 'For so infinite are the allurements of these amorous Calypsoes, that the fame of them hath drawn many to Venice from some of the remotest parts of Christendome, to contemplate their beauties, and enjoy their pleasing dalliances.'

The word *cortigiana* or courtesan came into vogue at the end of the fifteenth century to describe women similar to the hetairai of the Greek world. The courtesans were refined, gifted and much-courted ladies who captivated powerful men with their intelligence and their beauty. On the whole, they were highly cultured, often accomplished in literature and music. They were popular guests at parties for their informed and witty conversation, their charm, their stylish dress and their beauty.

The top-ranking courtesans became prosperous and entertained lavishly in their own apartments. These were like oversized jewel boxes, typically stuffed with velvets, brocades, inlaid furniture, musical instruments and carefully selected volumes of verse. Renaissance culture was a display culture, and the leading courtesans no less than any other members of high society made a point of parading themselves and their finery in public. They were assiduous church-goers and were welcomed as prospective penitents by some churches, where their numbers no doubt helped to boost the congregations. But their main purpose was publicity. Church-going was an excellent stage on which to advertise their beauty, their charms, their luxurious clothes, and to display their power and even, in a few cheeky cases, their piety. Crowds gathered around the church doors to watch as the leading courtesan of the moment arrived, like a Hollywood star at a movie première, preceded by several pages and manservants, surrounded by her admirers and with her hand on the arm of her current favourite.

Such a scene is described in a dialogue, thought to have been written by Aretino, between two women, Maddalena and Giulia. 'Did you see La Tortora's wonderful clothes when she went into S. Agostino? I didn't know her, I thought she was a baroness . . . And did you see the way her hair was done? It looked like one mass of curled gold on top of another. And that black velvet and gold robe, with gold cords interlaced over the velvet, and velvet ones over the gold. The work alone must have cost the world. And her rings and pearls and necklaces, and all the other beautiful things she had?' Giulia replies, 'Yes I saw it all, and I marvelled, because I remember La Tortora in Venice in an old sack of a dress, with her hands and ankles dirty, wearing old house slippers without heels.'

Wealthy cavaliers attracted by such showy displays were required to enter into long and complicated transactions if they wanted to strike up relations with a courtesan. Elegant love letters full of erudite literary references first had to be written, followed by verbal pledges of love. The great courtesans were visited by powerful and illustrious men, so the competition was fierce. Reaching her audience chamber, however, did not necessarily mean that they would reach her private chamber, let alone her bedchamber. For that the aspiring lovers would have to demonstrate further abilities, quoting fashionable poetry, playing madrigals, improvising songs and handing out expensive gifts. They had to be well-prepared to launch their bid for the bedchamber, and among the Venetians a class of agent-consultants known as the *mezzano* sprang up to furnish would-be lovers with the necessary weapons of seduction. Poems, sonnets and love letters could be provided, at a price, and when his client was fully prepared the *mezzano* would arrange the first meeting and, if successful, follow it through with the negotiations for the final bargain.

For their elegance, their wit and their learning, courtesans were considered to be a cut above mere prostitutes, and for a while in the sixteenth century some Venetian women born into good bourgeois families took up the career of courtesan. Sometimes they had been orphaned or widowed, or disowned by their families for becoming single mothers. Often the mere fact that they were single, in a city where 95 per cent of women were married by the age of eighteen, was enough to lead them into courtesanship as a socially acceptable solution to their awkward status.

One such woman was Veronica Franco, born in 1546, the only daughter among three sons in a bourgeois family sufficiently socially elevated to have its own coat of arms. Mystery surrounds the reason for Veronica's original entry into this profession. She is thought to have been married very young, but became pregnant by a wealthy lover when she was eighteen. She soon followed her mother into the profession and rose fast to become what her admirers called 'an expensive mouthful', who would not give a kiss for less than five or six scudi. Soon she was asking fifty scudi for what Montaigne graciously described as '*la négociation entière*'. She was reputedly very beautiful, with blonde hair dyed to the shade of gold supposedly desired by all the men of Europe. She had blue eyes, a heart-shaped face with a broad brow and a small pointed chin. Tintoretto, who was a friend of hers, painted a portrait of Veronica which is now lost; but an engraving of her made when she was twenty-three still survives in Venice. She looks slight, almost childlike, with an elfin delicacy of feature, carefully plucked eyebrows and rows of shining ringlets primped and arranged around her forehead to give her face its distinctive heart shape. Her eyes are sharp and her expression thoughtful: Veronica was clearly both attractive and intelligent. She was well versed in the classics, wrote fine letters and poetry in the style of Dante and became part of an intellectual salon run by the poet Domenico Venier, who acted as her literary adviser and critic. She played the harpsichord, and entertained clients and friends with fine concerts of madrigals, with word games and story-telling. She had several children, and was left interesting legacies by men of the wealthiest and grandest Venetian families. One bequeathed to her a feather bed and his annual income of four blocks of caviare and four sausages.

But it was in 1574 that Veronica's reputation as the most famous and gifted courtesan in Venice was sealed. On 18 July of that year, the 22-year-old Henri de Valois arrived in Venice on his way to be crowned King Henry III of France, after the death of his brother Charles IX. Always keen to throw their weight about in the company of monarchs, the Venetians put on a pageant of such grotesquely whole-hog extravagance and plutocratic vulgarity that no witness could doubt the city's legendary powers of raw wealth. Triumphal arches were designed by Palladio and decorated by Tintoretto and Veronese. Henry was carried to the city on a boat rowed by four hundred Slav oarsmen with an escort of fourteen galleys. The Ca' Foscari on the Grand Canal had been turned into a treasure palace for the king, full of rare marble and cloth of gold and hung with paintings by Titian, Bellini, Tintoretto and Veronese. For the principal banquet in the Doge's palace, two hundred of the most beautiful women of Venice appeared in dazzling white, their throats adorned with enormous pearls. The three thousand guests picked heroically at the twelve hundred dishes on the bill of fare and the feast was rounded off with three hundred different kinds of bonbon. When the king at last staggered out into the night, he found that a galley, shown to him earlier in the evening in its component parts, had been assembled outside. It was launched into the lagoon with a blast from a huge cannon which had been cast while he dined.

According to some historians, the king, who liked to wander around cities incognito, was never quite the same again. But he did take the opportunity between festivities to pay a visit to Veronica Franco, whom he had heard about from one of her admirers. The visit was supposed to be secret, but naturally all of Venice heard about it. We are told that they talked about Veronica's literary work. She later composed two sonnets and a dedicatory letter to the King. No thanks, she wrote, 'could possibly, even in part, requite the infinite kindness of your benign and gracious offers made to me about the book, which I am about to dedicate to you'. Henri's visit is unlikely to have been entirely for their mutual literary edification. He would probably have been aware of her reputation beyond poetry, and indeed Veronica had no shame in advertising her own abilities and comparing herself to the prototypical blonde, the goddess of love, Venus. She wrote in one of her love poems:

So sweet and appetising do I become when I find myself in bed with he who loves and welcomes me, that our pleasure surpasses all delight . . . Phoebus [Apollo] who served the goddess of love, received from her recompense so sweet that it meant more to him than to be a god, his bliss, to make my meaning clear, were those pleasures that Venus afforded him when she held him in her soft embrace: I too am versed in those same arts, and am so practised in the pleasures of the bed, that there I surpass by far Apollo's mastery of the arts.

Veronica died in 1591, aged forty-five, after a month of fever. Her last years had been financially difficult, and towards the end of her life her reputation began to wane. A scurrilous friend of the poet Aretino remarked that her breasts hung so low she could paddle a gondola with them, but still paid homage to how well she could sing.

Veronica remains one of Venice's most famous and distinctive beauties in a society which idolised beauty as an expression of sanctity. She was well-known in Venice and was probably painted by many of the city's leading artists. Two portraits attributed to the school of Tintoretto, *Portrait of a Lady* (Worcester Art Museum, Massachusetts) and *Portrait of a Woman* (Museo del Prado, Madrid), show beautiful young blondes with heart-shaped faces, dressed in sumptuous brocades, silks and velvets, each showing a bare breast. Some art historians believe that both portraits are of Veronica.

In an age when the codes of feminine beauty, based on the fabled glories of Venus, were so clearly laid down in the works of contemporary poets and painters, it is not surprising that leisured and wealthy ladies as well as courtesans desired to emulate the ideal. Blonde hair was the most effective key to beauty and in some ways it was the easiest element in the package to fake. Observant men were intrigued by the concerted efforts made by Venetian ladies to bleach their hair. Cesare Vecellio, a cousin of Titian's, described the elaborate arrangements in 1589:

The houses of Venice are commonly crowned with little constructions in wood, resembling a turret without a roof . . . During the hours when the sun darts its most vertical and scorching rays they repair to these boxes and condemn themselves to broil in them unattended. Seated there they keep on wetting their hair with a sponge dipped in some elixir of youth, prepared with their own hands or purchased. They moisten their hair afresh as fast as it is dried by the sun and it is by the unceasing renewal of this operation that they become what you see them – blondes.

Coryate, who was delighted to be granted 'a favour not affoorded to every stranger', watched the Venetian wife of an Englishman engaged in just this mucky business, noting that 'All the women of Venice every Saturday in the afternoone doe use to annoint their haire with oyle, or some other drugs, to the end to make it looke faire, that is whitish. For that colour is most affected of the Venetian Dames and Lasses.'

The case for the Italians as blonde fetishists ought not to be overstated, but it was certainly in northern Italy that the most active blonding took place. Fortunately a few of the many beauty manuals of Renaissance Italy survive, one of them being Giovanni Marinelli's *Gli ornamenti delle donne* (*Ways for Women to Adorn Themselves*) published in Venice in 1562. Volume II supplies various recipes for Venetian bleach, including one which recommends boiling up a kind of minestrone of vine ashes in pure water with sprinklings of barley shafts, twig bark, peeled and chopped licorice wood and a lime. 'Make a concoction of these ingredients; pour it off. Wash your hair, let it dry, then apply this liquid. Your hair will be shiny strands of gold.' Either that or you will be bald.

For hundreds of years sharp-witted Italian men flogged to a ravenous female public what they claimed were the ultimate secrets of blonde hair. Women were advised to comb olive oil and white wine through their hair, or ivy bark and hayseeds. Even horse urine was used. John Baptista della Porta's 1669 *Ninth Book of Natural Magick: How to Adorn Women and Make them Beautiful* opens with a series of recipes for dyeing hair blonde. 'Women hold the Hair to be the greatest ornament of the Body, that if that be taken away, all the Beauty is gone; and they think it the more beautiful, the more yellow, shining and radiant it is,' it begins. Eight recipes follow for blonde hair dye.

Modern readers armed with tubes of sweet-smelling unguents from L'Oréal or Clairol may be sceptical as to the efficacy of these disgusting potions. But evidence suggests that they were effective. Armand Brachet, in a treatise published in 1865, *Les Femmes blondes selon les peintres de l'école de Venise*, lists no fewer than thirty-six Renaissance recipes for preparing bleach, a solution known as *aqua bionda*. Konrad Bloch, a modern American chemist, has deduced that their ingredients would have combined to form potent bleaches, with hydrogen peroxide as the most likely active ingredient. Although hydrogen peroxide was not discovered until as late as 1812, 'there is a certain rationale', he says 'to the Venetian recipes; they cannot be discredited as alchemy.'

Potent they clearly were, but also damaging. John Bulwer records in his book *The Artificial Changeling* (1650) the cases of several unfortunate Italian bleach addicts:

The Women of old time did most love yellow Haire . . . The Venetian Women at this day, and the Paduan, and those of Verona, and other parts of Italy practice the same vanitie, and receive the same recompence for their affectation, there being in all these Cities, open and manifest examples of those who have undergone a kinde of Martyrdome, to render their Haire yellow. Schenkius relates unto us the History of a certaine Noble Gentlewoman, about sixteen or seventeen yeares of age, that would expose her bare Head to the fervent heat of the Sun daily for some houres, that shee might purchase yellow and long Haire, by anointing them with a certain unguent; and although she obtained the effect of her desires, yet withall, shee procured to her selfe a violent Head ach, and bled almost every day abundantly through the Nose . . . Another maid also by using this same Art, became almost blind with sore Eyes.

Clearly these ladies were not aware of − or preferred to ignore − the warnings of Giovanni Marinelli, who cautioned strongly against the use of hair dyes in his 1562 treatise upon the adornment of women. 'Permit me to remind you honoured and honourable ladies that the application of so many colours to your hair may strike a chill into the head like the shock of a shower-bath, that it affects and penetrates, and what is worse, may entail divers grave maladies and infirmities . . . We frequently see the hair affected in its essentials, or at its roots grow weak and fall off and the complexion destroyed through the use of so many injurious liquids and decoctions.'

This was fighting talk. But although many such warnings were issued, few chose to heed them when so much glory and power could be obtained from the universally accepted status of blondeness. Threats were still being hurled from the pulpit, too, but the ears of Italy's blonded beauties were deaf to them. Blonde hair was highly divisive and provoked extreme reactions. To some it was the epitome of sensual beauty. To others it was the sign of evil vanity and folly. Both swooning worship and thunderous denunciation hinted at calamities in the offing. But for the moment blonde hair still ruled unchallenged.

7

LIKE A VIRGIN

I T W A S Queen Elizabeth I's finest moment. On the morning of Sunday 24 November 1588, England's triumphant monarch set off from Somerset House for St Paul's Cathedral to attend the service of thanksgiving for England's mighty victory over the Spanish Armada. This was England's greatest victory since Agincourt, and the queen wished to acknowledge her debt to God and to Providence. She also wished to make a superlative statement, to fix in the minds of her people and of all Christendom her status as the greatest, most illustrious divine ruler, 'Eliza Triumphant'.

The public mood was especially jubilant that day. Tens of thousands of people clamoured for a glimpse of the queen and her cavalcade, cheering and waving banners. Snaking lines of scarlet-suited aldermen lined the route with gentlemen of the city dressed in their brilliantly coloured liveries. In front of the queen stretched a huge procession of blazing magnificence. There were heralds and trumpeters, judges of the realm, ambassadors, knights, barons, viscounts and hundreds of honourable gentlemen and ladies on horseback, all making their way towards the great cathedral amid the jangling of harnesses and the thunderous roar of hoofs. The queen, bejewelled and poised, the very image of a goddess, joined the cavalcade in an open carriage drawn by two white horses. Behind her head was a canopy laden with motifs: a crown, a lion, a dragon and the arms of England.

A procession of this scale and splendour had not been seen since the queen's coronation in 1558, and it was designed to match the magnitude of the event it celebrated. Pageants and ballads were performed in the queen's honour as she passed. Gifts of jewels and precious books were given and speeches made as the victorious queen made her way slowly down the paved Strand and then up muddy Ludgate Hill. She was dressed in one of her most dazzling embroidered robes, covered with a riot of gold braid and myriads of little jewels which sparkled and caught the light as she moved graciously to acknowledge the cheers of the crowd. Eventually reaching the cathedral at midday, she alighted from her carriage at the West Door, fell to her knees and 'made her hearty prayers unto God' before the enormous crowds. She entered the cathedral, which was hung with captured banners, and listened to a sermon before reading a prayer of her own and addressing the congregation. When she asked her people to have gratitude for their great victory, they replied with a deafening roar, shouting their praise of the queen. After a grand celebratory banquet hosted by the Bishop of London at the nearby Bishop's Palace, the queen's hundreds of attendants were marshalled again on horseback and with Elizabeth again poised in her open carriage like some magnificent living treasure, they made their dazzling return procession, this time 'with great light of torches', back to Somerset House.

Queen Elizabeth must have permitted herself a private glow of satisfaction. Her reputation had never been greater. Even her enemies, Pope Sixtus V, Henry III and the Ottoman sultan sang her praises, lauding her valour, her spirit and her courage. At home she was a goddess, hypnotic and untouchable, the very incarnation of divine majesty. Naturally a sitting was arranged for a portrait to mark the occasion. Three versions of the spectacular Armada Portrait survive, all following the same pattern. The queen stands, brilliantly lit, before two windows, one showing the sending of the English ships into the advancing Spanish fleet, the other showing the Spanish ships being dashed to pieces off the rocky coasts of Scotland. One elegant hand rests on a globe and on a table sits a heavily jewelled crown. But even that fades into the background next to the queen herself. She wears a magnificent robe of black and white, encrusted with huge pearls and starry jewels, stiff with gold thread, tasselled and spangled with a riot of bows and ribbons and finished off with eight ropes of enormous pearls which hang down to her waist. Her face is a smooth, pale and lustrous mask: despite her fifty-five years, she has the flawless complexion of a twenty-year-old. The face is poised on a stiff froth of lace, a cartwheel ruff, its circle completed by a halo of barbered golden blonde curls studded with enormous pearls.

Attentive schoolgirls may remember being told that Queen Elizabeth I had auburn hair. If we look at her early portraits, thought to be the most realistic records of her appearance because they were painted before she was ever considered seriously as a successor to the throne, her hair is indeed pale auburn. But by the time of the Armada victory it was actually well on the way to turning grey. She was wearing a golden blonde wig.

The Armada Portrait marks the beginning of Queen Elizabeth's transformation into a blonde. After her thirty years on the throne, generally recognised as a reign of exceptional prudence and felicity, the English regarded their queen as some kind of saviour sent by God. The Armada victory provided the final impetus for the creation of a Queen Elizabeth cult. She assumed the status of an immortal, and her image, spread by the work of sympathetic painters, turned her from something approximating to a human being into a spectacular jewelled icon, a hypnotic creature set apart from reality. She was a golden ruler of a golden age, and her blonde hair was part of this divine unreality. In 1588, to mark Sir Thomas Heneage's role in England's Armada victory, the queen gave him a specially commissioned miniature of herself, painted by Nicholas Hilliard and mounted in a case of enamelled gold, set with diamonds and rubies. It showed her as a dazzling young blonde.

Official images of the monarch were probably circulated more widely and seen by more subjects during Elizabeth's long reign than those of any previous ruler. Hundreds of paintings, miniatures, woodcuts and engravings were made during her life, some of them reproduced in vast numbers as frontispieces for Elizabethan editions of the Bible. In a country where the portrait was still a relative novelty to the majority of society, those images must have had an enormous impact as a political tool and focus of reverence.

For Elizabeth, blonde hair became an important element of her image and it fulfilled several functions. To start with it served as a cultural code which emphasised the queen's uncorrupted and untouchable virginity. Elizabeth had witnessed the disastrous marriages of both her sister Queen Mary and later her cousin Mary Queen of Scots. Many historians believe that Elizabeth had never had any intention of bowing to the rule of a husband, that she had probably resolved at quite a young age to rule alone. For years she had jousted flirtatiously with favoured courtiers at home and played the inevitable marriage games with strings of suitors from Catholic Europe, playing them off against one another. But in spite of the best negotiating efforts of her foreign policy ministers she had decisively rejected them all. When after a long period of coquetry she eventually dismissed the unfortunately pockmarked French Duke of Anjou, a man almost half her age whom she playfully referred to as her 'Frog', and he died in 1584, Elizabeth finally came off the marriage market. She was fifty-one years old and even the most optimistic of her supporters agreed that it was too late for her to produce an heir. Elizabeth had won. She was to remain a virgin queen; a bride, she reminded her subjects, wedded exclusively to her country. It was a typically brilliant piece of public relations and from then on the emphasis in Elizabeth's portraits was placed increasingly on a symbolically youthful virginity indicated by an abundant use of pearls (a symbol of virginity) and her blonde hair, a sign of her pure, unsullied femininity.

Elizabeth knew how to make the most of her gender. In August 1588 she had visited her army at Tilbury on the eve of the anticipated Spanish invasion and must have cut a stunning figure on horseback among her thousands of troops. 'I know I have the body but of a weak and feeble woman,' she told them, 'but I have the heart and stomach of a king, and of a king of England too'. With characteristically assertive self-promotion, she played on the supposed weakness of her sex to highlight her own courage all the more forcefully. Within months she was to tweak that image of femininity one notch higher by becoming a blonde. Edmund Spenser in *The Faerie Queen*, his long song of love for Queen Elizabeth, was to describe the aftermath of a battle scene in which Britomart, a valiant, chaste and queenly woman knight, removes her helmet to reveal long tumbling blonde hair 'like sunny beams', the proof of her gender and evidence of a courage all the greater.

Elizabeth's blonde hair played an important role, too, in her calculated styling as England's fairest maiden, the ultimate object of courtly love. This chivalric ideal, a leftover from medieval times, regarded chaste devotion to an elevated, beautiful and traditionally blonde mistress as a spiritually elevating thing. It served as a useful vehicle for devotion to the queen and perfectly suited Elizabeth's tastes and requirements. Elizabethan chivalry worked to inspire large numbers of fighting men in the Armada crisis. It also worked to encourage pleasing displays of loyalty and veneration on a day-to-day basis. The queen was a frequent and enthusiastic attendant at the royal Tilts, tournaments in which knights competed for her favour in jousting competitions. These were spectacular theatrical pageants, in which the knights appeared in inventive and often mythological costumes, and presented gifts to the queen as she sat with her ladies in the gallery overlooking a tiltyard sited on what is now Horse Guards Parade. The queen herself sometimes appeared in costume, too, dressed as Astraea, the virgin goddess of justice, as blonde Belphoebe, or in later years as Gloriana, the golden-haired Faerie Queen of Edmund Spenser's famous poem. Symbolically attired, she would acknowledge the homage of her gallant knights in this last flowering of medieval chivalry and then watch her champion defend her honour against all rivals.

But the most powerful message carried by the blonde hair of Queen Elizabeth's later years was in its reference to the halo of golden hair seen in images of the Virgin Mary. On the day that Sir Henry Lee resigned his title as the Queen's Champion of the Tilts in 1590, an altar was raised to the sacred English virgin queen and a verse sung by the royal lutenist which openly linked her with the Virgin Mary. 'Vivat Eliza! for an Ave Maria!' (Long Live Eliza instead of an Ave Maria) he sang, hailing Elizabeth as an alternative queen of heaven. An engraving of Elizabeth exists of roughly the same date, with the following couplet. 'She was, She is (what can there more be said?) In earth the first, in heaven the second Maid.' Elizabeth's virginity was working as a powerful magic conferring a miraculous purity which had become equated with holiness.

From the late 1580s onwards, the hair in the portraits became more fantastically blonde and the accompanying motifs prompting divine association became more obvious. Claims of miraculous healings at Queen Elizabeth's hands supported the comparison, and Elizabeth herself did not shy from occasionally presenting herself in her speeches to parliament as some kind of messianic saviour. Some of the imagery was magnificently unsubtle. In the elaborately illuminated manuscript for Foxe's *Actes and Monuments*, the opening letter C is decorated with an image of an enthroned Elizabeth receiving homage from three kneeling bearded men. The design unmistakably equates Elizabeth with the Virgin Mary.

Fate had favoured Elizabeth's deification not only in the date of her birth, the eve of the Nativity of the Virgin Mary, but also in the date of her death, the eve of the Virgin's Annunciation. And it was after her death that the image-makers went to work most assiduously. Three days after Elizabeth died on 24 March 1603, Dr King preached at Whitehall, referring to her as a second Virgin giving birth to the Gospel of Christ. 'Soe there are two excellent women, one that bare Christ and an other that blessed Christ; to these may wee joyne a thrid that bare and blessed him both. She [Elizabeth] bare him in hir heart as a wombe, she conceived him in fayth, shee brought him forth in aboundaunce of good workes . . .' Numerous elegies written to mark her death hailed her as England's own Madonna, and the artists, too, went to work, depicting her as the sacred Virgin in heaven, haloed by a circle of stars and sitting in celestial splendour amid billowing clouds. Representations of her tomb were erected in churches around the country. Beneath one of them are the verses: 'This was she that in despight of death Lives still ador'd . . .'

Elizabeth's carefully wrought apotheosis was complete. The construction of a persona along with its visual image had been entirely deliberate, a strategy designed in a newly Protestant England to immortalise her memory as a divine figure representing the advancement of her faith. While the sacred images of Christ and of the Virgin and saints had been removed from England's churches and rejected as idolatry, the sacred images of the Divina Elizabetha had spread rapidly across the land. In many ways it was a natural development in Protestant England for the cult of Elizabeth to replace the banished cult of the Virgin.

Image-making at the time of her death was nothing new. We know that Elizabeth had always tried to control images of herself. Even as early as 1558, when she succeeded the throne, she seems to have had trouble with her portraits. In 1563, Lord Cecil, her supremely powerful public relations officer, had drafted a decree complaining of the daily proliferation of unsatisfactory likenesses of the queen, of 'errors and deformities'. He proposed a kind of pattern book by which officially sanctioned artists would be able to produce 'correct' images. This explains why there were frequently several similar versions made of portraits, copied according to an approved pattern. It is not known whether Cecil's draft was ever executed, but clearly its censorship aims were not achieved. Towards the end of her reign, in 1596, unseemly portraits were sought out by government officers and there was an official bonfire of those judged to be of 'great offense' to the queen. Unedifying engravings were burned, too, over the years and one writer records that 'vile copies multiplyed from an ill Painting' were gathered in and for several years provided the cooks at Essex House with makeshift shovels for their ovens.

We can assume, though, that most of the surviving later images of Elizabeth had met with her approval. By the end of her life the gulf between image and reality must have been enormous. She had transformed herself from a grey-haired old lady with sunken cheeks and badly yellowing teeth (as we are told by an observant French ambassador) into a legendary blonde of imperishable youth. As well as giving her an image of goddess-like immortality, Elizabeth's fantastic youth was designed to symbolise the continuing peaceful and successful state of the nation. Like the face, this was of course a fiction. England at the end of Elizabeth's long reign was racked by economic hardship, by rumours of the Queen's illness and death, and by concerns over the succession. Amid these troubles, it was more important than ever for Elizabeth to develop a protective aura of remote sanctity.

The official portraits of Elizabeth done after 1590 portray an increasingly aloof and staggeringly unreal blonde diva. The Ditchley portrait shows a symbolically flawless creature hovering over a map of England, her tiny pointed toes directly above Oxfordshire. It was painted by Marcus Gheeraerts the Younger to commemorate the queen's visit to Sir Henry Lee at Ditchley in Oxfordshire in 1592. She wears an elaborately worked gown (one of nearly two thousand she owned at the end of her life), regal white and overrun with a lattice of pearls and jewels. Round her neck she has a pearl and ruby choker and looped over her bodice is the usual fistful of ropes of more fat pearls. Her wig is yellow-blonde. But by the time the portrait had been transposed to its pattern versions, one formerly at Blair Castle, another at Blickling Hall, it had been tweaked a couple of shades and become a stunning platinum.

Nicholas Hilliard painted many images of the queen in miniature in various shades of blonde and a few of brunette. But those done after 1590 were all subject to what is known as the Hilliard 'Mask of Youth' pattern. This was designed to reflect an idealisation of Elizabeth, a visual expression of the poetic worship of her beauty and loveliness during the last years of her reign. All of these depict Elizabeth as a pale yellow-blonde, several of them with her hair flowing loosely on to her shoulders like a young bride.

The painting attributed to Robert Peake called *Queen Elizabeth going in Procession to Blackfriars in 1600* shows a legendary queen dressed in a white gown studded with jewels and borne aloft in a canopied litter by her courtiers. She has pouting ruby lips, dark, sensuous eyes and the glowing complexion of a young girl. Her hair, dressed with jewels and pearls, is a fantastic shade of shimmering blonde. Massed around her are ageing courtiers and grandees strutting like peacocks and her dark-haired maids of honour, mere decorative foils to the queen's eye-catching magnificence. Stage-managing her image right to the last, Elizabeth floats ethereally above them like some luminescent celestial being. At the sunset of her glorious long reign, this was perhaps Elizabeth's most exotic and fantastic incarnation ever.

We know that the smooth face, the teenage eyes and the flawless hands are all blatant lies. But the hair might be truer than we at first think. Elizabeth had been wearing elaborately dressed wigs for twenty years when this painting was done, partly for convenience but also to conceal grey and thinning hair. By the 1590s Elizabeth had a substantial collection of wigs. In 1952, Roger Mountague, her silkman, delivered 'vij heads of haire to make attiers, flowers, and other devices for Attiers, Two periwigs of haire'; and in 1595 he supplied 'iiij lardge fayre heddes of heaire iiij perewigges of heaire'. In 1602, a year before she died, she was still buying hair for wigs.

Queen Elizabeth had always had a clear understanding of the language of clothes and hair. When she was engaged in foreign policy negotiations or being courted by potential suitors from Europe, she would wear varying styles of dress for diplomatic purposes as well as for reasons of fashion. Sir James Melville, the Scottish ambassador, noted in 1564 that some days she wore the English fashion, some days the French and other days the Italian. 'She asked me which of them became her best. I said, the Italian dress; which pleased her well, for she delighted to shew her golden coloured hair.'

Melville had been sent to England that year by Mary Queen of Scots to renew relations with Queen Elizabeth which had deteriorated to a point beyond even the pretence of friendship. During his stay he discovered a queen interested in very feminine rivalries:

> She entered to discern what colour of hair was reputed best; and whether my queen's hair or hers was best; and

which of them two was fairest. I answered that the fairness of them both was not their worst faults. But she was earnest with me to declare which of them I thought fairest. I said she was the fairest queen in England and ours the fairest queen in Scotland. Yet she was earnest. I answered they were both the fairest ladies of their courts and that Her Majesty was whiter, but our queen was very lovely.

The Elizabethan ideal of feminine beauty was the product of a mixture of poetic influences, contemporary paintings and the whims of Queen Elizabeth herself, whose appearance was imitated by society ladies as an expression of flattery. John Marston, the sixteenth-century poet and dramatist, gave a detailed specification for the ideal English beauty. 'The face should be round and ruddy, the forehead smooth, high and white, the eyebrows small delicate and marked with a pencil, the lips coral or like cherries ... the hair a rich golden yellow.' Marston's mother was Italian, so he may have been influenced by the Italian obsession with blonde hair. But he was not the only poet glorifying the blonde. This description of a yellow-haired beauty was written before Elizabeth's day, but the story was reprinted in England three times, the last edition appearing in 1567. The heroine was named Lady Lucres and looked like this: 'Her heare [was] plenteous, and lyke unto the goulde wyre, which hanged not downe behinde her, after the manner and custome of maydens, but in goulde and stone she had enclosed it; her forhed highe, of seemlye space, without wrynkell, her brows bente, her eyne shining like as the sun ... strayt as thriede was her noose. Her mouth smal and comely, her lippes of corall colour, her small tethe, wel set in order, semed Cristal.' Historians have taken this as the perfect Elizabethan beauty because we have her exact opposite described ironically by Shakespeare in Sonnet 130:

> My mistress' eyes are nothing like the sun;
> Coral is far more red than her lips' red;
> If snow be white, why then her breasts are dun;
> If hairs be wires, black wires grow on her head.
> I have seen roses damask'd, red and white,
> But no such roses see I in her cheeks;

Sonnets and love poems flooded the later years of Elizabeth, often written as gifts for the queen, singing the glory of the monarch and the beauty of the lady. The sonneteers, patriotic Englishmen entranced by beauty and nobility, all praise the queen's hair of gold and eyes like heavenly stars. These were stock compliments of the era, thought to derive ultimately from Petrarch's pure and blonde Laura, that most enduringly popular sonnet mistress. One sonnet by Robert Tofte, from a collection called *Laura*, praises: 'As burnished gold, such are my Sovereign's Hairs; A brace of stars divine, her blackish Eyes.' And Spenser's description of Belphoebe (who represents Queen Elizabeth) in *The Faerie Queen* gives her 'yellow locks, crisped like golden wyre' loosely shed about her shoulders. Poetry and picture were very closely allied during Elizabeth's reign, and Hilliard's Mask of Youth images of the queen, as the ideal Elizabethan beauty with her rosy complexion and her flowing yellow locks, perhaps corresponded most closely with the descriptions of the poets.

Ladies of rank modelled themselves on the queen's portraits

and on poetic descriptions of her, and those not blessed by nature with the admired requirements had to make good with artifice. Many resorted to hair dye. A book by Sir Hugh Platt published in 1602 entitled *Delightes for Ladies to adorne their persons* includes a selection of disagreeably tangy recipes to dye hair a 'faire yellowe or golden' colour.

Those squeamish about anointing their hair with putrid mixtures bought their hair on the street. This was, according to Philip Stubbes, 'either of horses, mares or any other straunge beastes, dying it of what colour they list themselves'. But as usual different rules applied for the rich, who simply pillaged the heads of the poor. 'If there be any poore women,' Stubbes tells us, '. . . that hath faire haire, these nice dames will not rest till they have bought it, or if any children have faire haire, they will entice them into a secret place, and for a penie or two they will cut off their haire, as I heard that one did in the citie of London of late, who, meeting a little childe with very faire haire, inveigled her into a house, promised her a penie, and so cutte off her haire.'

With such manifest fakery going on, it is not surprising that the satirists and wits had a field day, much as Ovid and his friends had done hundreds of years earlier. Ben Jonson's character Moria comments in *Cynthia's Revels*: 'I would wish to . . . know all the secrets of court, citie, and countrie . . . which ladie had her owne face to lie with her a-nights, & which not; who put off her teeth with their clothes in court, who their haire, who their complexion; and in which boxe they put it.'

Apelles, in *Alexander and Campaspe* by John Lyly, tells Alexander: 'If the haire of her eye browes be black, yet must the haire of her head be yellowe.' Shakespeare, too, could not resist

a few digs. Commenting in *The Merchant of Venice* on the fact
that 'All that glisters is not gold', Bassanio expresses his thoughts
on a woman's beauty, so often 'purchas'd by the weight'. He
goes on:

> So are those crisped snaky golden locks
> Which make such wanton gambols with the wind,
> Upon supposed fairness, often known
> To be the dowry of a second head,
> The skull that bred them, in the sepulchre.

Tease as they might, the satirists could do nothing to alter
the fact that blatant artifice was, as ever, no barrier to accepted
beauty. Ladies spent much of their day getting dressed and
preparing and repairing their hair and faces. In 1607 Thomas
Tomkis published a comedy, *Lingua*, in which a dozen maids
were asked to dress up a boy like a nice gentlewoman. There
was 'such doing with their looking glasses, pinning, unpinning,
setting, unsetting, formings and conformings, painting blew
veins and cheeks; such stir with sticks and combs . . .' and it
was claimed that the whole operation took five hours. This
was probably an exaggeration, but it is certain that ladies were
constantly preoccupied with the state of their faces and hair.

The much-admired pale skin that denoted breeding, leisure
and therefore wealth was attained with dangerous preparations
made from white lead. Borax was also used to give whiteness
to the skin and the surface was often glazed over with egg
white. Blue veins were sometimes pencilled on to the partially revealed bosom to display a refined 'blue-bloodedness',
although the results when done with a heavy hand more
often resembled Stilton cheese. Eyebrows were also plucked

or sometimes thickened with artificial additions, usually slivers of mouse skin. Age was clearly no bar to aspirational beauty, and those of particularly advanced years used a 'plumper' to lift their cheeks: 'a fine thin light ball which old ladies that have lost their side teeth, hold in their mouths to plump out their cheeks which else would hang like leathern bags'. One might call it a very rudimentary attempt at the face lift. Appealing to a similar constituency was the poem *The Folly of Love* which poked fun at the 'old madam' who tries to cheat time by the use of such devices as false hair, glass eyes and even artificial buttocks.

But it was the hair, a lady's acknowledged crowning glory, that perhaps received the most attention, being constantly dyed, powdered, curled, pomaded, perfumed and pinned in elaborate coiffures. Complaints were constantly heard that the popular beauty spent too much time on herself and would 'all the morning learne to dresse her head'. The Elizabethan quest for beauty was such that a whole new class of quacks sprang up to play the role of the cosmetic surgeon. In Marston's *The Malcontent*, Maquerelle asks Bianca: 'Do you know Doctor Plaster-face? by this curd, he is the most exquisite in forging of veins, spright'ning of eyes, dying of hair, sleeking of skins, blushing of cheeks, surphling [sulphuring] of breasts, blanching and bleaching of teeth, that ever made an old lady gracious by torchlight.'

Queen Elizabeth did not, of course, require the services of a Dr Plaster-face, for she had her loyal painters to render her appearance miraculously and painlessly just as she wished. And this is exactly what happened with a painting known as the Coronation Portrait. It was initially thought to have been painted in 1559, just after the coronation, but tree-ring dating has recently confirmed that the wood used for the panel is from trees felled around 1600, making this an image painted at the end of the queen's life. It shows the young crowned queen in her elaborate ermine-trimmed coronation robes, holding the orb and sceptre. The face is a flawless mask of cream and rose, her eyebrows barely a pencilled suggestion, her eyes dark and sensuous, her lips coral-red. And over her shoulders flows a loose mane of thick golden-blonde hair. In other words, every element of the ideal Elizabethan beauty is there, down to the delicate blue veins gently painted on to her white temples. The auburn hair that we can assume the 25-year-old Elizabeth still possessed at the time of her coronation has been replaced with golden blonde for the judgment of posterity, embodying the purity, the virtue, the beauty, glory and riches of her imperial golden age. This final refashioning of fact was the ultimate manifestation of the alliance between art and power, used by the queen with great effect to magnify and immortalise her most glamorous sacred mystique. Elizabeth had remained dazzling to the end.

8

SAINT-SEDUCING GOLD

T HE GLORIOUS aura of Elizabeth, England's blonde
goddess queen, who had astounded her subjects with the
occasional radiant glimpse during her last years, was already
out of date by the time of her funeral. Her portraits were
magnificently dated in style, possibly even, as Roy Strong
has suggested, deliberately archaic. Her impenetrable icon-like
mask of divine majesty was one which looked back to the
portraits of medieval kings and emperors who had been
God-ordained rulers. Her Coronation Portrait, one of the
last images thought to have been painted during her lifetime,
is done in the tradition of the High Middle Ages, and
bears remarkable similarities in style and conception to the
thirteenth-century portrait in Westminster Abbey of Richard
II. In artistic terms, Elizabethan England – insular in so many
ways and set apart by its faith – lagged well behind continental
Europe.

A distinct shift was occurring in Europe and had already
begun to spell an end to the supremacy of the blonde.
Italy was losing its leading position in arts and letters to
a growing French influence in both political and cultural
spheres which was to last until the early nineteenth century.
French artists of the early seventeenth century such as Simon
Vouet, Philippe de Champaigne and the Le Nain brothers

were painting with greater naturalism, clarity and calm, and with a cooler colouring. They were moving away from the heavily idealised Baroque styles of northern Italy towards a type of classical painting in which Poussin was beginning to set the standard. Although Poussin spent most of his life in Rome, he has been acknowledged as the undisputed leader of French art in '*le grand siècle*' and the standard-bearer of classicism. Poussin and his fellow French painters produced more rational images, reflecting the rationalism of French contemporary thought. They worked for patrons who were members of the educated bourgeoisie: merchants, bankers and civil servants. Though less influential and magnificent than the aristocracy, these men nevertheless played a powerful role in French cultural life. Poussin's genius, his intellectual depth and formal mastery, appealed to these men of taste and learning, and his paintings reflect their appreciation of the concept of the '*honnête homme*', the man of virtue and honour, unreliant on fripperies and vanities. His figures swoon less than those of his Italian predecessors. His angels appear in more human guise, without the aid of clouds and radiances. Their faces are more lucidly realistic. And they are predominantly dark-haired. Poussin's biblical paintings – some of his most beautiful and rarefied images – and his Arcadian works are peopled with the brown-, the black- and the auburn-haired. Although blondes of course still appeared in his and others' paintings, it could be argued that Poussin and the French painters of this period brought to an end the extreme fetishised cult of the blonde.

The court painters of Louis XIV, men such as Charles Lebrun and Pierre Mignard, showed in their portrayals of the pompous atmosphere of Versailles how the key personages of the aristocracy, the most powerful men and the most beautiful women, were all fashionably dark-haired. Louis XIV himself wore dark wigs in his early years on the throne and his two key mistresses were dark. Madame de Montespan had herself painted variously as a dark temptress and as a dark Goddess Diana, and Madame de Fontanges, 'beautiful as an angel, stupid as a basket', likewise stared appealingly out of a facial frame of dark curls. In matters of taste and style, the French were setting the fashion and the rest of Europe followed.

The new prominence given to the dark-haired was assisted by the work of a number of painters from northern Europe, figures such as Van Dyck, Rembrandt and Vermeer, whose paintings took on a new and penetrating intimacy which reflected the realities of female beauty. Blonde hair was on the way out. Dark hair was the new pinnacle of beauty.

By the second half of the seventeenth century, England too had caught on to the new fashions from across the Channel and blonde hair lost its aura of exclusivity. Ingredients for the most powerful blonde dyes, once the property only of the wealthy, had fallen in price. Blonding hair was becoming a bourgeois habit.

Samuel Pepys, that invaluable chronicler of London manners and mores of the seventeenth century, gives us some early indications of blonde hair going out of fashion. In March 1665, Pepys's wife, Elizabeth, acquired a pair of blonde hair-pieces. Pepys was not pleased. 'This day my wife begun to wear light-coloured locks, quite white almost, which, though it makes her look very pretty, yet not being natural, vexes me, that I will not have her wear them.' Two years later, Elizabeth was still wearing her blonde hair-pieces. '. . . and so away with my wife, whose being dressed this day in fair hair did make me so mad, that I spoke not one word to her in our going, though I was ready to burst with anger . . . and so took coach, and took up my wife, and in my way home discovered my trouble to my wife for her white locks, swearing by God several times, which I pray God forgive me for, and bending my fist, that I would not endure it'(11 May 1667). Pepys returned home and went 'without supper to bed, vexed'. The following day they argued again about the blonde hair and Elizabeth eventually promised, not before extracting some money from her husband to buy lace, that she would never again wear them while he lived.

Arch-social-climber that he was, Pepys had realised that fake blonde hair was by now considered cheap. It had cascaded too far down the social scale for his snobbish antennae not to be offended by it. The Earl of Sandwich, his employer, had a painting on his wall of a sophisticated titled beauty, her pale face framed with tumbling bunches of dark curls. This, Pepys realised, was what ladies of superior birth and background wore.

For the fashionable Restoration beauty, dark hair was now securely in vogue. In the late seventeenth century Sir Peter Lely, whose portraits can be interpreted as a barometer of contemporary attitudes to beauty, painted a series of stylish society ladies, almost all of whom linger palely, their eyelids sensuously lowered beneath a torrent of cascading dark brown or black curls. His portrait of Barbara Villiers, Countess of Castlemaine and Duchess of Cleveland, painted in 1670, shows one of the most flagrantly sensual women at court who became the archetype, for Lely and in the eyes of posterity, of the dark-haired Restoration Beauty.

Such glossy dark hair was not itself acquired without the

help of a little artifice. The contemporary *Ladies' Guide* listed numerous recipes for dyes to create the sort of black hair that would set off a fine pale-rose complexion. The most expensive ones, requiring 'powder of gold', once again set up barriers to protect the wealthy in their chosen displays from the hordes of bourgeois imitators. And soon dark hair was superseded in England by the fashion for wigs, fantastically expensive handmade pieces of sculpture which gave the rich another chance to display their means. These had come into fashion first for men when Charles II finally reached the throne in 1660 and his own mane of curly black hair turned grey. Wigs were initially dark (the king is said to have had a magnificent wig made out of samples from the pubic hair of his numerous amorous conquests) but before long, following the French fashion, they were worn powdered grey or white. By this time English ladies had abandoned the messy business of dyeing and opted instead for extravagantly powdered wigs. It is at this point at the end of the seventeenth century that we enter a period of extreme trichological fantasy and filth. Wigs were very expensive. In 1700 a fine wig sold for £140, seventy times a farm worker's annual wage. Many of the criminals sentenced at the Old Bailey were specialist wig thieves. But, in spite of attacks from thieves, the rich continued to display their wealth on their heads. As wig prices gradually fell during the eighteenth century, moneyed ladies turned up the competitive heat by wearing ever more elaborately mountainous hairstyles, rigged up on wire frames two or three tiers high. These were decorated with swags of false hair, thickly dusted with fine white flour and then trimmed with yards of silk ribbon, ostrich feathers, beads, pearls, pieces of fruit and fresh flowers in concealed bottles of water, shaped to fit the sides of the scalp. On top of all this the most ruthlessly fashionable added little figurines in blown glass, ships in full sail, horses, chariots, pigs with their litters or even scenes recreating allegorical poems or great battle victories of the American wars.

Such elaborate displays took many hours to create and, once dressed, were often kept for several weeks, the ladies in question having great difficulty settling down for a night's sleep. It was not unusual for ladies to have their hair dressed the day before a ball or court presentation and to sit and doze in a chair all night. Such hairstyles brought other unedifying costs. The *London Magazine* published a description in 1768 of the 'opening of a lady's head' after nine horribly itchy weeks. The writer observed 'false locks to supply the great deficiency of native hair, pomatum with profusion, greasy wool to bolster up the adopted locks, and grey powder to conceal at once age and dirt, and all these caulked together by pins of an indecent length and corresponding colour. When the comb was applied to the natural hair, I observed swarms of animalculas running about in the utmost consternation and in different directions . . .'

Fleas, lice and nits feasting on rotting floury powder and pomatum (a concoction made from beef marrow), layers of décor weighing up to two pounds, and accumulations so precariously high that women had to stick their heads out of their carriage windows or kneel on the floor on the way to the ball – as usual the rich suffered heroically in order to display their worth. But alas they also, as pointed out in a letter to the *London Magazine* in 1768, smelled most unsavoury even if they did look enticing.

Such ridiculous hairstyles could not last long. The French

Revolution effectively axed them overnight and ladies of leisure quickly developed a more tasteful short and natural look. This did not stop the wittiest of their hairdressers from inventing new styles à la mode. They combed their clients' hair up from the back, leaving the neck bare as if for the guillotine, and finished the arrangement off with a blood-red ribbon around the neck. But whimsical excess had had its day in England too. Powdered hair was quickly phased out when Pitt imposed a flour tax in 1795; and powdered wigs were abolished in the Army in 1799 when flour prices rocketed after a series of bad harvests.

For two hundred years blonde hair had been out of fashion. It had become so cheap and had acquired so many smutty associations that it could no longer hold on to its dignity. No more the rarefied glory, honoured and worshipped by the great classical poets. No more the sublime lustre of the Renaissance artist's dreams. No longer the sign of divine majesty. Blonde hair was now perceived as a warning – or convenient advertising – of a lady of cheap behaviour.*

Poets and playwrights, ever ready to expose and immortalise a secretive sinful passion, began to reach back to earlier assocations of blonde hair with a dangerously powerful eroticism. John Milton, when writing *Paradise Lost* in the 1660s, followed medieval convention in depicting Eve with

---

* A fascinating pocket-sized volume entitled *Harris's List of Covent-Garden Ladies: Or Man of Pleasure's Kalender for the Year 1788*, listing names, addresses, descriptions and speciality services of the most celebrated ladies available in London, reveals that roughly half of them were blonde, probably dyed. Many of them also, Harris tells us, had 'a noted affection for the brandy or the gin bottle'.

'wanton', 'dissheveled' golden ringlets with which to clutch
at Adam 'as the vine curls her tendrils . . .'. Shakespeare had
expressed the secretive fascination and fear of blonde hair in
The Merchant of Venice, giving Portia hair that is 'a golden mesh
t'entrap the hearts of men Faster than gnats in a cobweb'.

By 1694, *The Ladies Dictionary*, published in London, was
instructing ladies that hair of a yellow or shining golden colour
has been 'loaded with Obloquies, and is held as a sign of lustful
constitution. For it is a Fancy generally received that the Locks
can never sparkle with Golden Flames without, unless there
lodges some cherished heat of that kind within.' By the end
of the century a popular ballad with a similar message was
doing the rounds:

> The flaxen hath no good report,
> Tho many fancy the same;
> I know that most of that sort
> are notable Girls of the Game . . .

For the next hundred years, as Pope, Coleridge★ and others
wrote of the dangerous lure of blondeness, those unfortunates
with natural blonde hair were still doing their best to conceal
their predicament. A poem from 1772 made the point clear.

★ In his poem *The Ancient Mariner* of 1798, Coleridge painted his
apparition of Death as a hideous blonde.

> 'Her lips were red, her looks were free,
> Her locks were yellow as gold:
> Her skin was as white as leprosy,
> The Nightmare Life-In-Death was she,
> Who thicks man's blood with cold.'

'Alas, I'm sorry for the fair, Who thus disgrace the nation.'
And in 1775 in *The Lady's Magazine*, Dr John Cook offered
a recipe for disguising blonde hair.

> Time was when golden locks were looked upon as
> very beautiful, and even the lass of golden hair was,
> for that very reason, the more eligible, and preferred
> before those of the sex who bore any different colour;
> but now the case is changed . . . for the sake of those
> of the fair sex not so well satisfied with the present
> unfashionable colour of their hair, I freely proffer them
> the following short prescription, easily to be had, and
> as easily prepared whereby they may privately alter,
> whenever they please, the disagreeable yellow hue of
> their hair into an agreeable black, and that without
> either sin, danger, or shame.

Disagreeable yellow hair was already associated with shame,
but it was soon to become equally associated with stupidity.
In Paris in 1775, a beautiful courtesan named Mademoiselle
Rosalie Duthé acquired the dubious honour of becoming
the first officially recorded dumb blonde. She was a famously
vacuous creature who had taken the polite conventions of
feminine modesty to an extreme. She had developed a habit
of long pregnant silences. Perhaps she had nothing to say,
but her mystery and her secretive allure, combined with a
number of other more tangible attributes, meant that she
gathered appreciative customers from the highest social and
political ranks. She had established herself as a rich courtesan
living in considerable style by the time the programme of the
Saint-Germain-des-Prés fair listed her as a robot. 'Machine: A

very beautiful and extremely curious contrivance representing a handsome woman. It performs all the actions of a living creature, eating, drinking, dancing and singing as if it were endowed with a mind. This mechanical woman can actually strip a foreigner to his shirt in a matter of seconds. Its only difficulty is with speech. Experts have already given up hope of curing this defect and admirers prefer to study the machine's movements.'

Paris society, both high and low, who gathered for amusement at these boulevard fairs, began to giggle, and soon the playwright Landrin wove her character into a one-act play, *Les Curiosités de la foire*, which was performed in June 1775 at the Théâtre de l'Ambigu. Like all of the most prominent courtesans of Paris, Mlle Duthé arrived for the first night dressed in her greatest finery (she only ever wore pink), her blonde hair piled up high and laden with feathers and beads, her neck and ears dripping with her most glittering jewels. Having no idea what the play was about, she sat down with her lover, the Duke of Durfort, and was obliged to watch a representation of herself being lampooned on stage. Almost fainting from the embarrassment, she persuaded the duke to complain to the theatre manager, but he refused to take action. Her offer of a kiss for the first poet to redeem her reputation also went unanswered and the play kept Paris laughing for weeks.

It is ironic that, while blonde hair was being pushed out of high-class fashion by French cultural preferences and by its associations with strumpets, it should have reasserted itself as the very image of purity and spiritual integrity in the new literary world of fairytales. It was easy to tell the difference between the strumpet and the fairytale heroine. Mlle Duthé, arrogant, dyed blonde and vain, with strings of male admirers trailing after her aroma of knowing sexuality, was typical of a world far removed from the fairytale. You can instantly tell a classic fairytale heroine by her face and hair. She is young, pale and glowing, her milky northern European complexion tinged with rosy cheeks. Her blue eyes are wide and trusting, her nose delicate and her smile hopeful. Her abundant hair is naturally blonde, and in her manner you can often see an air of innocent virtue and charity, perhaps even a hint of the exploited skivvy waiting to be revealed in all her golden goodness.

By the late seventeenth century, the fairytale heroine had begun to add her dose of magic to the story of the blonde. An élite literary clique in Paris was transforming fairytales from a nomadic oral tradition, which had bounced around the world for centuries, into a literary print culture. Eavesdropping somewhat awkwardly on the tales told in the kitchens of their own grand residences, Charles Perrault, Baroness d'Aulnoy and others sourced their material from the ancient folkloric traditions of the common people. They extracted tales from servants and from maids, and they got hold of tales overheard in the natural nesting places of storytellers – the spinning rooms, the sculleries and by the well-side. The wealth of stories they amassed was the stuff of an illiterate people's culture, the resourceful entertainment of workers, often women, who were involved in the repetitive routine work of spinning, scrubbing, polishing and sewing. In between the revelations of gossip, dreams and news, these women spun stories loaded with all the universal motifs and lessons – of magic, fantasy, romance, generosity, and of greed, lust and cruelty.

With the exception of Snow White, who has always been distinguished by her black hair, the heroines of these fairytales were always blonde. These were not expensively dyed or manipulatively deceptive blondes. Such exotic creatures were unknown in the ordinary illiterate people's culture. These beguiling fictional blondes were entirely natural. Blonde hair cascaded through their stories in lavish quantities, acting as a signal of youth, innocence, purity and cleanliness. Its fairness was accepted, entirely symbolically, both as a sign of quality and as the imagined opposite of foul.

'La Belle aux cheveux d'or', one of the most pointedly loaded of Mme d'Aulnoy's stories, turns on the beauty, goodness and symbolic wealth of a princess's golden hair. 'Once upon a time there lived the daughter of a king, who was so beautiful that there was nothing quite so beautiful on earth; and because she was so beautiful, she was called Beauty with the Golden Hair, for her hair was finer than gold, and marvellously, wondrously blonde, all curly, and fell to her feet. She was always covered by her wavy hair, and clothes embroidered with diamonds and pearls, so that you could not look on her without loving her.' The story has a simple plotline about a poor and generous hero who, after accomplishing three impossible tasks, wins the heart of his princess by his courage and constancy. Being blonde, the princess is of course overflowing with the milk of Christian charity. She is also beautiful and fantastically rich; and her hair provides the source of his initial enchantment and later his married bliss. It is hard to imagine, had the princess been lavishly mousy for example, that the story would have survived for quite so long.

A blonde heroine was essential to a successful fairytale.

The stories of Giambattista Basile, Charles Perrault, and the *grande dames* of the Paris salons, Mme de Villeneuve, Marie-Jeanne L'Héritier de Villandon, Baroness d'Aulnoy and Henriette Julie de Murat, teem with blonde heroines, luminous princesses and generous-spirited girls whose rewards come – by this extraordinary colour-coded bias – as a result of their wealth of hair. 'Peau d'Âne', or 'Donkeyskin', published by Perrault in about 1697, is the tale of a father who wants to marry his daughter. After many failed attempts to escape her father's attentions, the heroine finally disguises herself with a filthy old donkeyskin and flees her home. At the climactic moment her golden hair reveals her worth to an appropriately princely hero and she is rescued from her distress. An exceedingly blonde Catherine Deneuve starred in the role in Jacques Demy's 1971 film *Peau d'Âne*, her hair glowing on screen like some kind of phosphorescent spiritual halo. The classic fairytale *Beauty and the Beast* (an early version of which was published in the eighteenth century by Jeanne Marie Le Prince de Beaumont), reappeared in Jean Cocteau's film *La Belle et la Bête* starring a classically virtuous blonde beauty. This theme of the beautiful, blonde and reluctant bride and the grotesque animal groom has shown great staying power over the centuries and has been the inspiration for numerous pantomimes and melodramas. Its kinkiest version yet is surely Hollywood's 1933 film, *King Kong*.

By the nineteenth century, in the stories of the Brothers Grimm, blonde hair as a colour code was still pouring from the pages. Again the source of the Grimms' tales was the culture of the common people. As children, the Grimm brothers had been lucky to make contact with the prolific storyteller Dorothea Viehmann. She used to stop by regularly at their home to tell a few stories on her way back from selling her farm goods at market. The two boys, Jacob and Wilhelm, used to sit at her feet in the living room of their Cassell home, enraptured as she wove all the classic fairytale ingredients – princesses, monsters, magic animals, magic sacks, wicked stepmothers – into fantasies which humbled the proud, elevated the good and glorified blonde hair. Close friends and relations later contributed similar tales. Wilhelm's mother-in-law produced thirty-six tales for the collection and Dorothea, the boys' sister, married into a family which provided another forty-one. The stories that the Grimms later wrote followed all the same patterns. The virtuous but wronged Rapunzel uses her long blonde hair to pull her lover up into her tower. In 'All-Fur', the mother declares, 'If you desire to marry again after my death, I'd like you to take someone who is as beautiful as I am, and who has golden hair like mine.'

Goldilocks, too, as her name implies, follows the convention of girlish blondeness; and in Cinderella we find the classic exploited skivvy eventually rewarded for her humility and virtue with a prince. At her wedding she appears with a properly coiffed head of blonde hair, signalling her newly revealed inner as well as outer beauty. Cinderella is consistently portrayed in children's books, in films, and in art as a beautiful blonde, her hairstyle changing with the fashions of the day, but her hair colour remaining in consistent contrast with that of her wicked stepmother and stepsisters.

That fairytales were described, in a respected German volume of criticism of 1811, as 'the wisdom of the peoples by which one lives', gives us an idea of the position they occupied in the literary and intellectual pantheon of their times. The sanctification of the Grimm brothers' stories had begun even before they were finally published in 1857. Fifty years earlier, the German poet Clemens Brentano had declared the growing collection a 'treasure'; and in 1842 another poet, Eduard Mörike, called it a 'golden treasure of genuine poetry'. By the late nineteenth century, the Grimms' tales and those of their contemporary Hans Christian Andersen were widely known and admired across the Western world and the values of their stories were becoming lodged in the imaginations of its children. Blonde hair had won itself a wholly new and eager constituency.

9

WRETCHED PICKLED VICTIMS

IN VICTORIAN England, blonde hair came tumbling back into prominence, less as a fashion among women than as a passion among men. If the blonde had been a preoccupation of Western art, literature and popular culture in classical, medieval, Renaissance and Elizabethan times, for the Victorians it became an outright obsession. In the paintings, poems, novels and other frantic outpourings of their period, the Victorians indulged in wild and fantastic images of hair, investing it with magical and symbolic powers. In the pecking order of obsessions, it was the blonde that triggered the most flamboyant responses. It kindled sentimental associations with cloying fairytale heroines; but it also re-emerged as a thrilling symbol of money and of sex, and became an expression of the notorious and unquenchable Victorian fascination with these consuming twin passions.

The Victorians were well versed in their divine and demonic blonde antecedents. They revelled in the saucy misdeeds of Messalina and of Poppaea. They pored over the perils of the Bible's two snakiest sorceresses, Eve and Mary Magdalene. They adored Botticelli's blondes and pondered the vanity, heartlessness and ravishing dominance of history's other notorious blondes.

For Victorian men this powerful blonde imagery was sinister, frightening, grasping – and irresistible. The quivering, glinting blonde locks worked on them like alcohol or cocaine; stimulating, exciting and deadly. In their fevered imaginations, fired by the prudery of Victorian society, blonde hair became the source of overt temptation, the most menacing sexual mantrap yet.

But could the Victorians always be sure that they were 'reading' their silky texts correctly? Like gypsies reading grave portents into their sodden tealeaves, Victorians studied, interpreted, worried over and eventually pawed women's hair to a degree not far off fetishism. Hair descriptions became so abundant and so important in literature that they acted as a method of shorthand character typing.

Elisabeth Gitter defined the types in her fascinating article 'The Power of Women's Hair in the Victorian Imagination'. Dark hair when straight, neatly combed and parted in the middle was typically the property of the virtuous governess or the industrious wife and mother. Tangled, disorderly hair represented the sexually and emotionally volatile woman. Artfully arranged curls denoted a girl-woman, immature and innocent, primped and preened for her man-father to embrace and protect. The more abundant the hair, the more combed, fiddled with, fluffed and displayed, the more obvious and potent the sexual exhibition.

Blonde hair had a particularly intriguing and exciting ambiguity of its own. It was a symbol in the Victorian imagination of the mythologised Victorian woman. When she was an angel, a fairytale child-woman, her blonde hair was a halo signifying her inherent goodness. When she was a demon, however her blonde hair was a sexual snare, invested with magical independent energy; enchanting, fascinating and ultimately devouring. Just as in the Middle Ages when the Virgin Mary's golden hair symbolised her incorruptible purity while Eve's represented lust, blonde hair in the Victorian era took on a similar duality. Was the Victorian blonde an angel or a demon? Context was essential for interpretation and Victorian literature frequently turned on the mistakes of men who, to their cost, misinterpreted her.

The innocent blonde is easy to spot in the novels of Charles Dickens. More than most other writers of the period, Dickens used the universal lessons of fairytales in his novels and created on his young girl characters a wealth of blonde hair signalling their spiritual integrity. His blonde women, cited by Elisabeth Gitter as the nearest descendants of the golden-haired fairytale princess, are doll-like creatures identified by their transcendence and purity. In the turbulent setting of *A Tale of Two Cities*, for example, Lucie Manette's long golden hair helps her amnesiac father to recognise her as he compares it to the golden strands of her dead mother's hair that he has treasured during years of imprisonment. Lucie uses her hair to warm his head, restoring him to life. Then, once married, she becomes the radiant angel, 'ever busily winding the golden thread that bound them all together, weaving the service of her happy influence through the tissue of all their lives'. Many such winsome young girls fill the pages of Dickens's novels, carefully drawn child-angels imbued with powerful contemporary ideals of innocence.

George Eliot's blondes are more deceptive. In *Middlemarch*, Mr Lydgate is led blindly into an infatuation with Rosamund Vincy's immaculate 'infantile fairness' which she blatantly uses, along with her swan neck, to seduce him. She 'turned her long neck a little, and put up her hand to touch her wondrous hair-plaits – an habitual gesture with her as pretty as any movements of a kitten's paw'. Married and trapped in the golden web of a woman who has turned out to be self-centred, indolent and narcissistic, Lydgate recalls his 'old dreamland, in which Rosamond Vincy appeared to be that perfect piece of womanhood who would reverence her husband's mind after the fashion of an accomplished mermaid, using her comb and looking-glass and singing her song for the relaxation of his adored wisdom alone'.

Clearly, Lydgate's knowledge of mermaids was a little patchy. As Thackeray pointed out in *Vanity Fair*, the stage for one of Victorian literature's most wicked blonde sorceresses, mermaids may look pretty enough sitting on rocks with their mirrors and combs, 'but when they sink into their native element, depend on it those mermaids are about no good, and we had best not examine the fiendish marine cannibals, revelling and feasting on their wretched pickled victims'. Thackeray's sandy-haired witch, Becky Sharp, is finally exposed as a monster: 'In describing this siren, singing and smiling, coaxing and cajoling, the author, with modest pride, asks his readers all round, has he once forgotten the laws of politeness and showed the monster's hideous tail above water? No! Those who like may peep down under the waves that are pretty transparent, and see it writhing and twirling, diabolically hideous and slimy, flapping amongst bones, or curling round corpses.'

Fascination with female hair was not confined to literature. In everyday life the Victorians developed a bizarre popular passion for hair and hair tokens which at its peak turned into an extraordinary cultural obsession. Ladies wore pieces of jewellery – necklaces of hair beads, earrings, bracelets and brooches – made out of the intricately plaited hair of family members, lovers and friends, sometimes living but often dead. The middle-class Victorian woman, supplied with a hair-working kit and pattern book, would while away hours by the fireside, weaving and plaiting hair into lockets, into larger basket patterns or nosegays, and constructing elegant landscapes with weeping willows to hang on the wall. Elaborate works of hair made by Messrs Forrer of Hanover Square were displayed at the Great Exhibition of 1851, and a full-length life-sized portrait of Queen Victoria, made entirely of human hair, caused a sensation at the Paris Exposition of 1855. The ubiquitous lock of hair, framed on the wall or enclosed in a locket, became an object of importance with an intrinsic value, a treasured repository of emotional attachment which contained something of the spirit within.

Hair was transformed into merchandise, a commodity which could be traded for wedded bliss, for sex or simply for cash. Robert Browning, writing to his future wife in 1845, nervously asks for 'what I have always dared to think I would ask you for . . . one day! Give me . . . who never dream of being worth such a gift . . . give me so much of you – all precious that you are – as may be given in a lock of your hair.' Elizabeth Barrett's timorous reply suggests that his request is so intimate it is tantamount to demanding her instant sexual surrender. 'I never gave away what you ask me to give you, to a human being, except to my nearest relatives and once or twice or thrice to female friends . . .' Browning finally got his coveted curl, set in a ring, and he was ecstatic. 'I was happy, so happy before! But I am happier and richer now . . . I will live and die with your beautiful ring, your beloved hair – comforting me, blessing me.'

The married Elizabeth Barrett Browning never forgot the power or the commodity value of hair. One of her sonnets opens with the unflinching image of hair for sale: 'The soul's Rialto hath its merchandise; I barter curl for curl upon that mart'. Her husband, in his poem 'Gold Hair: A Story of Pornic', takes hair as currency to its literal conclusion with the story of a beautiful and ethereal girl whose deathbed request is that her abundant golden hair remain undisturbed. The legend of her saintly life grows until many years later the floor of the church is taken up for repair and village boys begin digging for buried treasure. They find the remains of the girl and, wedged around her skull where her hair had been, are heaps of gold coins. The girl's golden hair, which everyone had assumed was a symbol of her inner sanctity, is revealed as her secret corruption, the sign of an appalling materialism and sinister filth.

In the Victorian mind, gold was filthy lucre, deceptively gleaming but tainted beneath with base dirt and death, a vice which should be hidden, hoarded and buried. Ruskin expressed special loathing for the power of money, used like golden hair as a snare: 'These pieces of gold . . .' he wrote in 'Unto This Last', 'are, in fact, nothing more than a kind of Byzantine harness or trappings, very glittering and beautiful in barbaric sight, wherewith we bridle the creatures.'

Yet commerce in blonde hair – and by extension in sex – was a theme that became as compelling as it was disgusting for the Victorian literati. Tennyson's poem 'The Ringlet' is rank with the perceived fallacies, deceptions and depravities of a woman's golden hair. Christina Rossetti's bewitching poem 'Goblin Market' depicts the frank sale of blonde hair for sex. Blonde Laura, longing for the goblins' fruit, laments her poverty. The goblins reply: '"You have much gold upon your head, /Buy from us with a golden curl." /She clipped a precious golden lock, /She dropped a tear more rare than pearl,/ Then sucked their fruit globes fair or red.'

Christina Rossetti's brother, Dante Gabriel Rossetti, illustrated the poem with the image of a voluptuous blonde Laura cutting a lock of her long, thick hair before an audience of salivating rodents. It was an appropriate subject for him. Of all the Pre-Raphaelite painters in his circle, Rossetti stood out for many reasons; but the most unusual was his obsession with hair. Stories were told of him panting through the streets of London in pursuit of a head of irresistible hair, or breaking off in mid-conversation at parties, as if hypnotised, on seeing a mass of gorgeous hair enter the room. His wife, Lizzie Siddal, and his other models, Fanny Cornforth and Jane Morris, are splendidly pallid and worshippable women who appear with obsessive frequency in his paintings. They all had strikingly beautiful hair, thick, opulent locks which in many of his pictures seem to take on an erotic life of their own. Morris had dark brown hair, Cornforth had blonde hair and Siddal had coppery gold hair. After Siddal's death in 1862, Rossetti wrapped her hair around first drafts of his early poetry which he buried with her. Seven years later, when he disinterred her body to retrieve his manuscripts, the hair, so the story goes, had grown and knotted itself around the paper, having to be cut away to release his work. Rossetti was shocked by the dead Siddal's assertive powers, and in his poem 'Life-in-Love' he pondered the terrifying supernatural radiance of her hair. 'Mid change the changeless night environeth, /Lies all that golden hair undimmed in death.'

By no means all of the beauties in Rossetti's paintings have blonde hair, but a large number of his *femme fatale* characters do.

His painting *Lady Lilith* of 1864 shows a sensuous heavy-lidded beauty of voluptuous, almost drugged intensity, langorously stroking her thick wavy blonde hair as if she were preening a pet tiger. Lilith, in Talmudic legend, was the first wife of Adam and a beautiful but evil woman. She appears in this picture as a classic Rossetti blonde, a deadly siren, ready to use her gold to tempt, corrupt and strangle. In case we hadn't got the message, on the back of a second portrait of Lilith, a watercolour of 1867, Rossetti copied out Shelley's translation of Goethe's description of Lilith:

> Hold then thy heart against her shining hair,
> If, by thy fate, she spread it once for thee,
> For, when she nets a young man in that snare,
> So twines she him he never may be free.

Rossetti's expressions of beauty in paint were perhaps a response to the unbeautiful broodings of his own mind, which spilled out in his caustically misogynistic poetry. Repeatedly he milked the sexual conceit of blonde hair. In 1859 he wrote a poem about a prostitute, a golden-haired temptress called Jenny, whose hair symbolises her lasciviousness and greed. The poem drips with ghastly combinations of lust, fear and avarice: Rossetti's narrator wrestles between desire and contempt as he lays gold coins in the sleeping Jenny's hair. In the end, Rossetti's own fantasy of dominance is revealed, and with it a fearful loathing of the womankind he desperately desires.

With all these Victorians spewing out page after impassioned page about prostitutes with blonde hair, can we assume that the hordes of women employed in this booming industry had continued the historic tradition, and did actually have blonde hair? One document published in 1883 for the edification of British visitors to Paris gives us a clue. Entitled *The Pretty Women of Paris. Their Names and Addresses, Qualities and Faults, Being a Complete Directory or Guide to the Pleasure For Visitors to the Gay City*, this enthralling little volume lists the prostitutes of Paris alphabetically. It gives comprehensive details of their careers, their men and their marriages, and merciless details of their attributes and their specialities, as well as Michelin-style 'worth a detour' recommendations. Among the nearly three hundred entries, there are roughly three times as many blondes as there are brunettes.

Clotilde Charvet, of 23 Rue Boissy d'Anglas, gets a reasonable star ranking. 'Youth and beauty are to be found united here – fine liquid eyes, well-cut features; small waist, and divine bust which proudly advances its twin riches – such are the charms of Clotilde. Her hair, naturally black, is dyed a rich gold, offering a strange contrast, when in a state of nudity, to the other hirsute attractions of her fair form.'

Valentine d'Egbord, of 12 Avenue d'Atnin, fares less well. She 'appears in our new Book of Revelations as a curiosity. Like a work of art, for marvellous preservation of remains of beauty, we treat her as such and request visitors "not to touch". Through the use and abuse of some cheap golden dye, her hair has fallen off, never to grow again, and has been replaced by an expensive arrangement of a rich, door-mat colour.'

Cora Pearl, the famous English courtesan who was once carried into her own dinner party on an enormous silver dish, naked but for a sprinkling of parsley, is listed as a blonde. In her heyday this harlot de luxe, who included Napoleon III and the Duc de Rivoli among her long 'golden chain' of customers, used to dye her hair to match her outfits, often appearing in a fetching canary yellow from head to foot. Her fellow British *grandes horizontales*, many of them stars of stage and bed, also cultivated an image of blondeness. Lillie Langtry claimed in her autobiography to have had naturally corn-coloured hair. Laura Bell, an ex-shopgirl from Belfast who in one night reputedly relieved the Nepalese envoy, General HRH Prince Jung Bahadur, of today's equivalent of £250,000, was known as a blonde; and Skittles was described, with some poetic licence, as a natural blonde by an aspiring lover, the Comte de Maugny. Dozens of these magnificent women, the 'yellow chignoned denizens of St John's Wood and Pimlico', as the *Pall Mall Gazette* described them in 1869, gathered every day in Hyde Park in their fashionable carriages, to be admired by wealthy gentlemen as well as dazzled wives and daughters.

Blonde hair had long been familiar as a symbol of sexual temptation and corruption – both in reality and in fiction. But only the Victorians could have turned it into an instrument of death. Bram Stoker's story 'The Secret of the Growing Gold' hinges on blonde hair as the tool of revenge of a murdered woman. The body is walled up in her former lover's fireplace, and her hair, humming with menace, continues to grow through a crack in the stone. Eventually it mysteriously kills both the lover's pregnant new wife and the terrified lover himself, who is discovered with a look of 'unutterable horror' on his face as he stares glassily at his feet, which have been entwined with 'tresses of golden hair, streaked with grey'.

The Victorian idea that blonde hair possessed terrifying powers was bolstered further by the slew of paintings of exotic blonde soul-stealers that poured from the brushes of Victorian artists. Lord Leighton's 1858 painting *The Fisherman and the Syren: from a ballad by Goethe* was first exhibited with a translation of the final lines of Goethe's poem 'Der Fischer': 'Half drew she him, Half sunk he in, And never more was seen.' The deadly siren wraps herself around the fisherman, who looks utterly drugged by desire, her long, sinuous fish tail coiled around his legs, her arms clasped round his neck and her streaming mass of blonde hair cascading provocatively down her smooth, naked back.

One of the most sinisterly grasping blonde seductresses of the period appears in John William Waterhouse's 1893 *La Belle Dame Sans Merci*. Based on Keats's poem, the painting depicts the kneeling armour-clad knight, spellbound by his enchantress, drawn down into a fatal embrace by the noose of golden hair she has wound around his neck. This extraordinary image passed on into opera, recreated in a scene in Debussy's eerie work, *Pelléas and Mélisande*. The love-struck Pelléas, symbolically accepting his own end, wraps Mélisande's golden hair around his neck in ecstasy as the music soars to climactic rapture.

For the average Victorian male idealist, a man perhaps a little frightened by sex, certainly troubled by the maelstrom of terrifying blondes depicted all around him, still deeply attached to his mother and assailed by religious doubts, home and the comfortingly unerotic devotions of a motherly wife became a sanctuary. As Britain raced into the modern technological age, society too had begun to change at an alarming speed. Some Victorians were intoxicated by the sensation of living in a new world of unlimited opportunities. But many more were anxious about the rapid advances of science and democracy while religious faith and political confidence ebbed away. With no apparent end to the hectic boom-and-bust cycles of the financial markets, and the development of the steamship, the locomotive and the electric telegraph, daily business life became an urgent, highly pressured and exhausting struggle. Middle-class men of rectitude were distressed by the new sense of material greed they saw around them, by the moral degeneration and by the harsh loss of tradition. They watched the exploitation of the countryside, with huge tracts of beautiful land being scarred by the smoke and grime of industrial development. They observed the exploitation of the workers. Few could ignore the growing social malaise: wealth for the few and squalor, disease and crime for the masses.

These men, plagued by the dark implications of their changing world, retreated to the home in search of the reassuringly warm comfort of uncorrupted goodness. Home was the psychological equivalent of slippers, 'the shelter', as Ruskin put it, 'not only from all injury, but from all terror, doubt, and division'. A quasi-religious picture of domestic decency and moral respectability became the anchor of their hectic lives. Home provided the solace of order and ritual. There were fixed mealtimes preceded by grace, daily prayers, evening routines of newspapers and needlework, perhaps readings from a novel. At the heart of this picture was a dutiful and devoted wife, free from all corrupting contact with the sins and brutalities of the modern world. The feminine archetype in the home was a creature of moral beauty, pure and immaculately unsexual. By the mid-century such saintly wives were being described as Madonnas – without apparent irony or impiety. Literary heroines characterised by unflagging moral integrity, wore their hair – fashionably dark – parted at the centre 'à la Madonna', a style influenced by Raphael's Madonnas. Dorothea is described in *Middlemarch* as 'the most perfect young Madonna I ever saw'. And Tennyson in his poem 'To Rosa' refers to Rosa Baring's 'madonna grace of parted hair', by which he implies her inspiring moral qualities.

Conditioned to bashful modesty and passivity, these women cultivated a becoming delicacy, wearing it like some kind of saintly halo. Many were actually enfeebled by frequent pregnancies, lack of exercise, an indigestible diet and the ludicrous fashion of dangerously tight corsets. How remote they seem, these controlled, centre-parted creatures, weaving and stitching away tirelessly at their hair pictures and their antimacassars. How sharply they contrast with the devouring, deceitful blondes of Victorian man's highly charged erotic imagination. It would be stretching the evidence, however, to imply such a clear-cut division. Nothing is ever quite this tidy, and there were of course dark seductresses as well as blonde wives of immaculate decorum and duty. But the broad pattern of character-typing by pigment is unmistakable.

Home and a Madonna-like wife of perfect devotion was not the only escape for anxious Victorian gentlemen caught in a rapidly changing society which was also repressive and excessively prudish. Children, too, particularly girls, became the subject of strange longings by grown men. Motivated by a nostalgia for lost innocence or perhaps by guilt at the despoliation of their world, these men regarded children as a hope for the future. Men who suffered perhaps from the failure of their own adult relationships, or from an emotional imbalance triggered by an over- or under-protected childhood, seemed particularly drawn to young girls. Those with angelic blonde hair represented a more obvious paradise of innocence, something precious which, like the colour of their hair, is lost by degrees as they grow up and gain experience, learn of sin and guilt, of worldly desires and expectations.

Victorian men of letters, men of the Church, men of great intellectual calibre and standing, enjoyed the easy and innocent pleasure of the company of young girls. John Ruskin was one of them. He was brought up on strict puritanical principles by a wealthy wine-merchant father and potently evangelical mother, who doted to an almost suffocating degree on their only son. As a child he was forbidden toys. Instead, his father read to him from Tacitus and his mother read him the Bible from beginning to end, several times. At eleven he wrote two thousand rhyming couplets influenced by Wordsworth, and by the time he had left Oxford, Ruskin possessed a mind which was, even by Victorian standards, prodigiously fine. But he was a loner and a dreamer, who was being gradually pushed by a stifling society into some truly eccentric obsessions. His disastrous adult romances with the young girls Adele Domecq, Effie Gray and Rose La Touche (all three of whom, incidentally, had blonde or pale mousy hair) have been amply documented; and there were many other young girls to whom he was attracted.

It was the fantasy imagery of the innocent young girl that seemed to appeal to him as much as anything else. Ruskin was particularly taken by the illustrations of Kate Greenaway. These cloyingly sweet watercolours depicted innocent little girls, often blonde and curly-haired, playing in a Regency setting. Childish innocence as beauty and the preciousness of childhood were themes much discussed by philosophers, artists and writers of the period. Ruskin would have been aware of the artworld view that the face of a child is the nearest thing to the ideal beauty of classical art. Yet with Greenaway's work,

Phryne Before the Tribunal, Jean-Léon Gérôme, 1861. The judges have abandoned all pretence of composure in their appreciative scrutiny of this classical blonde goddess. (Hamburger Kunsthalle/bpk berlin/Elke Walford 2002)

The Crucifixion, Masaccio, early 15th century. Mary Magdalene is identified by her long blonde hair flowing loosely over her red cloak. (Museo Nazionale di Capodimonte)

The Wilton Diptych (right hand panel), unknown English or French artist, *c.* 1395–9. (The National Gallery, London)

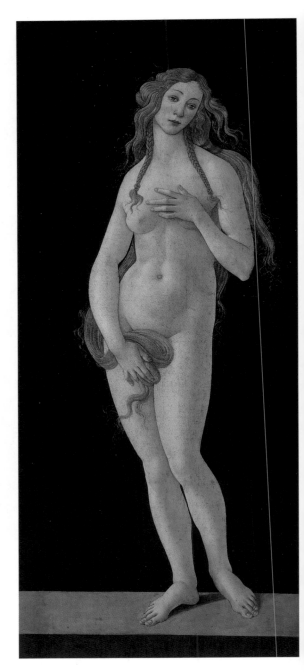

Venus, Botticelli Workshop *c.* 1486. The powerful sexuality of this image lies in the luxuriant golden-blonde hair. (Berlin Staatliche Museum/Preubischer Kulturbesitz Gemäldegalerie/Jörg P. Anders)

A Blonde Woman, Palma Vecchio, early 16th century. This woman, perhaps a Venetian courtesan, has dyed her hair blonde with only partial success. (The National Gallery, London)

Elizabeth 1, coronation portrait, unknown artist, *c.* 1600. Tree-ring dating has recently established that this portrait was painted some forty years after the coronation, at the end of Queen Elizabeth's life. Stage-managing her image right to the last, she had the artist alter her natural auburn hair to a dazzling shade of golden blonde for posterity. (The National Portrait Gallery, London)

The Fisherman and the Syren: from a Ballard by Goethe, Frederic Leighton, *c.* 1856–8.
Victorian painters were intrigued by the theme of seductive but destructive blonde sea
maidens. (Bristol City Museum and Art Gallery, UK/Bridgeman Art Library)

Hitler greets a group of blond boys. (Hulton Archive/Getty Images)

Stalin holds up a blond boy on a window ledge. (Keystone)

Roosevelt holds his
two blond grandsons
on his lap. (*New York
Times* Co./Archive
Photos)

Jean Harlow, Hollywood's first blonde goddess. She dyed her hair with a diabolical mixture of peroxide, household bleach, soap flakes and ammonia until it fell out and she was forced to wear a wig. (John Kobal Foundation)

Marilyn Monroe, the big chief of all blondes. She refused to allow other blonde actresses on the film set with her. (M. Garrett/Archive Photos)

Doris Day, one of the irrepressibly perky movie blondes of the 1960s. She was said to be so pure even Moses couldn't part her knees. (Archive Photos)

Tippi Hedren, the cool, sophisticated Hitchcock blonde. (Keystone)

Diana, Princess of Wales, who spent almost £4,000 a year having her hair bleached. (Keystone)

Baroness Thatcher, whose rigidly lacquered helmet of blonde hair was a demonstration of self-assurance, conviction and power. (Hulton Archive/Getty Images)

'Being blonde is definitely a different state of mind,' Madonna has said. 'I can't really put my finger on it, but the artifice of being blonde has some incredible sort of sexual connotation.' (Corbis Sygma)

in spite of his position as the leading art critic of the day, Ruskin allowed his sentimental inclinations to overcome his critical faculties. He delivered infatuated lectures on her art at Oxford and collected large numbers of her pictures.

Victorian prudery acknowledged so little but, by some upside-down logic, therefore sanctioned so much. Charles Dodgson, the Oxford mathematics lecturer better known as Lewis Carroll, was another Victorian with a freakishly fine mind and reverence for young girls. Carroll was a celibate cleric with a stammer and a somewhat eccentric appearance. His private world centred on the children, particularly girls, he pursued and befriended at social events, on trains, at the beach at Eastbourne, anywhere, from his twenties until his death at the age of sixty-six. In the company of these children he found that his shyness and stammer vanished and he was able to abandon his masculine world of strict logical sense and escape into a fantasy world of childish nonsense. As an author of children's books, he needed the company of children to help him understand the workings of the childish imagination. But he also seems to have needed the escapist indulgence of children as a prop for his psychological balance. On his summer holidays at Eastbourne he actively sought out children to befriend, totting up his score at the end of each holiday. In 1877, for example, he noted 'my child-friends, during this seaside visit, have been far more numerous than in any former year'. He then listed the names of twenty-six children from eleven families.

One of his favourite girls was Alice Liddell, the daughter of his neighbour the Dean of Christ Church. She was a lively and pretty girl with short, straight dark hair and a pixie face;

and she was the inspiration for his *Alice's Adventures in Wonderland*.

Carroll did some preliminary manuscript drawings of Alice for his books, but they look nothing like the impish scabby-kneed Alice Liddell. They show Alice as an angel instead of a child, a creature without real imperfections, a bride just out of reach, who has been transformed into an idealised, intensely ravishable beauty. Carroll drew long, luxurious wavy hair on his Alice. It was just like that of the blonde Helen of Troy painted by Rossetti, whom Carroll knew and whose works he admired and, in at least one case, owned. Carroll also owned a painting by Arthur Hughes, *Girl with Lilacs*, a rather blowzy celebration of feminine innocence in which a melancholic girl bends her head of thick blonde hair beneath a branch heavy with lilac flowers. Perhaps Carroll illustrated his own masterpiece while gazing up at this picture, which hung over the fireplace in his study, because the hair, dress and pose of the Hughes girl are almost exactly reproduced in his drawing of Alice growing under the influence of the 'Drink Me' potion. Carroll's nephew recalled that his uncle 'dwelt with intense pleasure on the exquisite contrasts of colour which it contained – the gold hair of the girl standing out against the purple of lilac blossoms'. Clearly, Carroll shared with Hughes an image of the perfect golden-haired female innocent that was inspired by visions of threatened virgin beauty.

In the first published edition of the books of 1865, illustrated by John Tenniel with an intrusive collaboration by Carroll, Alice is blonde. Carroll had sent Tenniel a photograph he had taken of his child-friend Mary Hilton Badcock, suggesting he should use her as a model for the Alice illustrations. In the photograph, Mary is a faintly grumpy-looking blonde sitting rigid as a peg doll in a hairband and the sort of puff-sleeved and crinolined party dress that Alice wears for her adventures. Tenniel probably worked straight from the photograph as he rarely used live models, and his illustrations set a high standard for all the many Alices to come.*

In almost all the post-Tenniel editions, artists have remained true to Alice's blonde colour-coding. Her hair colour became an essential marker to her character and to her powers of attraction – the innocent, unsullied child, open to the purest, most intense, most spiritual feelings and utterly receptive to the fantasy nonsense and anarchy of the stories she inhabits.

Most Victorians were probably unaware of the lustful under-tones in the Alice that finally appeared on the page in 1865. These same Victorians also barely flinched at contemporary poetry full of the urgent and flagrantly sexual desires of adults for children. Ernest Dowson in the fourth of his *Sonnets of a Little Girl*, wrote of a young blonde girl:

> . . . and in those pure grey eyes,
> That sweet child face, those tumbled curls of gold,
> And in thy smiles and loving, soft replies
> I find the whole of love – hear full and low
> Its mystic ocean's tremulous ebb and flow.

It seems extraordinary that this kind of sexually fraught material barely elicited comment. At the same time a multitude of harmless childish imagery was being produced on a prolific scale in art and literature to feed the more innocently mawkish

---

* One of the most original was the 1929 edition with illustrations by Willy Pogany showing Alice as a bobby-soxer with a blonde bob.

fascinations of Victorian society. Perhaps its huge popularity helped to make a sexual reverence for children seem more respectable.

Cherubic boys and girls were a popular subject for painters. John Everett Millais's most famous painting, *Bubbles*, of his blond curly-haired grandson, was used by Pears Soap as one of the first big advertising campaigns. If the public wanted pictures of pretty children, Millais reasoned, then he would give them just that. He made between £30,000 and £40,000 a year providing effusively sentimental images of childish purity and innocence.

Blonde hair's dual significance to the Victorians as a sign either of innocence or of bewitching sexuality gave it a dangerous ambiguity. But blonde hair had also begun to develop a third distinctive significance which was to lead in the early twentieth century to an inflammatory belief in its political superiority. This was to prove devastating.

THE ARYAN AWAKES

I N T H E glittering light of candles, a sentimental middle-class Victorian celebration of Christmas Eve is in progress. A tree stands in one corner laden with strings of glass beads and bright ribbons, sweetmeats and sugar-coated biscuits. Children in their best clothes are gathered around the piano singing 'Silent Night', their faces bathed with a pink glow of delicious anticipation. Perhaps they will have fairytales before bed, *Cinderella* or *Little Red Riding Hood*, but not until Papa has been indulged and allowed to sing his favourite *Lieder*.

The trappings of the fashionable Victorian Christmas in the mid-nineteenth century hardly presented a picture of true British culture. The idea of a tree was a German import, its dangling baked goodies of German inspiration too. 'Silent Night' was a translation from the German. *Cinderella* and *Little Red Riding Hood* were favourites from the German Grimm brothers' fairy-story collection. And Papa's melancholy renditions of Schubert and Schumann were certainly inspired by romantic dreams of the Rhine. All this was no coincidence, for Britain in the mid-nineteenth century was gripped by a cult of all things Germanic. In literature, art and music, Germany was proving to be an irresistible fashion-leader. Writers, historians, philosophers, musicians and artists flocked to Germany to suck inspiration from the country's great creative brains.

Thomas Carlyle was indefatigable in his translations and interpret-ations of Goethe and Schiller. George Eliot devoted the same efforts to Strauss. Turner romanticised the Rhine. British comp-osers and musicians migrated to Leipzig, Berlin, Munich and Frankfurt, the better to idolise the great German classical comp-osers, and to warm their bones with the music of the Romantic era, the sounds of Mendelssohn, Schubert and Schumann.

Germany was emerging as the powerhouse of Europe. It was producing the most exhilarating ideas in art and intel-lect, and it was gathering steam in the newly developing worlds of science and invention. At the same time, under Bismarck's glittering eye Germany was transforming itself into an industrialised economic behemoth. There were many contexts in which the peculiar genius and manifest destiny of the Teutonic race could be vaunted. By the mid-nineteenth century a self-flattering cult of things Germanic had begun to affect many British historians, who promoted the idea of the Anglo-Saxon race being part of a greater glorious Teutonic pedigree. The addiction to this crudely romantic view of Germany spread fast. Thomas Arnold in his 1841 series of lectures as Regius Professor at Oxford lauded the Germanic roots of the English nation and noted approvingly that 'half of Europe, and all America and Australia, are German more or less completely, in race, in language, or in institutions, or in all.' John Green, the author of the immensely popular *Short History of the English People* (1874), spread the perception that the Anglo-Saxons were really a Germanic people. Many more respected chroniclers continued the growing homage to Germany.

The contemporary fascination with the Anglo-Saxons' Teutonic ancestry, with its vigour, might and magnitude, its civilisation and freedom, conveniently came with a clear-cut identity. Teutonic blood, it was believed, gave the British their heroic mien, their noble height, their long, aristocratic faces, their blue eyes and their blonde hair. Sir Walter Scott's *Ivanhoe*, published in 1819, set out the accepted colour-coding of the day. The Saxon hero, Ivanhoe, has fair hair and blue eyes like his Saxon father; his wife, Rowena, is flaxen-haired and blue-eyed; but the beautiful Rebecca, a Jewish woman, has dark hair, dark eyes and dark skin. Responding, in the introduction to a later edition, to a reader's letter asking why Ivanhoe did not marry Rebecca, Scott exposed the unpalatable truth already current in his century: 'the prejudices of the age rendered such a union almost impossible'. Even in the mild medievalism of Scott's novels, ugly divisions were evident. Christian could not marry Jew; but more telling, in the rising heat of racialist thought, was the belief that the blonde and fair-skinned should not marry a member of a darker race.

Race was as important as any religious division. It was believed to determine levels of civilisation, success and power – everything, in other words, by which human beings ranked each other's affairs. Benjamin Disraeli in his novel *Coningsby* (1844) described the Saxons as a pure race. 'You come from the shores of the Northern Sea, land of the blue eye, and the golden hair, and the frank brow: 'tis a famous breed . . .' Openly exalting the Jewish race in his next novel, *Tancred* (1847), Disraeli also recognised the greatness of England: 'it is an affair of race. A Saxon race . . . has stamped its diligent and methodic character on the century. And when a superior race, with a superior idea to work and order, advances, its state will be progressive . . . All is race; there is no other truth.'

Nineteenth-century Europeans conceived easily enough of

race in terms of colour. Attitudes to people with darker skins were naturally affected by such well-publicised events as the Indian Mutiny of 1857–8 and the Jamaican Revolt of 1865. Misgivings about race were already prompting some Europeans to consider the more subtle gradations of worth believed to exist within the ranks of white men themselves. By the mid-nineteenth century most Victorian commentators agreed that, within Europe, the Teutonic peoples of the north and west were racially superior to the Latin hordes to the south and the Slavonic peoples to the east. The belief in the natural superiority of blonde-haired and blue-eyed northern Europeans was gradually gaining acceptance.

European racialist thought already had a long history. Back in 1799, the appropriately named Charles White in his *Account of the Regular Gradation of Man* had already singled out the white European as the most beautiful and intelligent of the human race, running on in eulogies about his 'nobly arched head' and 'quantity of brain', and bounding into flights of ecstasy over fair Teutonic womankind. Many eighteenth-century anthropologists had worked on the 'chain of being' in which humans were graded hierarchically from the lowliest creatures, the Negroes, bushmen and aborigines, to the yellow races and Slavs, until they reached the white race, the supreme species. Physical beauty was the most important way of classifying species within this hierarchy, and blonde colouring, supposedly derived from the sun, was believed to be a sign of greatness, together with blue eyes which reflected the sky.

Linguistic origins, too, were traced in an attempt to excavate the foundations of race. Scholars concluded that Sanskrit, as the basis of all Western languages, had been imported from Asia by the migration of Aryan peoples. It was here, at the end of the eighteenth century, that the word Aryan first made its appearance to describe, in the limpid imaginations of the Romantics, a superior people of honour, nobility, courage and beauty who had migrated west with the sun to find their own homeland. In 1855 Comte Arthur de Gobineau, a droopy-eyed aesthete with a weak chin but a volcanic eloquence, made use of linguistic and anthropological theories to spell out his awesome ideas in his 'Essay on the Inequality of Human Races'. De Gobineau finally anchored the Aryan in European history. He had always been interested in the antiquity and supposedly noble lineage of his own family (plain Arthur Gobineau's title was spurious) and this gave him a hierarchical outlook on the world which helps to explain his racialism. The Aryan as a beautiful, noble, chivalrous and freedom-loving aristocrat became his particular obsession. With the help of his like-minded friend Richard Wagner and the Bayreuth circle, his message was spread and popularised in Germany. After his death in 1882, de Gobineau's judgment of the black and yellow races was distorted and turned against the Jew. With an ideal blonde and blue-eyed human stereotype ready to do battle against a chosen public enemy, racialism and nationalism were beginning to fuse in the minds of a small but fiery minority. Yet the blonde Aryan was still no more than a racial myth.

Other racial thinkers took the message further, many of them integrating Darwinism and racism. Darwin himself was no racialist, but his ideas of 'natural selection' and 'the survival of the fittest' were open to subjective use by zealots who interpreted them as scientific backing for their theories of racial hierarchies. It was around this time that Darwin's cousin, Sir Francis Galton, began developing ideas of heredity which were to have an enduring if unintended influence on the blonde-versus-dark racial debate. In his most influential book, *Hereditary Genius* (1869), he explained how 'if I had to classify persons according to worth, I should consider each of them under the three heads of physique, ability and character'. Galton listed thirteen types of natural ability and classified the men of England accordingly – from judges down to wrestlers. He looked particularly at marriage, and argued that special help should be given to those couples who might produce children of greater than average 'civic worth'. He believed that the birth-rate of the unfit should be restricted and that of the fit encouraged. For the late Victorians, the concept of planned breeding of humans like that of cows or barley to improve the species had a strong appeal, and in 1885 Galton coined the term 'eugenics'. By 1900 eugenics had caught the popular imagination. The name Eugene was suddenly fashionable, and eugenics societies and journals sprang up all over Britain. Eugenics had gained both popular and scientific respectability. It was also, like Darwinism, with its ideas of superior and inferior humans, eagerly adopted by the ideologues of Aryan supremacy.

It was only a matter of time before a number of eugenics enthusiasts began making plans to establish new isolated settlements where a better and purer Aryan race could breed without infection from other less able races. In 1886, Elisabeth Förster-Nietzsche, sister of the philosopher Friedrich Nietzsche, arrived in the jungle of Paraguay with her husband, Bernhard Förster, and a party of fourteen German families of supposedly pure Aryan genetic extraction. They were there to found a colony, New Germany, which would become the core of a new Fatherland and would eventually grow into an empire covering the whole continent. In New Germany, so the theory went, a pure, blonde, blue-eyed race of Aryans would be allowed to breed, unhampered by the germ of Jewry. Eventually they would take their rightful place as the master race.*

Their motives were muddled at best. Förster, an unsophisticated, crudely anti-Semitic unemployed Berlin schoolmaster, believed he might play a part in saving the German race from destruction by the Jews. He also hoped his efforts might curry favour with Richard Wagner, the composer and founder of a powerful nationalistic and anti-Semitic circle at Bayreuth of which he longed to be a part. Elisabeth Förster-Nietzsche also mixed social advancement with political motives. Founding a new Aryan colony would in part satisfy her nationalism and her anti-Semitism. It would also, she hoped, help her to achieve her own ambitions to join the Bayreuth circle. They made a vivid pair: both stubborn, snobbish, fantastically egocentric and pedagogic. She was delicately pretty, with a *retroussé* nose and mousy hair; he was tall, handsome and lavishly bearded, with woolly eyebrows and a wolfish gaze.

The colonists had high hopes for their new world. Förster had heard with excited approval rumours of a wild Aryan race

* In 1871 the German Anthropological Society had carried out a survey of over 75,000 Jewish schoolchildren and found that 11 per cent were pure blondes, 42 per cent black-haired and 47 per cent mixed. The results were not, of course, well received. Although they should have silenced the racialists on the black and white categorisation of pure Jews and Aryans, the ideology of pure racial breeds had already been steeped in myths and stereotypes too long for abandonment and the concept of a racial enemy was too convenient to be easily discarded.

somewhere in the interior of the South American continent, fleshing out a theory which had long obsessed European explorers. 'I know not whether to believe the accounts,' he wrote, 'widespread but perhaps exaggerated, of a race consisting of wasted, blonde individuals . . . I am not in a position to say what truth there may be in these reports, which I have heard from many sides, but the existence of such a racially distinct group seems indisputable.'

When the Försters and their band of immigrants arrived at Asunción docks in Paraguay on 15 March 1886, their hopes were toweringly high. Each year they envisaged shiploads of new immigrants coming out to join their growing empire. The dream did not turn out quite as planned. A failure to purchase land for the colonists, bad soil, failed crops, corrupt leadership by the Försters, and a lack of subsequent supporting waves of colonists, led to the dwindling of the colony's fortunes and eventually to Förster's suicide. Elisabeth returned to Germany in 1893, having carefully concealed the facts with a face-saving fiction. She was disappointed but not defeated, and on her return threw her energies considerably more successfully into the business of myth-making around her brother, who died in 1900. New Germany still exists in Paraguay, a sad, largely deserted jungle settlement, inhabited by a handful of impoverished blue-eyed and in some cases blonde descendants of the original settlers.

Elisabeth Förster-Nietzsche had been accurate in her targeting of the Wagners as the group to which she might hitch her social ambitions. The cult they created at Bayreuth had indeed become a powerful force for the promotion of the Aryan racial myth. The Bayreuth Festival spirit and Wagnerism, born with the première of *The Ring* at Wagner's new opera house at Bayreuth in 1876, developed almost immediately into something close to a religious cult, with Wagner its high priest and Bayreuth its temple. From its very earliest days, it was nurtured by fanatics and presented as something uniquely German; and before long it was being moulded into a form of cultural nationalism, its operas enlisted to spread patriotic and racialist messages.

Two years after the founding of the Bayreuth Festival, the *Bayreuther Blatter* newspaper was launched as a vehicle for plugging Wagner's ideas among his patrons. Soon it was on the ideological rampage, spreading anti–Semitic, xenophobic poison. Wagner's operas, in particular *Parsifal*, were interpreted less for their artistic content than for their political imagery of German renewal as a nation purified of Jews, liberals and democrats. The Festspielhaus, the Bayreuth opera house, was described as a 'glorious Aryan fortress' and a 'temple of art for the renewal of Aryan blood, for the awakening of the general consciousness of the Indo-German nation and specifically for the strengthening of a healthy Germanness'. Critics insufficiently appreciative of Wagner's work were denounced as Jews. Artistic comment as well as performance had become overtly political.

Racialist zealots began recruiting Wagner's works to their cause. One of them was the fanatical Wagnerian and influential racialist Houston Stewart Chamberlain, the son of a British military family, who in 1908 had married Eva, one of Wagner's daughters. He was a passionate Germanophile, tall and bony with the craggy brows and ferocious eyes of an obsessive. His great life *oeuvre*, *Foundations of the Nineteenth Century*, heavily influenced by de Gobineau, was an interpretation of Western history in terms of racial struggle. Naturally, the Aryan race sat at the top of the heap. Published in 1899, at a moment when racialist thought was becoming widespread, the book's theories of Aryan-German supremacy and the Jewish threat seemed perfectly plausible to the racially insecure. To serious scholars, on the other hand, it was utterly risible. Chamberlain even turned Christ into a blond man with blue eyes, a Nordic carrier of light hailing from Aryan Galilee. His book was referred to as 'The German Bible' and was promoted by the All-German League, a group which included large numbers of teachers who spread its message in schools across Germany. An impoverished young Austrian watercolourist named Adolf Hitler was among many to be impressed by Chamberlain's theories of Aryan supremacy. Thirty-five years later some of them reappeared, slightly refashioned, in *Mein Kampf*.

European thought in the late nineteenth century was slowly being coloured by a small but relentlessly building tide of racialism. But Europe was by no means alone in this. In America, racial ideas were being imported directly from Western Europe and were developing to suit local conditions. America turned out to be a perfect breeding ground. Ever since the seventeenth century, white Americans, finding evidence of God's approval in the survival and prosperity of their tiny colonies, had cultivated the idea that they were a 'chosen people'. Until the outbreak of the Civil War, virtually all American settlers had come from northern or western Europe and considered themselves Anglo-Saxon or Teutonic in origin.

By the early nineteenth century, the colonists' determined drive westwards towards the Pacific was being presented as a mirror of the ancient mythical westward movement of blonde Aryan peoples following the path of the sun. When the 'children of Adam', many of them German, Danish and Swedish immigrants, finally arrived on the Pacific coast in 1846, their achievement was vigorously celebrated in the American Senate as one of the greatest events in the history of the world. Their triumphant 'circumambulation of the world' as the vanguard of the Aryan race was hailed across America and Europe, putting them 'in sight of the eastern shore of that Asia in which their first parents were originally planted'. That many of these 'children of Adam' fitted the stereotypical picture of the racial ideal bolstered white America's self-image further. Everywhere they looked, Americans saw Aryan progress and Aryans in charge. It is not altogether surprising that Aryan purity was becoming accepted as a source of white America's success.

By the 1850s America's Aryans were finding abundant proof of their superiority: in their growing material wealth, in their successful revolution against Britain, and in an economic growth spurt that had astonished the world. The presence of large numbers of blacks, Indians and Mexicans also meant that white American populations were receptive to ideas of racial hierarchies. As in Europe, such concepts were no longer restricted to an educated minority. By the turn of the century, the ideas of a succession of philosophers, sociologists, anthropologists and straightforward eccentrics had begun to reach a wider mass audience, promoting the idea that the blonde and blue-eyed ruled the world.

BODY POLITICS

IN 1898, Havelock Ellis, a British sexologist by profession, began a truly eccentric survey of the hair colour of the eminent men and women represented over six hundred years of British history in the National Portrait Gallery. For two years this tall, strikingly bearded fanatic wandered the galleries in his plus fours and long woolly socks with a step-ladder and magnifying glass, examining hair lines, roots, eyebrows and eye colour. 'I cannot regret the hours spent in the company of so many wise and noble and gracious personages', he later wrote. After many more months of analysis, he came up with an 'index of pigmentation' in which he ranked the eminent persons into sixteen groups in descending order of blondeness. His work, published in the *Monthly Review* in 1901 under the title 'The Comparative Abilities of the Fair and the Dark', was a remarkable, if unedifying, piece of fantasy which perfectly complemented its times.

Top of the table were the political reformers and agitators. 'These are not persons who reach the House of Lords,' Ellis informed his audience. 'Their opinions are too radical . . . but they possess in an extreme degree the sanguine irrepressible energy, the great temporal ambitions, the personal persuasive force, the oratorical aptitudes that in a minor degree tend to mark the class that rises to the aristocracy . . .' Ellis wrote lengthy explanations of the (rather poor) middle ranking achieved by the royal family (seventh after political reformers, sailors, men of science, soldiers, artists and poets), putting their lack of blondeness down to the 'intermixture with darker foreign royal stock'. The low position of the hereditary aristocracy (ranked twelfth) was also explained by infusions of foreign blood, and because 'peers have been in a position to select as wives . . . the most beautiful women, and there can be little doubt that the most beautiful women, at all events in our own country, have tended more to be dark than to be fair. This is proved by the low index of pigmentation of the famous beauties in the Gallery.' Dark hair was clearly still considered, by eccentric sexologists at least, as the acme of feminine beauty in 1901.

It was a *tour de force* of capillary extrapolation. Three years later, he expanded his extraordinary data and theories in his book *A Study of British Genius*, naming in an appendix the eminent men and women of an updated survey. Among those included in the fair category, his restless ruler types, he named Addison, Arkwright, Congreve, Frobisher, Gordon, Newton, Peel, Ruskin, Shelley, Smollett, Thackeray and Turner. Not even a snigger greeted its publication.

At the same time as Ellis was examining the hair covering Britain's greatest brains, a Swedish painter was beginning to put into tangible form an image of blonde idealism which was to spread across northern Europe, captivating the hearts and minds of a generation of aspirant blondes. Carl Larsson, born in 1853, came from a poor background in Stockholm and rose, in the manner of fairytale heroes, to become in the early twentieth century one of Europe's best-loved illustrators of an idyllic happy family life. Larsson painted bright watercolours of his wife, Karin, and their eight blonde children, romping, fishing and picnicking in sun-dappled bliss at the family's country home outside Stockholm. His work seemed to crystallise the dreams of many millions of Swedes and, outside Sweden, particularly of Germans. Larsson's publishers sold millions of reproductions of his paintings, which were pinned up in middle- and working-class homes, in nurseries, corridors and country cottages all over northern Europe. His books, too, sold by the hundreds of thousands. For their foreign sales, his publishers concentrated their efforts on Germany, where Nordic writers were enjoying great commercial success. His most famous book for the German market was the ingeniously titled *Das Haus in der Sonne* (*The House in the Sun*), which was filled with images of the blonde Larsson children larking about in the sun. This perfectly suited middle-class Germany's current obsessions with family solidity, health, fresh air, and a 'simple' life in the country, as well as their as yet little-acknowledged racial outlook. The book, published in 1909, had an overwhelming reception. As one critic wrote, 'You don't discuss Larsson – you love him.' Larsson won universally positive reviews and was presented, particularly in the provincial press, as the perfect 'Teuton', occasionally with racialist overtones. The painter himself matched the Aryan ideal, being tall, blue-eyed and blond.

Larsson began receiving enquiries almost weekly from Austrian and German art dealers wanting to offer reproductions of his watercolours for sale. He had already been fêted in some twenty-five separate exhibitions of his work in German art galleries. Massive numbers of reproductions were sold to German buyers and his images appeared regularly in mass-market German magazines. Larsson had tapped a singular nerve in the

German psyche with his pure, almost religious portrayal of the blonde ideal.

Larsson's work, which equated blondeness with special beauty and value, triggered a wealth of subconscious references, among which was the view that the blonde Larssen children were little angels, as sacred and innocent as the pure winged creatures of medieval painting. It may have been a sign of the gloom of the times that angels of a sort began appearing in Britain, too, when the Larsson clan's popularity was reaching its peak in the 1910s. A form of near-idolatory emerged in Britain focused on the blond hair of innocent and vulnerable young men trapped in the atrocities of war. Their attractions recalled the Victorian imagery of golden-haired boy-knights such as Tennyson's Galahad, and the beautiful boys of Victorian poetry such as the one in Oscar Wilde's 'Wasted Days': 'A fair slim boy not made for this world's pain, With hair of gold thick clustering round his ears . . .'

By 1914 these boys were both British and German, officers and men, and their blond hair shone like saintly haloes around their innocent faces. Wilfred Owen fondly recalled the beauty of a 'navy boy' met in a train compartment: 'His head was golden like the oranges/ That catch their brightness from Las Palmas sun.' Sassoon was struck by the attractions of a dead blond German. Finding a pile of German corpses, he was moved to lift and prop up the blond one against a bank. 'He didn't look to be more than eighteen . . . I thought what a gentle face he had . . . Perhaps I had some dim sense of the futility which had put an end to this good-looking youth.'

The universal horror at the futility of wartime sacrifice contributed to the association of youthful blonde hair with a special kind of sacred beauty. Perhaps this helps to explain the enduring worship of Rupert Brooke, whose sensitive good looks and blond hair became part of the myth surrounding his poetry and later his memory. Brooke was the first of the war poets, a quintessential fair young son of England, whose death in April 1915 embodied the justice of the cause for which the nation fought. Brooke's singular myth was immortalised in a poem written by Frances Cornford while he was still a Cambridge undergraduate:

> A young Apollo, golden-haired,
> Stands dreaming on the verge of strife,
> Magnificently unprepared
> For the long littleness of life.

It already contained the elements of the legend that was to develop during his life and then to grow unchecked after his death. Soon the golden-haired Apollo was made real in the famous photograph taken by Sherril Schell in 1913. It shows Brooke with bare shoulders and flowing blond hair and became the frontispiece to his volume of poems. Although Brooke's friends were appalled by the photograph, mockingly referring to it as 'Your Favourite Actress', few were impervious to Brooke's 'golden beauty'.

Rupert Brooke's golden-haloed image as the symbol of romantic British sacrifice had far-reaching effects. In an article in the *Eugenics Review*, written in 1920, G. P. Mudge waxed lyrical upon the great blonde race that is the English and the need to preserve it by means of eugenics.

Among the signs that England is awakening to the significance of her racial worth and all that it has meant in the culture, chivalry, justice and sportsmanship of the world, we cannot fail to recall the recent poems of Rupert Brooke . . . there is still with us a great reservoir of that English character we want, in the women of that type. England still contains a large percentage of the tall, well-built, blond, blue- or grey-eyed type, who recall to us the men that fashioned England, who were among the first to go to France in 1914 and 1915, and who laid the traditions of our national life, of our statecraft, and of our fighting services . . . For this is the type that must at all costs not only preserve itself against extinction, but must multiply until all the needs of the Empire are met.

A wave of rampantly racialist writing was now entering the *petit-bourgeois* consciousness on both sides of the Atlantic. The arguments of these Aryan apologists showed little sophistication. Using mostly clichéd phrases, they pounded the reading public with theories of Aryan or Nordic superiority, appealing to base mass instincts and often simply projecting educated middle-class values on to Nordic or Aryan man as if they were racial qualities. Blond hair – on men – was vaunted as the mark of the ultimate superior being.

Jörg Lanz von Liebenfels, a highly idiosyncratic former Cistercian monk and zealous anti-Semite, was one whose obsessions reached a wide audience in Austria and Germany. In 1907, Lanz (he was born plain Adolf Lanz but changed his name to indicate his membership of the Aryan ruling class) founded a religious order, the Ordo Novi Templi. Only blonds with blue eyes and blessed with an 'Ario-heroic' figure could apply to join, and successful applicants became part of an association designed to support the threatened blonde Aryan race in all countries of the world. They were expected to make racially appropriate marriages and to take part in a bizarre liturgy and calendar of mystical ceremonial. Lanz appointed himself prior and established the order in a romantically ruined medieval castle, Burg Werfenstein, perched on a sheer rock cliff above the River Danube near Vienna. He celebrated Christmas Day that year by hoisting a swastika flag on top of the castle tower.

Lanz's extraordinary views were already well known in racialist circles in Vienna, and the behaviour of his sect, with its bizarre and highly visible festivals and its pagan rites, brought him publicity in the national press. In 1905 he had launched his racialist periodical, *Ostara*, named after the pagan goddess of spring. Lanz was driven by the concept of a Manichaean struggle between the noble and virtuous blond and the bestial dark man, bent upon subversion, corruption and the destruction of the Aryan race. The filthy promiscuity of the barbaric and vice-ridden Jewish race would eventually, he believed, drag the Aryans down the evolutionary ladder.

Lanz's magazines were full of crazed notions of the dictatorship of what he called the blonde aristocracy. He published profiles of ideal Aryan blondes, paintings of blondes by approved 'blonde' Renaissance painters, and claims about the superior physical, intellectual and spiritual qualities of blondes. And he peppered his pages with slogans such as 'Are you blonde? Are you a man? Read *Ostara*, the journal for blond fighters for men's rights,' Right-wing contributors produced a few of the essays in *Ostara*, but Lanz wrote most of the numbers himself. They were distributed from city tobacco kiosks and had a respectable circulation, particularly strong in the numerous right-wing student fencing associations. In 1907, Lanz claimed an enormous circulation of 100,000 copies.

In *Ostara*, Lanz was in essence laying out his ideas for overthrowing the evils of modern mankind and paving the way for the domination of the blonde race. His solution involved a racial struggle in which inferior races would be deported, enslaved, sterilised or incinerated. Socialism, democracy, feminism and other corrupting emancipatory influences would be crushed. Elements of Lanz's bizarre fantasies are clearly reflected in the policies of the Third Reich. The extermination of inferior races, laws banning inter-racial marriages, the spread of pure-blooded Germans by way of polygamy, and the preferential care of Aryan mothers in the SS Lebensborn maternity homes were all anticipated in the pages of *Ostara*.

Not everyone was taken in by Lanz's absurd rhetoric, nor that of others writing in the same vein. In July 1930, Professor H. J. Fleure published an article called 'The Nordic Myth' in the *Eugenics Review*, pulling apart the supposedly scientific basis on which white superiority was based and exposing the 'sinister' political propaganda of those who peddled such theories. He denounced Wagner and his 'widespread expansion of egoism into racialism under the guise of a glorification of the fair-haired, blue-eyed white man'. He condemned Wagner's son-in-law Houston Stewart Chamberlain. He damned a good deal of modern writing as unscientific dogma; and he concluded that 'the idea of a tall, fair, Nordic type existing in purity in the far past as the indigenous stock of the region is as yet quite unproven. Nor is it by any means certain that the type which combines these characters is normally a highly superior one . . .'

Professor Fleure was fighting a losing battle. All across northern Europe and America the worship of the fair-haired blue-eyed white man had become a powerful force. In Germany you have only to look at the paintings of an early-nineteenth-century artist by the name of Fidus to get an idea of the blonde mania with which the Germans were already deliriously obsessed. Fidus himself was a dark, brooding, lupine figure. But his work, a kitschy cross between William Blake and modern-day Japanese comics, was dominated by the theme of the tall, solitary, molten-eyed blond hero. This superman tended to stand, inexplicably naked, on windy mountain peaks, his arms victoriously raised as he gazed up at the sun or out over a vast distant landscape, looking with the swirling fronds and tendrils of his yolk-yellow hair somehow like a capital letter in a richly illuminated manuscript. Fidus's men were invariably blond with lurid matching pubic hair. And his favourite portrayal styled them as Norse gods or warriors, with their requisite quota of suggestively undulating blonde maidens and who knows what strange thoughts of Aryan domination.

Germanic interest in the Nordic race had encouraged a general Romantic fascination with Scandinavia. The Germans had begun visiting the region as early as the 1820s despite poor transportation and accommodation. But tourists began to visit in greater numbers after Kaiser Wilhelm II began sailing every year from 1889 onwards to Norwegian fjords in his yacht, accompanied by a company of men who raved about their great Nordic past and pranced about on deck fancying themselves as the new Vikings. Scandinavian habits of outdoor exercise and gymnastics were brought back and enthusiastically embraced in Germany. After the stolid, overloaded style of nineteenth-century bourgeois living, people were drawn to the idea of a reformed life. They focused on new diets (including vegetarianism), outdoor exercise, gymnastics, natural healing and fresh air. Nudism, too, became a popular way of linking the body more closely to nature. In Germany the term *Nacktkultur* was coined in 1903 in a book by Heinrich Scham which established an enduring if questionable link between nudism, vegetarianism, social reform and 'racial hygiene', in particular anti-Semitism. Nudism had been used in the past by the German medical profession to combat diseases such as tuberculosis. But soon healthy Germans, many of them urban, took up the habit. The movement produced a lot of slightly repellent body-beautiful journals and by the late 1920s the streams of books on the subject, often enticingly illustrated with blonde beauties, had become hugely popular.

One particular book, *Der Mensche und die Sonne* (*Man and Sunlight*), written in 1924 by Hans Suren, was so popular it ran to sixty-eight editions in its first year of publication. No doubt the numerous photographs of attractive young nudes pursuing outdoor sports – running, gymnastics, volleyball, even skiing – accounted for part of the book's enormous success. There they were on page after page, lavishly bronzed and mostly blonde athletes (though predominantly men), cavorting in Arcadian flowered meadows, on idyllic beaches, in peaceful marshes and racing in goose-pimpled agony down icy Alpine slopes, in every case burnished by an omnipresent sunshine. But its text, an impassioned espousal of male health, strength and beauty justifying a new utopian culture, also appealed to a recently urbanised German population hungry for change.

The search for beauty, health and racial unity was all part of the appeal of nudism, and by 1930 there were more than three million members of nudist clubs in Germany, as well as 60,000 members of nudist schools who attended classes naked. In Britain, things had not got quite so far, but nudism had nevertheless produced a popular set of values supposed to banish inhibitions and to promote healthy open-air lifestyles.*

The British movement also pandered to political and racial as well as aesthetic prejudices. 'In this society,' wrote one keen British nudist, 'the notion is prevalent that the nordic blond type is much better adapted for gymnosophy [nudism] than the Mediterranean brunette type . . . these race bigots [the society's leaders] are bitterly antisemitic and would under no circumstances admit a Jew.'

While blonde nudists were proclaiming their vigorous superiority, other new aesthetic exclusivities were spreading their influence. One of them, linked to the powerful image of the burnished blond superman, was suntans. In the nineteenth century only outdoor labourers were tanned, and it was thought that long exposure to the sun roughened the sensibilities as well as the complexion. But by the early twentieth century, many low-status jobs involved working long hours indoors with little holiday, and so suntans became a way of displaying wealth and leisure for those who could afford to lie in the sun. The fashion for the suntan is said to have been invented

---

* British nudist societies began as rather pallid little gatherings in shady, ant-infested corners of isolated woods. Soon the expanding membership built luxurious camps and in winter they gathered indoors around sunlamps. Mass nudism, however, permitted no levelling of class distinctions: at the superior camps, butlers and waitresses providing refreshments of tinned salmon and lettuce were obliged to acknowledge their lower social status by wearing G-strings and aprons.

by Coco Chanel in 1923 when she descended the gangplank of the Duke of Westminster's yacht on the French Riviera, burnished with an apparently all-over tan. Fashionable tourists from the Scott Fitzgerald Beautiful People set, clustered in their particular colonies along the gleaming coast, quickly derobed and stretched themselves out in the baking sun to acquire matching tans. Within a few years no romantic hero was without one.

The Riviera set provided, as Harold Acton noted, a sporadic peep-show of changing society. Its new leaders were style-setters and self-made celebrities like Coco Chanel. As a hat-maker in fashionable Deauville in the early 1900s, Chanel had found that ladies would stop and chat to her during the day and then ignore her at society events after dark. But by 1920 she was being received everywhere and was photographed in cahoots with society ladies and on the arms and knees of titled men. Fashions were changing, too. On women, suntans, cropped hair, short dresses, beach pyjamas and sparse jewellery were in. White-powdered faces, constraining clothing, hats and jewels (except pearls) were out.

Hair colour was also changing. On men, the racial ideal in Europe and America had long demanded its heroes to be blond, tall and athletic, just like Hobey Baker, perhaps the most brilliant athlete ever to attend Princeton University. Baker's tall blond figure as captain of the football team in 1913 indelibly impressed Scott Fitzgerald in his freshman year, and became the model for Allenby, the football captain in *This Side of Paradise*.★

★ The novel, written in 1920, contains a conversation in which the key characters discuss why two-thirds of the members of every senior council over a ten-year period at Princeton have been blond, and why well over half the presidents of the United States were blond. They conclude that the blond man is a 'higher type'.

Baker may also have been the model for the noble, romantic and pointedly Anglo-Saxon statue of *The Christian Student* which stood until 1930 with its back to the library at Princeton, representing the official ideal of an American undergraduate.

If American men aspired to being blond, fashionable ladies in the 1920s most certainly did not. Dark, lustrous curls or smooth, glossy expanses of straight raven hair had been the ultimate expression of feminine beauty for something like ten generations. Despite the racial rhetoric of the time, the Victorian association of blonde hair with grasping duplicitous eroticism and with low-class promiscuity had kept it that way. The appearance of the first nude blonde calendar girl in 1913 had not helped the image of the blonde in the eyes of high society. The calendar pin-up was based on an oil painting by Paul Chabas of a blonde girl in a lake, which might have gone unnoticed if Anthony Comstock of the New York Society for the Suppression of Vice had not seen it in a gallery and demanded it be removed. A lively dispute ensued, the nude blonde gained notoriety and her image was immediately pirated by calendar companies and distributed by the hundreds of thousands. Reproductions eventually appeared on posters, cigar wrappers, sweet boxes, postcards and even on braces.

Within a few years, in the trend-setting microcosm of the French Riviera, divisions were breaking down and perceptions were being reshaped. Hydrogen peroxide dyes were being marketed for the first time and women were in a mood to experiment. The Americans had already successfully introduced the glamorous values of the jazz age, fast cocktails and an infectious indifference to tradition, and a number of amusing American women had begun making bold sexually liberated statements with their cropped bleached-blonde hair.

Florence Lacaze, who came over to Europe from San Francisco with her fabulously wealthy husband Frank Jay Gould, was a startling blonde force of nature who entertained lavishly, introduced waterskiing, collected art and held literary lunches in her vast Cannes villa, employing secretaries to do her reading for her. Her chic sun-bleached hair was met with approval by the Riviera luminaries of arts and letters, and with the waves of dukes and duchesses, kings, queens, princesses and counts and their assorted hangers-on who dropped in every summer.

From the smoothest, artiest, most *mondain* circles from which fashion often got its kick-start, Moise Kisling, the Polish-born painter known as Kiki, had married Renée Gros. She was a magnificent blonde blaze of unforgettable vitality. Sybille Bedford described her memorably:

> A head of rock-hewn features supported on a strong neck and powerful bronzed shoulders, large prominent blue eyes, heavy-lidded, thickly lined with kohl and a fat blue, honey fair hair, straight cut, savagely bleached and streaked by sea water and sun, a fringe covering one side of the wide forehead, a nose like a parrot's beak. Her clothes dazzled with strong plain colours; she dressed simply, a pair of sailor's trousers, bare-backed singlets, turquoise or scarlet, sea-shells about her neck, shell and ivory bracelets on her arms. It was superb. And when the monster smiled – proffering, it might be, a slice of melon – it was a smile of serene sweetness and sensuality.

Blonde hair, long the racial ideal cherished by anthropologists, eugenicists, sexologists, assorted cranks and their growing audiences, was breaking out into fashionable reality.

It still, however, carried exciting hints of sexual menace. At a party in Hollywood in the early 1930s, Margot Asquith was asked rather cattily by a blonde Jean Harlow how she pronounced her first name. 'The "t" is silent,' she replied, 'as in Harlow.'

12

THE MAN WHO WOULD BE GOD

I N 1931, *Platinum Blonde* opened in American cinemas, kicking off a capillary revolution. Jean Harlow, the star, had dyed her hair a dazzling shade of blonde. Her erotic glamour and salty delivery filled the cinemas of depression-hit America. She was astounding. Americans had never seen anything like it. Harlow slinked across the screen like some radiant hallucination draped in a series of voluptuous bias-cut satin dresses. But all eyes were fixed on her irresistible hair. Harlow had hair like a beacon and other women wanted it. Jean Harlow fan clubs sprang up, and across the country women reached for the peroxide on the shelves of their local drug stores. Soon heads of platinum-blonde hair could be seen vamping up and down fashionable boulevards from Los Angeles to New York. Before long virtually the entire pantheon of America's goddesses, the stars of Hollywood, had followed Harlow's lead and mutated into luminous blondes. In America, blonde was best. It was glamorous and highly attractive. It was also a tacit signal of a superior racial type. Two years later in Germany, Hitler's National Socialist Party came to power. Here, too, according to the Nazi racial ideals of the time, blonde was best. Germany's gods were blonde.

For much of the first half of the twentieth century, the world's three most dynamic nations – Germany, the United

States and the Soviet Union – held beliefs about race which, although pursued quite distinctly, were derived from the same origins. In Germany the Aryan blond was vigorously promoted as the noble, virile and godlike racial ideal, demanding as its corollary the vicious demonisation of the Jew. In white America, a historic belief in the superiority of the Aryan, combined with a persistent strain of anti-Semitism and an antipathy towards blacks, Hispanics and Asians, encouraged the development of a radiantly sunlit blonde American ideal, the WASP American dream. In the ethnically disparate Soviet Union, racial antipathy towards Jews and other minorities, coupled with the need to centralise and energise an ethnically sprawling state, led to a similar creation of a dynamic blonde Soviet ideal, the representative of a new, healthy and vigorous nation.

In each case, by the time war loomed at the end of the 1930s, blonde hair had acquired symbolic trappings of purity and moral cleanliness. It represented an unchallenged physical and intellectual superiority; and it was beautiful. Naturally the top wartime box office female film stars in all three countries were blonde. In the Soviet Union it was the elfin Lyubov Orlova, who made her debut in the 1934 film *A Petersburg Night*, and became the darling of Soviet cinema audiences during the war. In America, the uncontested cinematic pin-up queen for GIs around the world was the bubbly blonde Betty Grable, pure, unthreatening and innocent. And in Germany the spotless blonde maiden Kristina Söderbaum topped the box office for many years.

Germany's blonde ideals had ominous origins dating back to the race theories of the eighteenth and nineteenth centuries. But under the Nazis, the concept of blonde Aryan supremacy was taken with great efficiency to such innovative and diabolical political extremes that it still exerts a horrifying fascination. The Nazi leaders were obsessed with their semi-religious belief in a superior race of blond German godlike men and their mastery of a world in which inferiors had been exterminated. The imagery of the pure blonde Aryan provided the Nazis with the basis for the major themes of their ideology: the contrast between good and evil, pure and impure, order and chaos, salvation and destruction. Himmler calculated that, with the strict application of Nazi laws on racial hygiene, the German people could be gene-coded into a pure-blooded blonde 'Nordic' race within a period of 120 years.

Hitler himself had been an interested follower of blonde supremacy theories from at least as early as the 1910s, when he was an impoverished painter in Vienna. By the time he was plotting his political ascendancy he had elevated this racial ideal to a heroic holy grail. He was well versed in the ideas of Aryan superiority put forward by nineteenth-century racial theorists. Standard biographies demonstrate that he had also read the works of Guido von List, a cultist believer in the future world domination by a blonde Aryan German race. List was a prolific turn-of-the-century writer who helped to popularise the swastika, an ancient Hindu symbol for the sun which he reinterpreted as a sign of the unconquerable Germanic hero. Hitler was also well acquainted as a young man with the crackpot blonde-worshipping ideas of Jorg Lanz von Liebenfels.

Hitler's own obsessions with Aryan racial purity corresponded closely with those of Lanz. In *Mein Kampf*, Hitler laid out his political philosophy based on a violently nationalistic theme of race. His arguments urged the suppression of Jews and Marxists and the squashing of such contaminating ideas as democracy, liberalism and feminism. He presented the blonde Aryan Germanic race as the superior race of genius and devoted many embittered pages to his contempt for the Jews, damning them as parasites in the bodies of other peoples. The 'contamination of our blood, blindly ignored by hundreds of thousands of our people, is carried on systematically by the Jew today. Systematically these black parasites of the nation defile our inexperienced young blonde girls and thereby destroy something which can no longer be replaced in this world.'

Hitler's rhetoric was tailored to suit the prevailing climate of xenophobia, to engineer and use existing hostilities towards the Jews. Unfortunately for the Nazis, few Jews fitted the stereotypical image imposed upon them, and some flouted it to an unreasonable degree. In her memoir of wartime Warsaw ghetto life, Lisa Appignanesi described how the hair colour of her Jewish parents had profound consequences on their lives. Her father was dark, but her mother had inherited her family's persistent natural blondeness. In the horrifying circumstances in which they lived, the psychological results of this genetic accident were striking. Her father was fearful, her mother fearless. With her various acquired Aryan aliases, she could simply pass as a gentile woman and her honey-coloured hair and blue eyes became a means of survival for the entire family. 'Blondeness meant everything that was desirable, strong, powerful; darkness was weak, shameful, uncertain. Since she was blonde power itself, my mother's narrative about her life was never one of fear . . .' Others, too, managed to evade capture and death by dyeing their hair. Ruth Langer, for example, an Austrian-Jewish Olympic swimmer escaped from Austria to England in 1938 by bleaching her hair and carrying a false baptismal certificate.

It seems absurd that the logic of Nazi racism rested so heavily on the vulnerable and easily undermined logic of appearances. Most galling for the Nazi leadership was the fact that the appearance of the German population itself fell far short of their fetishised ideals. Hans Günther, one of Germany's most popular racial theorists, known as 'Rassen Günther' to his friends, had calculated that a mere 6–8 per cent of Germans were pure Nordics. Pure Mediterraneans, he said, made up 2–3 per cent of the population and pure Baltics and Alpines a further 2–3 per cent each. The remainder was a racially muddy mixture.

The relatively small proportion of pure Nordics confirmed Hitler in his idea that Germany's noble blonde race was being destroyed by parasitic Jews. The overriding necessity, as the Nazis saw it, was to nurture and boost the idealised Aryan elements within the population. This, they reasoned, would lead to the rightful European and later world domination by the German Nordics. The Nazis resolved to achieve their aim in two ways. On one level, a cultural one, they conjured up by means of distorting propaganda an image of pure Aryan blondeness for Germany. On another level, they developed two 'curative' population strategies. The first was an Aryan breeding programme by which racially and physically acceptable men and women worked to 'make a child for Hitler'. The second was an abduction policy by which blonde babies and children were taken from their parents in parts of the nascent Nazi empire and brought back to the homeland for Germanisation.

The population programmes were Himmler's responsibility. He planned to breed a whole nation on the model of the élite blond SS superman. In 1934 he appointed the Agriculture Minister, Walther Darré, an Argentine-born former chicken-breeder, as the head of his SS Race Office. Darré was the author of a book called *Blood and Soil*, published by the Nazi party in 1929, in which he posed the thesis that the true German race was one of exceptional quality which should be encouraged to breed productively. His philosophy complemented Himmler's perfectly:

> Just as we breed our Hanoverian horses using a few pure stallions and mares, so we will once again breed pure Nordic Germans by selective cross-breeding through the generations. Perhaps we will not be able to keep the whole of the German people pure through breeding, but the new German nobility will be pedigree in the literal sense of the word . . . From the human reservoir of the SS we shall breed a new nobility. We shall do it in a planned fashion and according to biological laws . . .

Within two years, Himmler had founded the Lebensborn organisation and opened the first of the Lebensborn homes as a medical centre and maternity home. It catered for unmarried (or married) Aryan mothers giving birth to genetically valuable babies fathered by SS men and other racially impeccable Germans. Stories abound of SS men of abundant Aryan genes being singled out as part of the programme and sent off to perform their patriotic duty as 'conception assistants' with blonde Aryan women who, so the theory went, would eventually present the Führer with an Aryan son.

There were twelve Lebensborn homes in Germany and more were set up in occupied territories: three in Poland, two in Austria, and one each in Belgium, Holland, France, Luxemburg and Denmark. In Norway, where the blonde women were considered particularly good breeding stock, nine homes were established. The German High Commissioner for Norway, SS Lieutenant-General Rediess, in his pamphlet *The SS for Greater Germany – with Sword and Cradle*, declared in 1943, 'This is a Germanic people, it is our duty to educate its children and young people to make the Norwegians a Nordic people again, as we understand the term. It is definitely desirable that German soldiers should have as many children as possible by Norwegian women, legitimately or illegitimately.' Few German soldiers were inclined to disobey such explicit orders for patriotic promiscuity.

It is not clear exactly how many children were born as a result of the Lebensborn project – most historians put the figure at 12,000 or fewer. But Himmler himself recognised that it would not, alone, make a significant contribution to the immediate demands of the war nor to the long-term requirement for a fully Nordicised Germany. His second Aryan population-growth scheme was based on the capture of racially acceptable children from conquered territories (judged largely by their blonde hair and blue eyes) who were young enough to allow complete brainwashing and ethnic acceptance as Germans. Following a comprehensive racial and physical examination, the selected children were brought to Germany where their names were changed and all links with their parents severed. Adopted by Nazi families or sent off to live in orphanages or boarding schools, thousands of blonde children were expected to turn themselves into patriotic Germans.

One of the victims, a young Polish girl named Helena Wilkanowicz, later recounted her capture from a Polish orphanage in 1943. 'Three SS men came into the room and put us up against a wall. There were about a hundred children altogether. They immediately picked out the fair children with blue eyes – seven altogether, including me, though I do not have a drop of German blood in my veins. I was twelve years old at the time – somehow I managed to survive. Perhaps it was because I'm blonde, I don't know.'

Himmler's two blond-obsessed population programmes blighted the lives of hundreds of thousands, but did little to Nordicise Germany. If Germany was yet to turn itself into a nation of blondes in practice, the Nazis resolved in the meantime to make it one in theory. Hitler and his Minister of Public Enlightenment and Propaganda, Joseph Goebbels, set about creating a propaganda machine which would gain supremacy over education and the arts and turn Germany into a country teeming with ideologically acceptable blondes. Nazi orthodoxy was instilled at every level. Teachers were required not to convey truth but to promote the official doctrine of Aryan supremacy. Children were encouraged to play not 'Cowboys and Indians' but 'Aryans and Jews'.

Under the eye of the pugnacious Goebbels, the visual arts were systematically purged and remade according to a new aesthetic which endorsed and illustrated Nazi racist policy. The new canon called for the abolition of all forms of 'degenerate' modern art. This meant art associated with social 'degeneracy', in particular Bolshevism, Jewry and speculative capitalism. It included anything abstract, from expressionism to cubism, as well as anything intimating the debauchery of Berlin, all the jazz, high heels, bobbed hair and foxtrots that Hitler loathed. At the same time the Nazis installed in its place a crudely stereo-typed depiction of the noble and heroic blonde German race.

In 1936 Hitler appointed Professor Adolf Ziegler, a promi-nent painter and President of the Reich Chamber of Visual Arts, to lead a purge tribunal to confiscate specimens of morally impoverished degenerate art from over a hundred German museums. The following year a selection of the confiscated paintings was shown in Munich as the first stop of a touring exhibition of Degenerate Art. It was the most popular art exhibition ever staged in the Third Reich. More than two million visitors came to stare at the unframed paintings, displayed in a confused muddle and captioned with filthy jokes; and the venomous Goebbels employed actors to mingle with the crowds and pour scorn on the paintings. The exhibition amounted to the public pillorying of culture associated with politically unacceptable ideology. The Nazis' perceived cleansing of their aesthetic world nicely mirrored their intended racial cleansing of the real world.

The exhibition was part of a heavily staged political showdown in the confrontation between the superior and the inferior race, giving the two opposing sides a clearly defined visual image. The art of the superior race – made by carefully straitjacketed Nazi-approved artists – was promoted at the same time with a loudly trumpeted show entitled the Great German Art Exhibition, displayed nearby in a specially constructed neoclassical 'temple of German art'. Although less successful, this exhibition did establish the unmistakable trends in Third Reich art of the aesthetically sanitised racial ideal. Pompous Nordic heroes dominated the displays, monumental male bodies with the chests of supermen, striking virile poses. They were strangely banal figures, matched by full-bodied Amazonian women with naked skins of corset-like impenetrability, two-dimensionally, lifelessly perfect, who managed to appear both sanctimoniously asexual and pointedly fecund.

The Great German Art Exhibition was a showcase of Nazi paranoia. Hitler's embrace of racialist myth had nurtured in him an obsession with the rural German family of 'noble simplicity'. Accordingly, the exhibition included plenty of images of racially approved rural life. Sylvan idylls teemed with robust blonde peasant families, wielding scythes and sheaves of wheat, dancing round maypoles, positively oozing honesty and virtue and displaying a utopian lifestyle of timeless simplicity far removed from reality.

One of Hitler's pastoral favourites was the 1937 painting *Sower* by Oskar Martin-Amorbach which hung in his headquarters in Munich. A monumental peasant figure with peroxide-blond hair strides across the fields contentedly casting seeds into the bosom of mother earth. In the distance a rainbow hangs above a team of farmers using a primitive plough pulled by cattle. A brilliant light illuminates the unspoiled horizon, symbolising the goodness of a pure and honest life. The painting wilfully ignores the high levels of technology that powered mechanised farming in Germany by this time, the very mechanisation that the Nazis believed was eroding the ethnic features of Germany's glorious classical history. It was only later, once war had become a reality, that Nazi art began depicting the nation's vast and unassailable war potential, churning out images of zealous factory workers forging weapons for the fighters on the front line.

A respectful obeisance to antiquity was another key theme demanded by the Nazis' aesthetic tastemakers. Countless heavily blonded versions of Danaë, Leda, Venus and the Judgement of Paris were churned out, giving a Nordic wash to the classical myths. Themes of youth, health and vigorous outdoor sport were also encouraged. Albert Janesch's *Water Sport* of 1936 depicts fourteen blond supermen in skintight white shorts rowing and canoeing on a river. Each one is a steroidally muscular automaton, and even the cox has the bloated musculature of a bodybuilder. Hitler reserved this one for his private collection.

The cream of Aryan mankind had well-considered templates. Lanz von Liebenfels in his *Ostara* periodicals and many other racial anthropologists had furnished their readers with detailed physiological characteristics in their hymns of praise to the perfect Aryan. In 1926 a committee of German anthropologists and physicians sponsored by the publisher J.F. Lehmann had actually announced a prize to find 'the best Nordic head', both male and female. This was Germany's first official blonde beauty contest. Readers of the most popular racial journals were invited to send in photographs of individuals they considered best represented German Nordic man or woman. When the contest closed on 1 October 1926, 793 male and 506 female photographs had been received and the prizes were duly awarded. A year later a book containing a selection of the photographs was published. *Deutsche Köpfe Nordischer Rasse* is a breathtaking display of self-conscious racial virility. The men are earnest, most of them dressed in sober suits, one in his medal-laden First World War uniform, one sporting a bare hairless torso and gazing towards a future of unassailable Aryan domination. The women are exemplary blonde maidens, piously posed with an eye to the coming German Millennium, their hair plaited and pinned up over the head, or loosely knotted in buns, some in ballgowns, some in peasant blouses, and all fantastically serious as if undertaking a task of supreme national importance.

The Nazi cult of blonde beauty was an essential part of

Goebbels's propaganda campaign.* Given that only 6–8 per cent of Germans were pure blondes, mendacious shufflings of the pack were engineered to turn up blondes with unrealistic regularity. Official photographs and posters of the Hitler Youth showed vigorous young blonde girls and boys striding about like miniature Nazis, cheerily bounding up mountains, performing heroic gymnastic feats, marching beneath swastikas and undertaking exemplary boy-scout-type good deeds.

All these healthy young blondes symbolised the youth of the Nazi regime, its future and its hopes. But the Nazis did not appreciate the irony of lauding qualities that its own leaders did not possess. Hitler was fifty at the start of the war and manifestly not blond, although a portrait in the Imperial War Museum painted by Heinrich Knirr in 1937 gives him some nice golden highlights. Several Nazi supporters attempted to reconcile the image of their leader with the Nazis' ideal racial picture, and some dissembled to a comical degree. A certain A. Richter wrote in a pamphlet entitled *Our Leaders in the Light of the Racial Question and the Study of Prototypes*: 'Hitler is blond, has rosy skin and blue eyes, and therefore is of pure (Aryan) Germanic nature, and all other rumours concerning his appearance or personality have been sown into the soul of the people by the black or red press . . .' Goebbels's mastery

---

* The influences of the Nazis' Nordic aspirations have been felt in some unexpected quarters. Arthur Koestler, as a Jew persecuted during the war, later felt that his badge of acceptance was to be seen with blonde women. According to one of his biographers, Koestler had a preference for blonde women for the rest of his life.

of propaganda was infectious, creating and fetishising the very thing that was lacking in reality.

Only one senior Nazi possessed a physical appearance that fitted the racial ideals of the Third Reich. He was Reinhard Heydrich, Himmler's second-in-command in the SS and later Deputy Reich Protector and Hitler's representative in Czechoslovakia. Heydrich was tall, athletic, blond and blue-eyed, a highly intelligent, calculating man with a menacing streak of cruelty. He appeared to be the perfect Nazi. Ironically, he was also believed to have Jewish ancestry. Tormented by this stain on his pedigree, which was tactically used by both Hitler and Himmler, Heydrich became a driven man, stealthily climbing the ranks of the Nazi party. By the age of thirty-two he was in charge of state security and one of the most powerful men in the country. His awed subordinates referred to him as 'the Blond Beast'. He had proven himself a supreme political manipulator with considerable tactical and psychological skill and in many ways he embodied the SS state completely. Official photographs show an aquiline figure of startling thinness with a lean profile and long almost bloodless fingers. He looks bony and possessed, the poisoned viper of the Third Reich. Yet he was also a family man. One photograph shows him in his weekend Bavarian costume, dressed in leather shorts and playing with his blond infant son. He is lovingly watched over by his blonde wife, Lina, who is done up as Heidi in a dirndl dress.

After Heydrich was assassinated in May 1942 by Czech resistance fighters in Prague, Hitler described him in a funeral address as 'the Man with the Iron Heart'. In inner Nazi circles, he had been talked of as Hitler's successor; and as Joachim Fest points out in his fascinating book *The Face of the Third Reich*, the blond Heydrich was a symbol, perhaps the representative figure of the Third Reich at the peak of its internal and external power. He, more than any other senior officer, represented the youth, vigour, fearlessness – and evil – of their ideals.

Nazi Germany had fashioned an image of itself which was built almost entirely on fantasy; and the parallels with the Soviet Union are clear. Although there were obvious political, ethnic, geographical and demographic differences, Hitler's Germany and Stalin's Soviet Union to a great extent shared fantasy racial self-images.

Stalin faced a far wider ethnic diversity within his borders than did Hitler. The Soviet Union of the 1930s was a colossus made up of a staggering variety of populations, ranging from the largely Slavic Russians (who accounted for by far the largest proportion of the total population), Ukranians and Belorussians to the Turkic peoples in the south, the Latvians, Lithuanians, Mongols, Tartars, Khazars and Moldavians, as well as the Soviet Iranians, Koreans, Chinese, Kurds, Finns, Germans, Greeks and others. In order to promote state unity, and in spite of his own origins in Georgia, Stalin introduced in the 1930s a deliberate strategy of rigid centralisation based on the elevation of the Russians to occupy a core unifying role. Russian history and Russian heroes were aggressively celebrated across the entire Soviet Union. The Russian language became compulsory learning in all schools. A month into the Second World War, *Pravda* referred to 'the great Russian people' as 'the first among the equal peoples of the USSR'. At the same time, in the growing climate of paranoia and xenophobia, a new category of 'enemy nations' deemed to be traitors was created which led to severe recriminations against individuals and entire nations simply on the basis of their ethnic identity. During the late

1930s and early 1940s, hundreds of thousands of Estonians, Latvians, Lithuanians, Poles, Kurds and Chinese, as well as Chechens, Tartars, Ingush and others, were either deported to Siberia and Central Asia or arrested and executed.

Stalin's policies of forced assimilation and national repression rested on the chauvinistic promotion of the Russians at all times. He introduced an aggressive policy of Russocentric propaganda in the mid-1930s and Russians became highly visible as the 'Elder Brother' nation. Visual images were paramount, and their themes, texts and designs were dictated to artists from a single government department, closely regulated by official censors and supervised by the Central Committee. Paintings were turned out in large numbers and reproduced for distribution; and posters were printed in huge editions so that in urban and rural areas, in factories and collective farms, in huts, houses, dormitories and apartments, virtually every person in the state was confronted with the image of the ideal Soviet citizen, both male and female.

The emphasis for this chosen ideal was on the youthful, vigorous and clean-cut look. Given the obsessively pro-Russian bias, the faces in these posters were not Tartar, Mongol or Siberian. The preferred face was of course Russian; but from within the variety of ethnically Russian faces, a particular kind was chosen with fine bones, pale skin, blue eyes and blonde hair. Stalin's ideal citizen was definitely an Aryan. That only a small proportion of Russians, and an even smaller proportion of Soviet citizens nationwide, were actually blonde does not seem to have bothered Stalin and his propagandists. Blondes cropped up more frequently in these propaganda images than any other kind of Russian, each one a vision of divine Aryan superiority. Stalin's new blonde Soviet gods were attractive and enthusiastic workers energetically building a dynamic Soviet paradise of abundance and harmony.

Stalin sourced his propaganda models in unlikely places. Like many Soviets, he was infected with *amerikanomaniya*, hypnotised by the shimmer and power, the methods and products, of the world's most advanced capitalist economy, America. Stalin was attracted not only by its production lines of gleaming tractors and other symbols of technological progress, but also by the powerful appeal of the wholesome, clean-cut, healthy young blondes seen in America's films and news-reels. Stalin himself was an avid fan of Hollywood movies, and it is not surprising that the aura of the glamorous blondes he admired on screen fed into the propaganda imagery of his ideal Soviet citizen. Stalin was also, like Hitler, not young – he was seventy by the end of the war – and for him the vision of superior blonde Aryan youth was crucial in setting a theme of hope and future prosperity for his regime.

Healthy and tanned, displaying mouthfuls of stunning white dentistry, the young blonde men and women of the Soviet Union were depicted accordingly in art and propaganda posters cheerfully building a technological future for the USSR. Beneath flawless blue skies they worked away tirelessly on building sites, tunnelled metros, and brought vast acreages of the steppes under fertile control with combine harvest-ers, threshing machines and other marvellous technological advancements. Stakhanovite worker-heroes were particularly singled out and celebrated. Aleksandr Samokhvalov's 1937 painting *Woman Metro-Builder with a Pneumatic Drill* is typical in its portrayal of a superhuman woman, an epic athlete of the building site, blonde, busty, with broad hips and a gorgeous

Hollywood profile, nonchalantly resting with her drill, looking out towards the light.

Another painting of 1934, by Serafima Ryangina, entitled *Higher and Higher* shows a young man and woman poised like triumphant mountaineers as they climb pylons high above the country in the drive to build an electricity network across the state. The picture could be the cover of a Mills and Boon romantic adventure. He is dark and rugged, she is blonde and cosmetically perfect, smiling euphorically as she looks up towards her country's sunny future.

Posters, too, played a powerful role in proclaiming the newly invincible Soviet state. One colourful work of 1933 shows two slim and strong young women both displaying peroxide-blonde hair under their headscarves, marching happily off to help with the harvest, rakes slung over their shoulders. 'Collective Farm Woman, Be a Shock Worker of the Harvest', exhorted the text. Following Stalin's declaration that Soviet life had become merrier, workers in posters were required to smile. A muscle-bound blond labourer happily cheers the completion of the Dneprostroi Dam in a poster of 1932, and in another of 1934 a pointedly blonde farming family gathers with broad grins round a gramophone with their giggling golden-haired toddler, the books and certificates in the background proof of social advancement and prosperity gained through hard work. As one poster critic wrote in 1933, the image of the worker should include a 'healthy, lively, intelligent, intellectual face. He is the prototype of the new man, a combination of physical strength, energy, fortitude and intelligence.' But a braver reviewer disapproved of the grotesque unreality of these images, particularly the two slim blonde women setting off for the harvest. The artist 'wanted to present healthy, jolly, pretty and intellectual faces, to show the new person who combines in herself physical strength and energy with a high level of culture. But it must be recognised that the artist did not succeed. The *kolkhoznitsy* [collective farm women] are not typical. We have instead some kind of "Mashen'ka and Dasha", pretty and rosy but completely uncharacteristic of the *kolkhoz* masses.'

Of course, all these images were grotesquely unrepresentative of reality. The tractors, drills, combine harvesters and electrical pylons were precisely the things that were missing in Soviet life. In the ruined Soviet villages of the 1930s, a tractor was as rare as a decent meal. Peasant lives were brutish and short, eked out in the squalor of fly-ridden hovels with thatched roofs and mud floors. Millions of emaciated farmers tilled the soil with wooden ploughs. Many more Soviets lived a nightmarish existence of collectivisation and servitude, dealing with communal kitchens and loos, intimidation and informers. City life was oppressively overcrowded, with scarce, rationed food supplies at the ends of long queues, the results of Stalin's policy of exporting grain from the starved countryside in exchange for Western technology. The workers who struggled in ironworks and on assembly lines to achieve Stalin's targets were ill-equipped, inadequately trained and half-starved, typically driven by terror. They were far removed from the blonde bombshell imagery churned out by Stalin's well-oiled propaganda machine.

Yet Stalin saw himself as the very embodiment of progress. There was to be no compromise in his determination to whip his weakened country into shape and catch up the fifty to hundred years he estimated it lagged behind the advanced nations of the West. Stalin was engaged with his country in a struggle for survival and he knew that he badly needed the help of the bourgeois West to succeed. While he enthusiastically and freely adopted the imagery of Hollywood blondes for his propaganda models, he had more difficulty getting hold of the Western technology that was going to enable his Russian socialist state to survive. The capitalist world was also in crisis. The Great Depression had affected every country with which the United States did business, creating ugly scenes of poverty, hatred and war. Roosevelt, like Stalin and Hitler, was to take shelter behind the propaganda of manufactured optimism, in an enhanced world that teemed with racially acceptable blondes.

13

BLONDE VENUS

WHEN ROOSEVELT rolled into office as President of the United States in 1933, serene, dignified and confident, with his elegant cigarette holder and his calculated 'eternal smile', he was taking on a country crouching under a dark cloud of impending bankruptcy, starvation and fear. Within his first hundred days he had averted disaster, restored a psychological balance to the nation and reinvigorated the country with a new sense of purpose and dynamism. In a blizzard of legislative activity the financial sector was shored up with federal support; private enterprise got an injection of public spirit and public money; public works projects were initiated; and work camps were set up for the young. Like Stalin's Soviet Union and Hitler's Germany, America became a planned economy of a sort. Yet it was ruled by neither socialism nor totalitarianism, but by a state capitalism aimed at national prosperity.

In its initial stages, Roosevelt's New Deal was both lauded and cursed. Many of his measures were unpremeditated and incoherent. He created dozens of new agencies, designated by their initials (the CCC, the NRA, the TVA and many more) which frequently confused even the President himself. These agencies were riddled with anomalies, their efforts overlapped, their staff engaged in feuds, and their output was of only partial success. Yet it was with this aura of rapid constructive action that Roosevelt managed to revitalise the United States, injecting new energy and hope into his electorate. He was compassionate and confident. He made courageous speeches. He appeared to be engaged in a great heroic adventure. He convinced millions that he was the heaven-sent man of the hour. In the end, he managed to turn the emergency into a personal triumph.

Roosevelt had an intuitive grasp of the importance of the mass media in modern politics. During his first year in office he gave the first of his nearly 1,000 presidential press conferences, the first of his pioneering 'fireside chat' radio talks, and ensured that he was seen week in week out on the cinema screen, a commanding and vigorous presence which exuded optimism and carefully disguised his infirmity from polio. Film played a key role in the campaign to sell the New Deal to Americans, and in many cinemas the FDR newsreels, glorifying the President with flattering camera angles and friendly sound-bites, were given more time than the accompanying feature film.

In all three countries – the United States, Germany and the Soviet Union – where power was supported or enforced by means of elaborate illusion, the silver screen became the most important myth-making medium of the age, the perfect surface on which to project political fantasy. But when it came to the business of weaving fantasies, no organisation could compete with the dazzling power of Hollywood. America was the ultimate maker of myths, and movies became the most effective expression of American culture. From the 1930s up to the end of the Second World War, Hollywood churned out thousands of films for international audiences which endorsed and illustrated the prevailing racial preference for the Aryan.

Some of them went to extremes in their portrayal of the incorruptible blonde as a symbol of white American superiority. During the early 1930s, a series of what have been called racial adventure films was produced in Hollywood. Shot mainly on backlots in Los Angeles, these films charted the travels of white Americans to darkest Africa, exotic Asia and other hazardous territories. The results were risible in terms of ethnography, but they revealed much about American racial paranoia, focusing on the steamy allure of racial mixing, both cultural and sexual – but mainly sexual.

The typical plot hinged on the wildly arousing violation of a beautiful and innocent blonde by a dark beast of massive sexual potency. Posters advertising *The Blonde Captive* of 1932, for example, showed a gorgeous bare-breasted blonde being dragged off by a simian aborigine. *Trader Horn* of 1930 tells the story of a missionary's daughter kidnapped as a child by cannibals with less than chivalric intentions. She grows up to rule over their tribe, her voluminous blonde hair acting both as an improvised halterneck top and as a symbol of white superiority amid black savagery. And in *Blonde Venus* of 1932, the blonde goddess Marlene Dietrich, who insisted on wearing $60 worth of powdered gold in her wig to give herself a little extra sparkle, appears in a gorilla suit among a chorus-line of gyrating blacked-up beauties. As she peels off her skin she sings 'Hot Voodoo', voicing subliminal desires of miscegenation.

But the film offering the most outrageously heavy-handed dose of racial paranoia was *King Kong*. This grew from an impressively kinky image in the mind of producer Merian Cooper, of a colossal racially coded beast, a gorilla, 'so large', he told the *Hollywood Reporter* in February 1933, 'that he could hold the beauty in the palm of his hand, pulling bits of her clothing from her body until she was denuded'. In the voodoo steaminess of Skull Island, the beautiful blonde Ann Darrow, played by Fay Wray, is kidnapped by natives and sacrificed to the beast, who whisks her away and defends her from dinosaurs and other hideous primeval predators. Acting on his rights of possession, King Kong begins to peel off scraps of her dress, ratcheting up the sexual tensions until eventually he is subdued by white technology, a gas bomb. Chained and enslaved, the gorilla is taken to America, where he escapes to run amok in New York City, throwing cars at the New York Stock Exchange, smashing trains, chewing New Yorkers and eventually climbing the Empire State Building, still clutching his blonde. The film was a box office bonanza and went on to become a global hit. But there was one exception. In Germany, Goebbels banned the film on the basis of the ape's alluring power. But through neutral Sweden he obtained blackmarket copies for the Führer and himself to enjoy. It was still one of Hitler's favourite films at the end of the war when he used to sit in his bunker on the eastern front, watching screenings late into the night.

King Kong was made in 1933, but within a year of its production, American cinema had changed. In July 1934, the Production Code Administration, under its chief censor Joseph Breen, began systematically to regulate the content of Hollywood films. The red-blooded diet of raw sex, vice and violence, offered in a frantic attempt to drum up trade in the face of plummeting depression-hit audiences, was reined in by a new rulebook dedicated to public restraint and social control. Portrayals of abortion, incest, miscegenation, drugs and excessively lustful kissing were banned, as well as the words 'damn', 'God', 'floozy' and 'sex', and any bedroom scene unless both parties had at least one foot on the floor. Comic confusion resulted. While MGM was handing out false breasts with erect nipples to any of its actresses who needed them, the censors were ordering Disney to remove the udders from its cartoon cows.

Pre-code vamps, the blatantly erotic Jean Harlow and Mae West and their dozens of blonded imitators, who had been specifically coloured and shaped as the comically vulgar sales-women of sex, were forced to transform themselves in the new puritan climate. Harlow succeeded in changing herself from modern brassy bad girl into a softer, more wholesome blonde. She became something of a ditzy screwball heroine until she died unexpectedly in 1937 at the age of twenty-six. Some newspaper reports claimed she had been poisoned by the toxic hair dye that for years she had applied every few days to her scalp. Harlow had in fact worn a wig during her last years, having reduced her own hair to the consistency of bristles using a diabolical mixture of peroxide, household bleach, soap flakes and ammonia. But that hair, wig or not, with its numinous screen magnetism, had already irreversibly transformed cinema and with it the self-image of women. Harlow's hair has been imitated with varying degrees of knowing irony ever since.

Mae West, America's hip-swaying queen of sexual innu-endo, for a while fared more successfully in dealing with Hollywood's new codes. Having built herself up as a sassy, sexy, fast-talking comic vamp, West refused to change. She fought with the censors for hundreds of lines, and, even when she lost, the censors could not control her suggestive sing-song delivery. She was even banned from radio after her lubricious rendition, as Eve, of the line 'Would you, honey, like to try this apple?' With a censor stationed on set for each of her films after 1934, checking every line and intimation she inserted, West's public image was gradually being cleansed around her. That year she posed for a Paramount publicity shot as Liberty, in a clear blueprint of the new cleaner blonde look. She stands alone against a black background, boned and corseted into her clinging dress. Her crown is lit up to proclaim her position as twentieth-century American woman. She is a camera creation, a lustrous blonde parody beauty queen, one hand on the contours of her rolling hip, the other holding the symbolic flame, her face gazing up in the smiling knowledge that Paramount Pictures, and indeed the whole film industry, would survive the Great Depression. She is one of America's first blonde pin-up girls.

Mae West's appearance as a clean-cut blonde was a sign of things to come. Within a year, a monstrous, perpetually sparkling golden-haired child actress by the name of Shirley Temple had bounced on to the Hollywood stage. Temple was the archetype of the banal, cuddly doll-blonde whose manufactured optimism was designed to lift a depressed society. She set to work immediately to bludgeon the home front into a state of good cheer. Hollywood's film producers, an ardently pro-Roosevelt clique, had been directly instructed by Washington with the task of cheering up America. They took their orders to an extreme with Shirley, who was allowed to reign as a focal point of Hollywood from 1935 to 1938. The irrepressibly chirpy Shirley leaped out of bed each morning trilling songs or reciting the lines she had memorised for her day's work. She received $10,000 a week, an almost inconceivable sum to the twenty million Americans on relief; but she barely knew the difference between a nickel and a dollar.

Ideological pressures shaped the themes of Temple's films. Her typical role, carefully positioned as the orphan or adopted child, was to soften the hard hearts of the wealthy, to encourage them to charity, and to intercede on behalf of others more needy than herself. It was no coincidence that dimple-cheeked Shirley and her capacity to encourage love and generosity appeared at a moment when public sources of charity were drying up. Shirley always ended up with the person who needed her unlimited supply of love most. Whoever possessed her owned a magic wand whose touch changed darkness into light. And her golden hair played a vital part in her fairytale goodness. It signalled riches, represented her promise of plenty, symbolised her status as treasure. Arthur Miller, the Fox Studios cameraman entrusted with the young Shirley's look, recalled, 'I always lit her so she had an aureole of golden hair. I used a lamp on Shirley that made her whole damn image world famous.' The Roosevelts were not blind to Shirley's golden ability to tap-dance the public out of their depression, and when Eleanor Roosevelt invited 'film folks' to the White House to lend FDR a touch of glamour, Shirley was among the chosen. Roosevelt was projecting himself as a man discreetly in touch with the cultural and racial expectations of his time.

In the Soviet Union, too, film reflected political imperatives. Stalin considered the cinema to be an excellent instrument with which to spread his message to the people, and he aimed to use it more than any other artistic medium for creating the 'new Socialist man and woman'. With the decision in April 1932 by the Communist Party Central Committee to force the doctrine of Socialist Realism on all the arts, Stalin was able to pursue his desire to create a Socialist state cinema which would extinguish all the experimentation and distinguished avant-garde work of the 1920s. The vision, poetics and intellectual scope of this earlier Soviet cinema, which had turned it into the most innovative film industry in Europe, were replaced by uncritically affirmative social stereotypes. A few film-makers were brave enough to circumvent bureaucratic pressures and preserve their integrity, but most applied the doctrine blindly and produced films of extraordinary tedium and official conformity. In 1935, Stalin wrote an article for *Pravde* congratulating the Soviet cinema on its fifteenth anniversary. 'In the hands of Soviet power, cinema constitutes an enormous and invaluable force. With unique opportunities for spiritual influence over the masses at its command, cinema helps the working class and its party to educate the workers in the spirit of Socialism . . .'

Although the heavy hand of the party was already visible in Soviet cinema, its audiences were not discouraged. They craved movies. They wanted to be whisked away from their everyday miseries into some shining fantasy world peopled by the beautiful and the heroic. They also wanted hope. Going to the cinema was one of the few forms of entertainment available to the urban masses and Stalin catered carefully to their hunger. Historical spectacles were churned out, great epics such as *Aleksandr Nevsky* and *Peter the Great*, which were designed to rekindle patriotism with old-fashioned appeals to national glory. The Revolution was also reviewed as a theme, hammering home the rightful establishment of Soviet power; and there were numerous films set in the contemporary world. In spite of the paramount importance of economic propaganda, surprisingly few were set in factories, considered even by the party to be too barren for good cinematic fun. But plenty were set on collective farms, many of them musical comedies which gave the impression that life in the countryside was a constant merry round of dancing and singing. Grigori Aleksandrov's *Volga-Volga* of 1938 was one of these, made at the height of the Stalinist purges. Some of the people who worked on the film were exiled, their contributions never credited. But *Volga-Volga* is said to have been Stalin's favourite film and to have received a certain amount of his personal guidance. It starred the blonde Lyubov Orlova, the most glamorous and most popular actress of Soviet cinema, in a classic fairytale story of a girl from a small town who carries a letter to the capital and successfully challenges and confronts the capitalists who have taken charge of an amateur theatre.

Lyubov's dazzling career as top Soviet blonde was not harmed by her marriage to her director, Aleksandrov. He, like Stalin, was an ardent fan of Hollywood and its products, and had travelled to America in the early 1930s as assistant to Sergei Eisenstein. He had been particularly impressed with the volume of output of the Hollywood studios, and also by the lavishly choreographed productions of Busby Berkeley, full of crystal chandeliers, endless corridors of mirrors and pyramid patterns of smiling, scantily dressed blondes. Back home he set out to develop the Soviet musical as a combination of entertainment extravaganza and ideology. He began casting Orlova in leading roles and within a couple of years she had captured the spotlight in his 1936 film *Circus*, playing the dazzling Marion Dixon, a blonde circus performer. The film incorporated some memorable dance numbers, redolent of the Busby Berkeley routines, and featured songs which became some of the most popular of the period. But it was Orlova, with her intoxicating blonde hair, bright eyes and abundant charisma, who from this time on became the darling of the screen and the embodiment of Stalin's ideal Soviet woman.

By the time Aleksandrov cast Orlova as the star of his musical *Shining Path*, in 1939, Stalin was actively involved in Soviet cinema. From the mid-1930s he had routinely interfered in the scripting and casting of films, often changing their titles and endings. But by the late 1930s he had become the supreme cinematic censor, who watched and approved every film released. He micro-managed the industry, supporting favoured directors and actors. When Aleksandrov's 1939 musical was dismissed by the party censors as unsuitable, Stalin countermanded them and not only approved the comedy for release, but thought up twelve different titles for the film, eventually choosing *Shining Path* in preference to *Cinderella*. It is a classic Soviet rags-to-riches tale, in which Orlova plays a simple weaver in a textile factory near Moscow who becomes an exemplary worker and ends up in the Kremlin, where she is awarded the highest Soviet medal, the Order of Lenin. Sent by her comrades to train as an engineer, she is finally elected as a member of the Supreme Soviet. The film represents the epitome of Stalinist glorification.

In Germany, too, film played a key role in the political agenda. Under the Nazis the German public thrilled to the medium of cinema. They flocked to see historical romances full of bewigged courtiers, First World War heroic epics, pastoral tales of creamy milkmaids in dirndl dresses and plaits, soul-warming stories of bullied adolescents making good as members of the Hitler Youth, and accounts of the sisterly solidarity of wives left behind by men at the front. Comedies were churned out as well as adventure stories, crime thrillers and musicals which imitated Hollywood's troupes of high-kicking showgirls. Over a thousand films were made during the Third Reich and they met every monumental cliché of Nazi ideology. Good German girls and heroic lads were blonde; Jews and enemy forces were dark.

Subtlety was not a renowned characteristic of Nazi cinema. Typical of the standard fare is *Annelie*, a romantic drama set in the 1870s starring Luise Ullrich, which tells the story of a young German girl, bright-eyed, blonde and bedirndled, who rebels in adolescence, but then grows up and is transformed into a heroic wife and mother. This patriotically heart-warming film was one of the most successful made during the Nazi era and took 6.5 million marks at the box office. But there were many more repulsive vehicles for Nazi ideology. In 1936 Paul Diehl made a puppet film of the familiar Grimms' story 'The Tale of One Who Went Forth to Learn Fear'. The boy leaves home, sleeps under a gibbet, enters a haunted castle, breezily defeats a succession of monsters over the course of three nights and survives to claim his reward, the hand in marriage of the princess. The boy is blond, his assailants are hook-nosed, dark and swarthy, and the princess is an uncanny premonition of the Barbie doll, blonde and kookily wide-eyed with perfect bee-stung lips. The film was used as a propaganda vehicle for racial indoctrination and for inculcating fearlessness in the Hitler Youth.

Many of the leading German actresses of the 1930s and early 1940s were, or made it their business to be, blonde. Lois Chlud, Carola Höhn, Trude Marlen, Dorit Kreysler and Hilde Weissner all gaze out of their publicity photos with the fine arched eyebrows and knowing superiority of Aryan goddesses. Zara Leander, a dark-haired actress with a remarkably expansive *décolletage*, stood out as the exception. But she made her way towards the top playing foreign women, not quite pure, who indulged in adulterous affairs. For a party aristocracy almost entirely devoid of allure, these stars were dazzlingly attractive and many were invited into top Nazi circles to lend a little of their sparkle.

Hermann Goering, the wildly sybaritic economic leader of the Third Reich, was the one senior Nazi who did go to great lengths to develop his own personal glamour. He bred bulls on his hunting estate, owned the biggest model railway in the world, and had a pot of diamonds carried near him at all times by a special servant in case he felt the urge to run his fat fingers through the sparkling stones. After his first wife, the beautiful blonde Swede Carin von Kantzow, died of tuberculosis in 1931, Goering married a second deluxe blonde, an actress by the name of Emmy Sonnemann. In Heinz Paul's 1934 film *Wilhelm Tell*, Sonnemann played the heroine in peasant smocking, her blonde hair carefully plaited and wreathed over her head. It was one of the few Nazi-period films that became a success in America.

Germany's top star was the blonde Kristina Söderbaum, an aristocratic, pretty and talented performer possessed of a sexy purring accent. She became a star overnight with her debut in 1938 as the heroine in *Jugend*, married the director, Veit Harlan, and within a few years had become the most popular actress on the German screen. She starred as the stereotypical pure Nordic maiden in dozens of films, but her most memorable role was as the heroine of the crudely racist film *Jud Süss* in which her ravishment by a Jew is the climax of the film. For good measure, Söderbaum was made to commit screen suicide to atone for her own defilement.

In Germany the cinema's function was, as anywhere else, escapism. Rising cinema attendances throughout the Third Reich demonstrated a national desire for such 'entertainment' and the annual number of cinema-goers quadrupled to one million between 1933 and 1942. Of course, their diet of films was minutely controlled according to strict rules laid down by Goebbels's ministry. No film could go into production before its plot had been presented − in thirty-four nineteen-syllable lines per page of typescript − to the ministry for inspection and approval.

Hitler was fully aware of the power of the medium, particularly its indoctrination potential, and even attributed Nazi victories to the strengthening and morale-boosting powers of the cinema. Like Roosevelt and Stalin he arranged for propaganda newsreels to be shown as part of every cinema programme and became something of a film nut himself, occasionally intervening in casting decisions. He used to watch films late into the night, often those of Marlene Dietrich, his personal screen goddess. (That Dietrich had deserted Nazi Germany to join America's booming film industry in Hollywood seems not to have affected the Führer's admiration for the star.)★

Arriving in Los Angeles in 1930, Dietrich had entered a world already familiar to her from Germany, in which racial politics and popular entertainment had seemingly fused in

★ Goebbels tried to lure Dietrich back to make films in Germany but she refused all offers unless, she said, she could get close enough to the Führer to shoot him.

the highly visible symbol of the blonde film star. In an industry whose first principle was profits, Hollywood studio policy and audience expectation dictated a constant flow of long-limbed blonde women on screen to represent the American dream. The image of women in film was being dictated by the blondes. In the footsteps of Harlow and West came Joan Blondell, Ginger Rogers, Lana Turner, Alice Faye, Marion Davies, Constance Bennett, Miriam Hopkins, Carole Lombard, and the occasional blondes Marlene Dietrich, Irene Dunne, Bette Davies, Barbara Stanwyck, Norma Shearer and Joan Crawford.

By the time America entered the Second World War, Hollywood was teeming with racially superior and socially well-behaved blondes. Shirley Temple had already brought the newly tamed blonde down to baby level; and in 1941, a new grown-up clean-cut blonde appeared on the scene. *Life* magazine pinned down the precise moment of her arrival. 'The 49th minute of the movie *I Wanted Wings* is already marked as one of the historic moments of the cinema. It was the moment when an unknown young actress named Veronica Lake walked into camera range and waggled a head of long blonde hair at a suddenly enchanted public ... Veronica Lake's hair has been acclaimed by men, copied by girls, cursed by mothers, and viewed with alarm by moralists. It is called the "strip-tease style", the "sheep-dog style" and the "bad-girl style" (though few except nice girls wear it), but to most movie-goers it is simply the Veronica Lake style.' *Life* went on to inform its readers that 'Miss Lake has some 150,000 hairs on her head, each measuring about .0024 inches in cross-section. The hair varies in length from 17 inches in front to 24 inches in back and falls about 8 inches below the shoulders. For several inches it falls straight from the scalp and then begins to wave slowly.' The magazine completed its list of essential Lake data with the gem that 'her hair catches fire fairly often when she is smoking'.

The unrivalled pin-up girl of the war period was another clean-cut blonde, Betty Grable, who ruled the film lot at Twentieth Century-Fox and became the number-one box-office attraction in the country. The Grable of *Pin-Up Girl*, *Coney Island* and *Song of the Islands* attracted filmgoers in their largest-ever numbers. Grable grossed $100 million at the box office during her peak years and was in many ways a perfect propaganda vehicle. She was blonde and banal, tall, well-scrubbed and ever ready with a chirpy song-and-dance routine. Far from the luxury-loving vamp charged with high-voltage eroticism, Grable was warm and safe, nostalgic and virtuous, a girl with a heart of gold who was prepared to roll up her sleeves and do her bit for the war effort.

In her most famous incarnation, her pin-up shot looking back over her shoulder above a pair of legs insured for $1 million, she became a symbol of everything that American boys longed for. Twenty thousand copies were sold every week to GIs and her trite smiling image accompanied them everywhere they went, tacked up over barrack beds in thousands of Quonset huts. For the the American fighting man, the pillowy blonde Grable, clean, loyal, beautiful and unthreatening, became the antithesis of war, an idealised dream just out of reach. The power of her appeal was sufficient to raise $40,000 in war donations in 1943 in exchange for a single pair of her nylons.

Racial attitudes go a long way in explaining the American

desire for this new generation of wholesome wartime Hollywood blondes. Black American populations had long provided
the most visible racial fears in America; and in the run-
up to the Second World War their civil rights demands
were aggravated by the blatantly discriminatory employment
policies of the military establishment. But black American
racial problems were considered a home-grown issue. In
the years before America entered the war, public opinion
studies found that, despite the usual excess of xenophobia
and jingoism, there was little public antipathy felt towards
German-Americans who were well-assimilated. It was found,
however, that Americans distrusted Jews more than any other
Europeans except Italians. Prejudice was rampant. Jews and
Italians were considered inferior stock, dark and swarthy
elements which threatened the Nordic purity that was taken
to be America's strength.*

After the Japanese attack on Pearl Harbor, the key target of
racism shifted and the most poisonous expressions of prejudice
were directed at the Japanese-Americans. The Governor of
Idaho, who announced that 'they live like rats, breed like
rats and act like rats', suggested that they should all be
deported back to Japan and that American power should
then sink the archipelago. In the end more than 100,000
Japanese-Americans, two-thirds of whom were American
citizens, were rounded up from three West Coast states and
packed off far inland, their civil and material rights withdrawn.

* Racial stereotyping of Jews was so common that one Jewish
professor of medicine, in an attempt to refute it, classified the
noses of 2,836 New York Jewish men and found that only 14 per
cent of them had the stereotypical 'Jewish' hooked nose.

J. Earl Warren, the Attorney General of California, explained the rationale: 'We believe that when we are dealing with the Caucasian race we have methods that will test the loyalty of them . . . But when we deal with the Japanese we are in an entirely different field and we cannot form an opinion that we believe to be sound.' It was an interesting manifestation of the colouring divide: the fair and light-skinned we can deal with, the dark we do not trust.

Jingoism and prejudice did much to reinforce the American belief in blonde superiority;* and Hollywood did its best to make it manifest. In spreading its pervasive aura of whiteness, its pin-up girls had to cleanse their bodies and their behaviour of indications that whites traditionally associated with minorities. The most startling example of this transformation occurred in the career of Rita Hayworth, a wartime pin-up of such bombshell potency that her image was painted on an atomic bomb used in a test to obliterate Bikini atoll in the South Pacific. Rita was Spanish, born Margarita Cansino. Until her epiphany, she had starred as a seethingly passionate Latin-dark heroine in the Charlie Chan films. But in 1937 she married a former used-car salesman named Edward Judson who realised that, like the cars in his showroom, his wife needed a 'new front'. He shamelessly set about remodelling her as the essence of perfect white beauty for wartime consumption. First he changed her name to

* In 1921 the first Miss America had been Margaret Gorman, a fifteen-year-old blue-eyed high-school girl with blonde hair. Roughly one in three of all the Miss America contestants over the years has been blonde, few of them natural. The first Jewish Miss America was Bess Myerson, crowned in 1945.

Hayworth, redolent of the agrarian dreams of homesick GIs. Then he dyed her hair strawberry blonde and had her hairline altered with electrolysis. Finally he arranged elocution lessons to eradicate all traces of her Spanish accent. Hayworth was photographed against idyllic American rural backdrops, wearing patriotic star-spangled red white and blue. She went on to become one of America's top box office stars.

While domestic glamour accounted for the majority of Hollywood's wartime output, the studios also managed to portray the all-American girl participating directly in the war. One of the most enthusiastic vehicles was Paramount's 1943 film *So Proudly We Hail* in which three de luxe stars – Veronica Lake, Paulette Goddard and Claudette Colbert – replicated, not entirely convincingly, the lives of a group of nurses dug in against Japanese attack on the island of Corregidor in Manila Bay. Putting aside the dehumanised, battle-hardened reality of nurses living in tunnels 400 feet beneath the surface of the bombed island, Paramount retained the soft lighting reserved for its most sumptuous female stars, but filmed them with a severe minimum of make-up. The climax of the story centres on Olivia, played by Veronica Lake, a Jap-hating fury whose fiancé has been killed at Pearl Harbor. The women are trapped in their quarters by the Japanese, cut off from their escape vehicle and with a single grenade to repel the advancing enemy. Olivia steps forward and grabs the grenade with the words 'So long, Davie, thanks for everything . . . it's our only chance . . . it's one of us or all of us . . . good-bye.' A long close-up of her face focuses on the sacrificial resolution in her eyes. She lets down her blonde hair, pulls out the pin and then walks slowly towards the enemy. With her back to the camera, the aroused Japanese move in around her like ants lured to a honeypot. Moments later the grenade destroys them all. Her blonde hair has become the ultimate *femme fatale* attraction, one might say the biggest blonde bombshell of the war.

14

DIRTY PILLOW SLIP

T HE BIG chief of all blondes was of course Marilyn
Monroe. She was the wiggling embodiment of every
adolescent male fantasy. All glossy blonde curls, ripe hips,
cartoonishly ballooning bosoms and that moistly receptive
deep red mouth, she was a fabulous bodily projection which
invited the slavering gaze and became the ultimate object of
illicit sexual desire.

Monroe was a construct, a carefully moulded vehicle for
male voyeurism, whose job was to light up the 1950s and
make herself available to the world. This modern professional
dumb blonde first took shape under the insidious influence of
the Californian sunshine when the head of the Blue Book
modelling agency, a woman by the unlikely name of Emiline
Snively, persuaded Norma Jean Mortenson to dye her mousy
hair blonde. The story goes that she also advised her to cut a
quarter of an inch off one heel to create the wiggle. Groucho
Marx immediately spotted her luminescent magic and devised
a cameo role for her in his film *Love Happy*. 'She's Mae West,
Theda Bara and Bo Peep all rolled into one,' he raved. The
male star-making machinery of Hollywood rapidly took over
and transformed a promising model into a devastating angel
of sex called Marilyn Monroe. By the time she had signed
her first contract as a starlet with Twentieth Century-Fox,

the studio publicists were sending out pin-up photos and arranging magazine features. Every statistic of her shapely body and every detail of her unhappy background was enlisted for the campaign, highlighting all the themes that were to become central to her popular image.

The type was established early and it stuck. Monroe's exquisite package of curves and blonde hair (she chose a shade called 'Dirty Pillow Slip'), her half-closed eyes and her innocently whispered sexual innuendos turned her into the world's first international bulb-popping Movie Star. She was a natural and entirely self-possessed exhibitionist, and she nestled happily into her assigned playmate role. She won starring parts, married Joe DiMaggio and learned how to make love to the camera. With popular culture in 1950s America still characterised by a near-Victorian prudery which equated sex with depravity, Monroe's open, innocent and unqualified sexual abandon was simply sensational.

But her status and pay were increasingly at odds with her popularity. Locked into a 'slave' contract with Twentieth Century-Fox, she was virtually powerless to determine her own career. The dumb blonde routine had brought her fame, but she needed to convince people that there was a serious actress under the fluffy curls. In spite of setting up her own production company and turning out several subtly nuanced comic performances, she never did throw off the winsome dumb baby act. Daryl Zanuck, the production chief of Twentieth Century-Fox, always referred to her as the 'strawhead'. And judgments of her as the hottest piece of sex on earth ran hand in hand with judgments of her as the ultimate dumb blonde. When George Axelrod's comedy *Will Success Spoil Rock Hunter?* opened on Broadway in 1957 it became a reminder that many people saw Monroe as a joke. Attending the premier of the play, Monroe sat through the story of a dumb self-obsessed sex symbol 'whose golden curls and fantastic behind have endeared her to moviegoers the world over'.

The concept of the dumb blonde that emerged in 1950s America in the unforgettable shape of Marilyn Monroe was – consciously or not – a creation of men and for men. It was made at least partly in response to the growing assertiveness of America's women. In 1945 American men had returned from the war to find their women more confident and more independent than ever before. Hundreds of thousands of women, already eager to work outside the home, had come forward and taken up job vacancies left by men who had been drafted. They had worked competently, many of them on production lines in the auto and electrical plants central to the war effort. They had earned their money (albeit less than men) and proven themselves capable of doing men's jobs. They had gained power, status and a new assertiveness. When returning veterans realised this, they saw the props of a crucial social support system being kicked away. At stake was the myth that women are made only for marriage and motherhood.

Polls taken at the end of the war revealed that between 60 and 85 per cent of American women in non-traditional jobs did not want to relinquish them. Two months after the war ended, two hundred women picketed a Ford plant in Detroit with placards reading 'Stop Discrimination Because of Sex'. A small and heavily embattled group, these women were determined to maintain their sense of empowerment and to spread an awareness of gender inequality. Even if levels of pay and representation still lagged far behind those of men, a legacy of expectation had been established.

The political climate was deeply inhospitable to ideas of social change. The men who ran Hollywood – and they were all men, many of them Jewish – whose job it was to anticipate and reflect the social (male) desires of the day, reacted by creating a film star in a completely new mould whose job was subconsciously to subvert this growing female independence. They banished all those sensibly shod career woman role models from wartime movies, strong self-confident women who rolled up their sleeves, did without make-up, and got things done. In their place they put Monroe. She was the perfect backlash. She was vulnerable, dreamily soft and dependent, a colossal baby-doll whose lack of self confidence meant that she needed the approval of men for everything she did. She was feminine and adored. Her generous sexuality made her the subject of women's imitation and of men's dreams. And, given that Hollywood's men seem to have been among the most slavish adorers of blondes, she was blonde.

It was Monroe's luminescent hair that generated the extraordinarily powerful erotic charge of her sexual persona. Billy Wilder recalls that she was entirely aware of this. 'She knew it. There was another girl in the band [in *Some Like It Hot*] who had blonde hair. And she said to me: "No other blonde. I'm the only blonde".' When a brunette played a scene with Monroe, she might as well have been painted on the backdrop. Again several years later, during filming of *Let's Make Love* with Yves Montand, Monroe complained to the director that a minor actress had put blonde streaks in her hair. She refused to report to the studio until the hair colour was changed or the actress dismissed. Monroe herself invested more time and more money on her hair than on any other aspect of her appearance. Details of her peroxide habit can be found in Simone Signoret's autobiography:

> Every Saturday morning the hair colorist of the late Jean Harlow would board her plane in San Diego and arrive in Los Angeles, where Marilyn's car would be waiting for her at the airport and would bring her to our kitchen, or rather the kitchenette of Bungalow No. 21. Before allowing her to remove the bottles from her old carrying bag, Marilyn would ply her with food from a buffet – a combination of brunch and cocktail party ingredients – she had carefully prepared. The old lady would indulge with gusto. Marilyn would knock on my door, telling me to bring my towels, and then the hair-dyeing party would begin . . . When she left the two of us would be impeccably blonde – Marilyn platinum and I on the auburn side.

Blonde was the colour of the Hollywood sex goddess. She was already a well-established fantasy figure in magazines, in fiction and on the stage. She was a favourite subject of the illustrator Varga, whose improbably shaped blondes became the most popular calendar pin-ups of the 1930s and '40s. P.G. Wodehouse wove her appeal into his novels: 'Like so many substantial Americans, he had married young and kept on marrying, springing from blonde to blonde like the chamois of the Alps leaping from crag to crag . . .' And Raymond Chandler created a rich archive of dangerously alluring blondes such as this one from *Farewell, my Lovely*: 'It was a blonde. A blonde to make a bishop kick a hole in a stained-glass window.' By the mid-1950s, there were dozens of actresses lining up to mould themselves in the curvaceous image of its most pungent archetype, Monroe. The Swedish-born Anita Ekberg succeeded in building her fourth place in the 1951 Miss Universe contest into a tentative film career, bolstered by a leonine mane of platinum-blonde hair, a 102cm bust and a lucky break taking Monroe's place on Bob Hope's 1954 tour of US bases. Four years later she arrived in Rome with her husband, Anthony Steel, and their flirting, all-night drinking, barefoot dancing and public skirmishes gave the city's paparazzi their best subject-matter for years. Ekberg's hair and her Minervan proportions immediately endeared her to Federico Fellini, who cast her as Sylvia in *La dolce vita*. No one who has watched the film will ever see the Trevi Fountain in the same light again.

Diana Dors was Britain's contribution to the buxom blonde species. She caused a sensation at the 1956 Cannes Film Festival, arriving in an open pink Cadillac, displaying much of her ample body and trailing voluminous dyed blonde hair and a fine line in hot chat. Promoted initially as a sex symbol, she refused to accept the connotations of dumb sexuality. Instead she skilfully manipulated her career, strewn in the best Hollywood tradition with personal scandal and professional disputes, towards an enduring television personality. The French fielded Brigitte Bardot as their leading example of the breed, a glamorous and generously proportioned ex-model who dyed her long brown hair blonde and became known as 'the Sex Kitten'.★

★ In 1957 when she starred in *Et Dieu Créa la Femme* (*And God Created Woman*), the magazine *Cinémonde* reported that a million lines had been devoted to her in the French dailies, two million lines in the weeklies, and that this gush of words had been illustrated with 29,345 photographs of her. It also claimed that she had been the subject of 47 per cent of French conversation.

She went on, after several disastrous marriages, to live with a large number of cats. One more Monroe acolyte frequently dismissed as a dumb blonde was Jayne Mansfield, whose hair, breasts and general vulgarity won her a flimsy film career for a few years. As Bette Davis said of her, 'Dramatic art, in her opinion, is knowing how to fill a sweater'.

Increasingly the subject of joyous ribaldry, the numerous blonde mammary women engineered and sent out on to the screen in the 1950s and 1960s were nevertheless highly professional sex symbols who fulfilled Hollywood's requirements as popular saleable commodities. Hollywood moguls, most of them vain, exploitative, megalomaniac pocket dictators, tended to equate good movies with big profits – and that usually meant a big, bosomy blonde star. When Monroe died in 1962, it is said that a frantic Harry Cohn, the lecherous head of Columbia Studios, yelled, 'Get me another blonde!' For years his line-up of blondes continued to reduce grown men to a state of wobbly pubescent longing.

Except for one. During the 1950s and early 1960s there was a film director in Hollywood who made a profession out of torturing blondes. Over and over again, Alfred Hitchcock picked slim, elegant blondes to star in his films, fine-boned ethereal actresses with a glint of repressed sensuality lurking beneath a smooth surface. Madeleine Carroll, Ingrid Bergman, Grace Kelly, Kim Novak, Eva Marie Saint, Janet Leigh and Tippi Hedren – physically and psychologically they were all of a type. There was something about the delicate features, the vulnerable ladylike control and the blonde hair that excited Hitchcock. 'Suspense', he said in 1957, the year he made *Vertigo*, 'is like a woman. The more left to the imagination, the more the excitement . . . The conventional big-bosomed blonde is not mysterious. And what could be more obvious than the old black velvet and pearls type? The perfect "woman of mystery" is one who is blonde, subtle and Nordic . . .'

Hitchcock's favourite actresses were all blonde, subtle and Nordic-looking, and to their polished refinement he introduced a conflicting brutal sensuality. 'Tear them down at the very start,' he said, 'that's much the best way.' He delivered the sardonic, the sadistic and the savage with a famously impassive relish. He stripped them naked psychologically. He manipulated them, broke them down and then feasted on them like a vampire. 'Blondes are the best victims,' he explained. 'They're like virgin snow which shows up the bloody footprints.' Tippi Hedren began filming *The Birds* as the silky champagne blonde Melanie, her hair twisted up into a smooth chignon, her elegant suit and glistening maquillage perfect. But by the end, both she and Melanie were a wreck. She was terrorised by the seven days required to film the horrifying sequence for the climactic attic scene. 'They had me down on the floor with the birds tied loosely to me through the peck-holes in my dress. Well, one of the birds clawed my eye and that did it; I just sat and cried. It was an incredible physical ordeal,' she recalled later.

'Torture the women,' Hitchcock once joked. In *Vertigo* he has James Stewart psychologically torturing Kim Novak; and in *Marnie*, Sean Connery does the same to Tippi Hedren. There is also a story of how Hitchcock once terrified Hedren's young daughter by giving her a tiny coffin. Inside it was a doll, a perfect replica in miniature of her mother, down to the suit she wore in *The Birds*, and a perfectly crafted smooth blonde chignon wig. Blonde hair seems to have been erotic fixation for Hitchcock. Many of his films contain lingering shots of a woman's hair, but there is obsession beneath the aesthetic pleasure. His Jack the Ripper in *The Lodger*, a London film from 1926, assaults and murders only blonde women. In *Marnie*, our first glimpse of Hedren's face comes just after she has washed swirls of dark brown dye out of her hair and re-emerged as a blonde; and in *The Birds*, the bottle-blonde Hedren swabs her wounds with a bottle of peroxide. In her superb short book on the film, Camille Paglia notices that the chemical revives her like some magic elixir. Paglia notes too that Hitchcock has jokingly seated her beneath a sign reading 'Packaged Goods Sold Here'.

He considered his women captivating but dangerous, their blondeness a beautiful but false colour that hid something dark and threatening. It was as if the camouflage of the hair expressed the camouflage inherent in the character; and this was profoundly exciting to Hitchcock. His own dreamlike nature repeatedly invented an urgent fantasy of being trapped in the back of a taxi with one of his *soignée* blondes at the moment when her armoured personality opens up and her dammed-up sexual energies are finally unleashed. Whatever his personal pleasures, the effect of Hitchcock's films was to present beautiful blonde women as ruling goddesses whose triumphs eventually turn them into victims to be tortured and violated.

When Paglia first saw *The Birds* in 1963, 'blonde sorority queens ruled social life in most American high schools, a tyranny I accepted as their divine due. Melanie Daniels [Hedren] has the arrogant sense of entitlement of all beautiful people who sail to the top, from Athenian stoa and Florentine court to Parisian salon and New York disco. Nature gives to them, but then nature takes away.' Hitchcock didn't just take away. He ground down his blondes and destroyed them. In the climate of postwar America, this too, like the creation of the dumb blonde, amounted to an attempt – conscious or otherwise – to subvert the growing power of women.

But these were dangerously insensitive strategies, even if they were subconscious. Hollywood depended on women. Seventy-five per cent of America's cinema audiences were women, and to repulse them with too many images of tortured or dumb blondes was not good business practice. By the early 1960s Hollywood was suffering the effects of the rise of television, and its ruthless tycoons knew that their future lay in the indoctrination of teenage girls. They set out to seduce America's daughters. Before long a third species of blonde emerged – again created by the male controllers of Hollywood – who had a greater aspirational appeal to young women. They were the chirpy, peppy girls-next-door represented on screen by the ineffably winning characters of Debbie Reynolds, Doris Day and Sandra Dee. These girls added a further convenient blow to the tender shoots of female emancipation. Loving and innocent, they were slightly more grown-up versions of Shirley Temple, monstrous pink dollies professionally bursting with girlish exuberance. There were dozens of them in Hollywood in the early 1960s, bland and sweetly snub-nosed Daddy's girls, almost indistinguishable from one another; and they perfectly reflected the docile role that most men preferred women to play in postwar American society.

They made the buxom fantasy Monroe, with her complex self-interests and dark demons, look like a dirty joke; a tantalising dish, certainly, but no good as a wife or mother. These perky blondes, on the other hand, were inoffensive girls with a resolutely clean and unthreatening sexuality. Doris Day was said to be so pure, even Moses couldn't part her knees.

Dwight Macdonald wrote about this American Dream Girl in his 1969 book, *On Movies*:

> She is as wholesome as a bowl of cornflakes and at least as sexy. She has the standard American figure: long-legged, tallish (everything is on the ish side) with highish smallish breasts and no hips or buttocks to speak of. And the standard American (female) face, speaking in terms of aspirations rather than of realities: Nordic blonde, features regular, nose shortish and straightish, lips thinnish, Good Bone Structure . . . She has the healthy, antiseptic Good Looks and the Good Sport personality that the American middle class – that is, practically everybody – admires as a matter of duty. Especially the females. No competition.

So the blonde – whether buxom, coolly elegant or bland – was still the dominant female type in Hollywood and as such covered the aspirational ground for much of America. Naturally, the attentions being lavished on blonde goddesses had begun to rile large numbers of women who were not blonde. In 1955, Eleanor Pollock wrote caustically in *Good Housekeeping*:

> In my studies of blonde behavior, I have seen yellow-haired dynamos who can repair cars, run offices, talk knowingly about the H-bomb, do anything a man can do and do it better. So long as there are no men around. Let one appear, and our golden-haired expert becomes as fragile and helpless as a doe caught in the headlights of an automobile at night. This happens almost overnight, even to blondes by choice. What's more, it works. I'd

like to see any brown-haired damsel get away with it. She'd be treated as if she had rocks in her head. But not our little yellow chickadee.

Carol Channing found when she starred in the 1949 musical version of *Gentlemen Prefer Blondes* that men sat on the edges of their chairs to hear what she thought about the weather. 'I didn't have to be bright; I wasn't expected to.' She told *Good Housekeeping* in 1955. 'All I had to do was be blonde.' Many more dreamed of following her lead.

For a woman, being blonde in 1950s America was part of a dream of being desirable to men. It was also part of a dream of inclusion. For those still excluded from the highest levels of American society by virtue of a background which was not northern European, the development of new and more effective home hair dyes brought the possibilities of assimilation closer to reality. They introduced the arousing idea that you could slip from one identity to the next with no more ado than twenty minutes in the bathroom. Now anyone could begin to acquire the trappings of the established affluent class, which still included a head of blonde hair.

In 1956 Clairol brought out a new hair-colour product which made it possible to bleach, shampoo and condition in one step, and at home. In the words of Bruce Gelb, who ran Clairol at the time, it was to the world of hair colour what computers were to the world of adding machines. But there was still the slight stigma of blonde hair being associated with fast women. Malcolm Gladwell describes the dilemma in his fascinating 1999 *New Yorker* feature on hair dye and the hidden history of post-war America. Clairol handed the advertising account to Foote, Cone & Belding, where a junior copywriter named Shirley Polykoff came up with the teasing line 'Does she or doesn't she? Only her hairdresser knows for sure.' The message effectively justifed a convincing fake. The new product flew off the shelves. For her next campaign for Lady Clairol, Polykoff came up with 'Is it true blondes have more fun?' She followed that with one of the most famous lines in advertising history: 'If I've only one life, let me live it as a blonde.' Blonde was no longer just a look; it was a whole psychology. In the summer of 1962, just before *The Feminine Mystique* came out, Betty Friedan was so 'bewitched' by that phrase, according to her biographer, that she dyed her hair blonde. David Hockney was equally attracted by the dream. After watching the commercial late one night on television, he rushed out to his nearest all-night chemist, bought a tube and bleached his hair.

Clairol bought acres of advertising space and filled it with sentimental images of pretty and tastefully dressed blonde women, contentedly preparing delicious dinners for their husbands, or lying happily on the grass beside their matching blonde children. The idea was to make bleaching hair as respectable as possible. One of the key changes in the perception of dyeing was a subtle semantic one. Just as wigs were coyly renamed 'transformations' to gain respectability in the 1920s, when Clairol banished the word 'dye' and replaced it with 'tint', women all over the country silently cheered and began experimenting with this once-scandalous process. By 1957 *Look* magazine was reporting that 55 million American women were adding colour to their hair. In the twenty odd years when Polykoff wrote copy for Clairol, the number of American women colouring their hair rose from 7 per cent to more than 40 per cent.

Polykoff herself, the brown-haired Jewish daughter of a tie salesman and a housewife, believed that a woman should be allowed to be whatever she wanted, including being a blonde. Ever since the age of fifteen she had dyed her own hair blonde. When her daughter turned thirteen and her natural blonde hair began to darken, Polykoff started bleaching that, too. She believed in appearances, in becoming fictions and self-reinvention. As a teenager, Shirley Polykoff had applied for a job as an insurance agency clerk and been turned down. When she tried again at another firm, as Shirley Miller, she got the job. Such efforts at assimilation in 1950s America were par for the course for Jews, Italians, Irish — all of them trying to win acceptance in a nation which was still racially insecure. Polykoff's 'Does she or doesn't she?' campaign was all about how no one could ever really know who you were. According to her daughter, 'It really meant not "Does she?" but "Is she?" It really meant "Is she a contented homemaker or a feminist, a Jew or a Gentile — or isn't she?"'

The desire to be white and preferably blonde was still powerful in the early 1960s. In California, the source of national and often international trends and assumptions, America's youth culture was devoting itself to sun, surf and endless summers. For them tanned skin and blonde hair was a symbol of perfection. The Beach Boys sang about blonde girls, and beach bunnies gathered in fluffy little clusters on the sand, dedicating hours to bleaching their hair in the sun and the surf. For those without time for the beach, there was always Clairol, or a visit to Raymond, one of the first hairdressers of repute to develop his own blonde dyes. He made a speciality of turning hair of any colour ash-blonde by first bleaching it, then colouring it with very strong coffee or tea, finally adding two drops of clove oil to conceal the peculiar smell. Blonde was the aspirational standard of American beauty.

Young American girls soon had a distinct model on which to base their appearance: a stick-thin doll with pointy toes called Barbie, crafted in durable pink plastic by a military weapons designer, an expert on missile casings. When Barbie and her cruise missile breasts were launched into popular culture with that mass of long hair, the shopping habits, the ballerina outfits and the pyjama parties, she was an emblem of the 1960s American Dream. She symbolised the ideals of affluence and material comfort that were shaping America's developing consumer economy. This was outwardly a time of conservatism and conformity centred on the ideal family popularised by the media. Father was the breadwinner, mother was the homemaker, and they lived happily with their two to four children in a sunny suburban home. Barbie was the natural role model of the daughter of the house. But in spite of the impression of happy families, rigid gender roles as well as barriers of class and social conformity were already under assault. The looks, sounds and ideals of a previous generation were being energetically overturned, and much of the momentum was coming from London.

15

OF PRINCESSES, PUNKS AND
PRIME MINISTERS

THE NOISE was deafening at the Ad Lib in Soho, the hottest nightclub in London. Red, green and blue lights straked back and forth across the pulsating crowd, cutting through a thick fog of cigarette smoke. Models with cropped blonde hair and men in tight black Carnaby Street trousers draped themselves around each other at the bar. An energetic beat group pounded out radical numbers and on the dance floor, a frenzy of long legs in short skirts, perhaps Julie Christie and Marianne Faithfull among them, vibrated close to the scruffy young bloods of the moment, David Bailey, Terry Donovan, maybe Terence Stamp or Michael Caine if they happened to be in town. At the corner table, more or less permanently reserved for the Beatles, Ringo made eyes at Maureen. In the surrounding streets, dozens more clubs throbbed with the energy of dashing young bodies gyrating late into the night, every night; Annabel's for the elegant and titled crowd, The Scene on Great Windmill Street for the Mods, Ronnie Scott's for the jazz and The Flamingo for the beat crowds.

What was it that created 'Swinging London' in the 1960s? When John Crosby, an American journalist, did his research for an April 1965 feature in the *Daily Telegraph*, he discovered the answer:

It's the girls. Italian and Spanish men are kinky for English girls ... The girls are prettier here than anywhere else ... They're more than pretty; they're young, appreciative, sharp-tongued, glowingly alive. Even the sex orgies among the sex-and-pot set in Chelsea and Kensington have youth and eagerness and, in a strange way, a quality of innocence about them. In Rome and Paris, the sex orgies are for the old, the jaded, the disgusting and disgusted. Young English girls take to sex as if it's candy and it's delicious.

The goddesses of the scene were mesmerising blondes. Julie Christie had won an Oscar in 1965 for her performance in *Darling*. Marianne Faithfull was the reigning queen of rock chicks. Veruschka painted herself gold all over and Ursula Andress and Catherine Deneuve simply smouldered beneath their thick blonde manes. The power of the blonde was magnetic. And then in 1966 Twiggy became the most famous model in the world with her meagre child's body (Barbie without the breasts) and an immaculately dyed golden gamine hairdo that took eight hours to perfect and made her look like a cross between an angel and Greta Garbo. Twiggy as the beautiful blonde child was a devastating combination of innocence and sexuality. Thousands of girls rushed out, blonded and chopped off their hair and squeezed themselves into Op Art mini shift dresses and PVC boots. Twiggy went to America on a wave of English fashion fever and prompted Mia Farrow to chop off and bleach her hair, too. The look had somehow become caught up with Britain's drastic redefinition of social and cultural attitudes and its infectious belief, for a while, that, crazily, anything was possible.

In America, too, hair colour was becoming unexpectedly significant. The years between the late '50s and the early '70s had marked a strange period of social history in which hair dye and the campaigns used to sell it became intimately linked with the politics of assimilation, with feminism and with women's self-esteem. 'Women entered the workplace, fought for social emancipation, got the Pill, and changed what they did with their hair,' wrote Malcolm Gladwell in the *New Yorker*. 'To examine the hair-color campaigns of the period is to see, quite unexpectedly, all these things as bound up together, the profound with the seemingly trivial. In writing the history of women in the postwar era, did we forget something important? Did we leave out hair?'

It seems that we did. The women's movement was gaining momentum during this period and, strangely, hair colour was playing a part. By the mid-1960s, American women born in the Depression era were experiencing tensions between reality and ideology. Most of the media, educators and policymakers continued to laud domestic fulfilment for women, assuming the voluntary full-time dedication of married women to their families. Their message, relentlessly repeated, was that women did not need careers and that their role as mothers was completely self-justifying. But their message ignored reality. In an era of apparently exhilarating possibilities defined by the rise of the youth counterculture, with more women educated to university level, smaller families as the baby boom slowed down, growing financial and intellectual incentives to seek employment, and more clerical, sales and teaching jobs available, women were becoming vaguely, guiltily, aware that they were hungry for more experience of life. In the absence of a visible feminist movement and in the face of the imagery everywhere of fulfilled and enriched full-time mothers, they could only interpret their frustrations as personal.

While a huge 96 per cent of housewives polled in 1962 described themselves as extremely or very happy, 90 per cent of the same sample hoped that their daughters would not lead the same life as they did. The daughters hoped they would not, either. By the late 1960s, with mass demonstrations and the spread of texts such as *The Feminine Mystique*, explicitly feminist women's groups had been set up in most urban centres throughout America, furious at the government's trivialisation of gender discrimination. They began to press for an opening-up of public debate on equal rights reform. Middle-class women were beginning to identify with the women's movement. But their demands for equality were often ignored. At one national conference of the New Left in 1967, a women's group won a place on the agenda with great difficulty. When their turn came, the chair refused to call on them and patted their representative, Shulamith Firestone, on the head, saying, 'Move on little girl; we have more important issues to talk about here than women's liberation.'

In the early 1970s, the daughters of these women were entering their twenties, well-educated and facing life choices that were likely to involve some degree of sex discrimination. One of them was Ilon Specht, a college dropout from California who was working as a copywriter on Madison Avenue. She was a young woman working in a business dominated by older men. Every time she wrote a line of copy that included the word 'woman', a man would cross it out and write 'girl'. In 1973 Specht joined a team working on a commercial for L'Oréal which was trying to win a share of the American hair-dye market from Clairol. They were having trouble getting the right image for a new blonde dye named 'Preference'. Interviewed by Malcolm Gladwell, she explained how their particular problem reflected precisely the wider social problems of the era. 'They had this traditional view of women, and my feeling was that I'm not writing an ad about looking good for men, which is what it seems to me that they were doing. I just thought, Fuck you. I sat down and did it, in five minutes. It was very personal. I can recite to you the whole commercial, because I was so angry when I wrote it.' She lowered her voice to recite the text: 'I use the most expensive hair colour in the world. Preference, by L'Oréal. It's not that I care about money. It's that I care about my hair. It's not just the colour. I expect great colour. What's worth more to me is the way my hair feels. Smooth and silky but with body. It feels good against my neck. Actually, I don't mind spending more for L'Oréal. Because I'm' – and here Specht struck her chest with her fist – 'worth it.'

The commercial was a potent and uncompromising readjustment of Clairol's message, switching the emphasis from that of a dependent woman looking good for the benefit of men to one of a sassy, independent woman looking good for the benefit of herself. Such a barefaced equation of hair colour with self-esteem had never been aired before. But L'Oréal had, in one short phrase, captured the particular feminist sensibilities of the day, just as Shirley Polykoff had done twenty years earlier. Preference sailed off the shelves and immediately began challenging Clairol's dominance of the market. The advertisement was so successful that some years later L'Oréal took the phrase and made it the slogan for the whole company. Dozens of blondes have been auditioned over the years to say the line and been rejected. 'There was one casting we did with Brigitte Bardot,' recalled Ira Madris, a campaign copywriter from the period, 'and Brigitte, being who she is, had the damnedest time saying that line. There was something inside her that didn't believe it.' Brigitte's 'Because I'm worth it' had no conviction. She was a cuddly doll-blonde of the old school who dyed her hair for men, not for herself.

Hair dye had become a strange symbol of women's liberation. Young women were dyeing their hair for themselves, unperturbed by what men might think of it. And those men still living among the outdated sexist ideas of automatic male dominance were clinging to the blonde bimbo. Concerted efforts were being made to maintain the dumb blonde and she was increasingly represented by the blonde joke. Why do blondes have TGIF on their shoes? Toes Go In First. What do you call a blonde with two brain cells? Pregnant. Dumb blonde jokes began pouring out of pubs and clubs in the 1970s, joining the streams of Irish jokes that had been around for years.

As late as 1977, the *Listener* magazine published an article entitled 'The irresistible dumb blonde'. 'This is a creature', wrote Charles Marowitz, 'who makes no pretence at being well-read or intellectually genned-up. She does not enter into sophisticated word play. She has no concepts to juggle; no theories to espouse. Her most salient points are physical, and imbued with a kind of irresistible sexuality . . . she protrudes in the right places. Her flesh invites animal approaches. Her aura suggests she has been anatomically constituted for the exercise of pleasure. Her small-talk, her trivia, even her drivel are, in a way necessary attributes, and actually enhance her other attractions.'

To keep the dumb blonde alive, dozens of blonde sex symbols were still being engineered by the moguls of Hollywood and the new tycoons of television. In 1977, Farrah Fawcett, a toothsome blonde with a body toned and tanned to perfection, appeared in the leeringly sexist series *Charlie's Angels*. At a stroke she created The All-American Look for the next ten years. Her long Californian sun-streaked hair was layered and fluffed until it looked 'wild, free and natural', and it became the basis of international myths of eroticism, success and adventure. Eight million people bought copies of the poster in which Farrah posed, bursting pleasingly out of an unzipped wetsuit. Her sexuality was clean and unthreatening and just about powerful enough to make a thirteen-year-old boy try out his first ogle. 'I think she's the worst actress in the world,' said one New York fan, 'but I love her hair.' It was a judgement shared by many. Farrah's wild and free hair captured the essence of California, its cult of the golden body-beautiful, and its obsession with health, vigour and the sexual appeal of total fitness. Farrah became an icon of her times, the embodiment of the American fantasy of success and beauty.

In Britain, by the time women fans of *Charlie's Angels* had begun teetering through damp suburban streets displaying their doomed imitations of Farrah Fawcett's hair, the look was already under attack. A new young generation was gathering in a tribal cavalcade of disaffected adolescents, drawn by the romance of anarchy and infamy. Brought up in the relentlessly grey economic recession of the '70s, many of them were unemployed, depressed and poorly educated working-class teenagers, and they celebrated their self-imposed exile from society with flamboyant sartorial obscenities.

The cult of punk had taken root in the mid-1970s in a small

but sensational shop in London's King's Road called SEX. Its name was brazenly spelt out in huge letters of padded pink vinyl, displayed like a vast spongy pop-art sculpture above its front window. It looked terrifying. Beckoning the customer inside were piles of naked headless mannequins draped over each other as if indulging in an orgy. Those brave enough to enter found themselves in a kind of fetish gymnasium, the walls lined with pale pink rubber, and bars hung with whips, handcuffs and other exotica glorifying the sordid, the inappropriate and the tasteless. Presiding over this provocative little emporium were two ruling blondes, the two icons of the punk movement, Jordan and Vivienne Westwood.

Jordan was the daughter of blameless working-class parents from Seaford, a sleepy Sussex seaside town whose genteel and largely retired population pottered along in ignorance of the vitriol boiling up in the King's Road. Jordan was not like them. Every morning she joined soberly suited commuters on the train ride into London, dressed typically in stilettos and ripped black fishnet stockings held up by suspenders. Her black vinyl leotard was accessorised with a harness of chains. Her hair was peroxided to a violent shade of platinum blonde and teased into a rigidly lacquered beehive. To give extra zest to her public project of *épater les bourgeois*, she carefully ringed her eyes every morning with lavish quantities of kohl, and painted her lips in a macabre black or dark purple. 'If you want the epitome of imposing and intimidating,' she recalled, 'that's what I was. You had to have courage to walk into that shop.' Standing beside a double bed covered with a rubber sheet, clad in her shop gear – a studded leather bra and thigh-high boots – Jordan goaded her customers to clamber into skin-tight rubber suits and leather harnesses. Frequently asked to model the clothes herself, she became a billboard for SEX and later, as the punk star of Derek Jarman's film *Jubilee*, a recognised emblem of the punk movement.

Vivienne Westwood was her boss, the proprietor with Malcolm McLaren of the shop, and designer of a range of customised clothes which later formed the core wardrobe of the Sex Pistols. Posing like Jordan as the intimidating dominatrix, Westwood wore kinky leather fetish gear and spike heels and modelled her own slashed and safety-pinned T-shirts nonchalantly emblazoned with the most provocative images she could think of. The severed head of the queen, swastikas and male genitals were her basics. To ensure a maximum shock aesthetic, she aggressively peroxided her hair and razored it into spikes, gelling it to stand erect in a style which David Bowie later adopted.

The bottle-blonde look was deliberately repulsive. It was designed to look subversively artificial, chemically enhanced with visible dark roots, a vicious reaction against the dazzlingly healthy, natural and girlishly compliant look of Californian beauty. Quickly associated with all that was cheap and taste-less, it had gained an additional evil slur from the notorious photographs flashed around the world a few years earlier first of Ruth Ellis and then of Myra Hindley, their bottle-blonde hair parted to reveal slashes of slovenly dark roots.

In the context of the mid-1970s, when sexuality was not something that was openly discussed, even less flaunted, the impact of SEX and its two blonde punks was deeply and perversely shocking. Westwood had always had an itch for revolt and her ideas were eagerly embraced by anguished or bored adolescents. Soon suburban teenage girls were spotted parading down the King's Road in peroxided hair, heavy black make-up and T-shirts featuring Snow White surrounded by seven sexually aroused dwarfs. Chrissie Hynde remembers noticing boys in other parts of London in black leather jackets and bleached blond hair. Parents, teachers and elders were satisfactorily outraged. When Debbie Harry began conquering the world's rock charts in the late 1970s with her high-adrenalin band Blondie, sporting peroxided blonde hair with a strip of anarchic dark roots down the middle, the look became the height of alternative chic and the emblem of female rebellion.

Ten years later, Vivienne Westwood, the renegade eldest daughter of a cosy, ballroom-dancing, working-class provincial couple who once ran the Tintwistle Post Office in Derbyshire, posed on the cover of *Tatler* as Margaret Thatcher. Beneath the image read the banner headline 'This Woman Used to Be a Punk'. It was a convincing and highly subversive likeness. Michael Roberts, the photographer and stylist, remembers that Vivienne did not initially want to be part of the spoof because she hated Margaret Thatcher. But, once convinced of its shock appeal, 'she did it so well it was creepy'. Dressed in a conservative suit, pearls and a bouffant blonde wig, she imagined herself leaning over a child in a hospital bed and telling herself, 'I care, I really care.'

History does not relate what Margaret Thatcher made of the April fool cover of *Tatler* that year. While Westwood had decisively dunked her dark hair in the peroxide in the early '70s, pulling out a head dripping with rebellious vitriol, Mrs Thatcher's change from mousy to power-blonde was a more gradual mutation. It also coincided with a broader social change. Ever since the war, the typical uniform of the quintessential Tory woman had been a muted twin-set and pearls with sensible shoes. But by the early 1980s, things were changing. Colour schemes became vibrant. Blonde highlights began to appear in hairstyles. Heels got higher and pads sprouted in the shoulders of executive suits. More women were in employment, some of them in executive roles, and they were confidently creating their own look. Far from the days of Monroe's dependency on male approval, these power-blondes were doing things just as they wished. Any man foolish enough to call them dumb would have been laughed at.

Mrs Thatcher was one of the most powerful of power-blondes. An early unsuccessful job application at ICI had produced a personnel report saying, 'this woman is headstrong, obstinate and dangerously self-opinionated'. As a young MP she was much the same, but hid it better. Nevertheless, no one told her what to do, still less how she should do her hair.

The hairstyle took a while to evolve. As Mrs Thatcher climbed up the ranks of the Conservative Party, her hair gradually became more regimented. When still a new MP in the early 1960s her dark hair had been softly brushed back and allowed to curl freely. As a minister it had been dyed a violent blonde and backcombed to give her a rigidly lacquered helmet. By the time she was leader of the opposition in 1975 it was being inflated further into a formidable sphere, every hair smoothed into submission. And by 1979, when she walked into Downing Street, her hair was styled into a huge imperial halo, golden and utterly uncompromising, a demonstration of self-assurance, conviction and power. The shampoo-and-set look was resolutely anti-fashion; like the queen's shampoo and set, it was a way of signalling the unassailability, longevity and immutability of her reign.

Mrs Thatcher's long-term regular haircolourist, Brian Carter, says that blonde hair softens the features and helps women to fight the effects of advancing age. He was engaged in 1979 to tone down Mrs Thatcher's violent platinum colour and to give her look more authority and dignity. But there were other reasons for Mrs Thatcher's mutation from mousy to blonde. Just as Queen Elizabeth I and many other powerful women had used both the beacon-like effects and the sexual attractions of blonde hair to their advantage, Mrs Thatcher realised that her golden halo gave her advantages. It harnessed the light. It demanded attention. It demonstrated her status and wealth. It was the perfect model for the nation. As Grant McCracken notes in his hilarious anthropological study, *Big Hair*, Mrs Thatcher's hair 'was profuse and celebrated the abundance of Tory policy promised in 1980s England. (Ronald Reagan's profuse hair had this same significance for 1980s America.) And it was coherent, the very picture of a nation bending itself to a single will.'

Mrs Thatcher obviously had not read, or had chosen to ignore, the words of John Molloy, a 'dressing engineer' whose 1980 book, *Women: Dress For Success*, was designed to help the newly emerging executive woman to create the right look around the male-dominated boardroom table. Women were advised to look 'serious' for work; that is, not too feminine. Long hair was to be avoided as too feminine and too sexy, while curly or wavy hair lacked authority. As for dyed blonde hair, that was an absolute no-no. 'While blondes may or may not have more fun, brunettes definitely have more authority. Dark hair means power and blonde hair means popularity, so any attractive small blonde reading this book may want to decide whether she would rather have more fun or more power.' Throughout the 1980s Mrs Thatcher enjoyed a great deal of power and a certain amount of fun. With her thrusting embonpoint, her basilisk stare, her large handbag and that uncompromising blonde helmet, she had no trouble keeping her rowdy cabinet and the rowdier opposition benches firmly under control, and whenever she went abroad she was trailed by a wake of admiring foreign statesmen.

During Mrs Thatcher's reign, other assertive women restyled their mousy selves as blondes, untroubled by charges of dumbness, and climbed the ladders of their professions or simply rose to greater power and influence. Hillary Clinton was one. Like Mrs Thatcher, she had spent her early political life in dull brown obscurity; but by the time of the 1992 presidential election she had radically restyled her image. She started wearing make-up. She ditched her glasses in favour of contact lenses. She had her hair cut more flatteringly and she began to use blonde highlights. By the time the Clintons were established in the White House, she was a fully fledged blonde. Over the years the style has changed, but the colour has not. Hillary is blonde for the same reason that Thatcher is blonde: it makes her look younger, it demands more attention, it is sexually attractive and it signals status and control. Never was a hair colour used to greater advantage than when Hillary appeared on the cover of *Vogue*, blonde, cool and controlled, at precisely the moment when the public was being fed images of the tousled and curly-black-haired Monica Lewinsky. It was not so much a good–bad dichotomy as a contrast between a self-disciplined woman and her husband, a man out of control.

For the same reasons of youth, beauty, status and power, other prominent women have performed similar mutations from brunette to golden blonde – Tina Brown, Jennifer Saunders, Kiri Te Kanawa, Camilla Parker Bowles and many

251

more. The very blonde Denise Kingsmill, a powerful employment lawyer and author on behalf of the government of the Kingsmill Review on Women's Employment and Pay, visits her hair colourist to have her roots dyed twice a week. Nobody would call her dumb.

Fifty years after Marilyn Monroe burst panting on to the screens of cinemas all over the world, do 'blonde' and 'bimbo' still necessarily go together? The answer is it depends what sort of blonde. The crisply cut, carefully tailored executive blonde does not trigger thoughts of dumbness. Quite the opposite. Her hair signals calculating control. But the long-haired or bouffant blonde who also displays enhanced lips and bosoms, wide eyes and skimpy clothes is still likely to attract the bimbo label. Pamela Anderson, Claudia Schiffer, Caprice, Dolly Parton and Ivana Trump are all examples of the type and all seem to bear an alarming resemblance to blow-up dolls. They are fashioned to appeal to men. They may have the highest IQs in the world, but the way they look is a mark of submission.

Hugh Hefner has a soft spot for this kind of blonde. He shares his Playboy Mansion in California with seven girlfriends, Katie, Tina, Tiffany, Cathi, Stephanie, Regina and Buffy. Hugh is seventy-five, his girlfriends are aged between nineteen and twenty-eight. All seven of them have long platinum-blonde hair, big painted puppy eyes, bubbly personalities, orthodontic smiles and breasts which burst like melons out of their matching bikini tops. They might have been cloned to order. In 2001 Hefner explained to *Vanity Fair* that he is in his Blonde Period. 'There is something cute and sweet about the way they all have this kind of blonde-girl-next-door look . . . We do all kinds of wonderful things together. We go to Disneyland together. We go out to the movies, and we go out to the clubs . . .'

At seventy-five, post-stroke and still, with the help of Viagra, performing as he says like a 'class act', Hefner's personal Bunny world is still swinging. His girls idle away their time adrift in a sunshiny world of clubs, parties, expensive clothes and compliant bodies. They share rooms decorated with Barbie dolls and *Playboy* centrefolds. Most of them seem to be on long-term audition for a centrefold of their own.

The popularity of the blonde Barbie look is remarkably enduring. Cindy Jackson runs a consulting service in London for people considering cosmetic surgery, and has had more than twenty operations herself to achieve her goal of looking like Barbie. For Cindy, Barbie is the pinnacle of feminine beauty. The doll's best traits, she insists, are her vulnerability, her long legs, small chin, wide eyes, soft skin and long blonde hair. The hair is essential to the look, but it is the easy part: regular highlights every month. In addition, to complete the picture, she has had multiple dermabrasion, nose jobs, chemical face peels, breast implants and removals and liposuction vacuuming work. A mole on her cheek at nose level used to be down near her jawbone: it travels north each time her face is lifted. Her obsession with looking like Barbie began in 1988 when she went to a surgeon asking for a face lift. At the time she wanted beauty, glamour and power. Now, with the whole Barbie package in place, she says she has running after her the kind of men whom most women would die for. After fifteen years and $100,000 spent on cosmetic surgery, Barbie has won herself the dubious reward of securing James Hewitt as her boyfriend.

Hewitt's previous amours include one of the world's most famous blondes. Princess Diana was a woman who, like many of the others, had been blonde as a child, had turned darker in adolescence and then in adulthood took steps to reverse the process. She became increasingly blonde as she acquired power. Hers was a classic case of blonding to heighten her sexual attractions, to look younger and to attract more attention. As she became more powerful, more manipulative of the press, more heavily dependent after her divorce on her public image, Diana became more brazenly blonde until by the time of her death in 1997, she was a heavily bleached platinum. In her final years, Princess Diana was a devious combination of saint, martyr, avenging Amazon and little girl. For each one of her roles, she needed to be blonde. She wanted to look innocent and portray herself as the wronged wife. She wanted to attract attention to fight her corner, and she needed to be loved.

Diana had always traded on her appearance, relying on the world loving her for her glamour. After she married in 1981, the faintly dumpy and apparently camera-shy Sloane with mousy hair blossomed quickly into a burnished glamorous blonde, a tall, often provocatively dressed royal fashion model who knew very well the value of photographic publicity. According to her friend James Gilbey, Diana could sniff a camera at a thousand yards. She seemed to enjoy the limelight and the adoration of the public, and she traded on her increasingly evident sex appeal to get it. Her wardrobe was transformed from one of fussy Sloaney outfits to a sleeker image of tailored lines and plain colours. Soon after her marriage, Kevin Shanley at Headlines in South Kensington started adding highlights to her mousy hair, returning it to the blonde shade of her early childhood years. According to many commentators, from that moment she seemed to grow in confidence. The shy hunch-shouldered posture disappeared for ever. As her preoccupation with her appearance increased, she moved on to two of London's top stylists, Sam McKnight, who cut her hair every six weeks, and Daniel Galvin, who touched up her highlights at his Mayfair salon. By the mid-1990s, she was spending £3,600 a year on dyeing her hair blonde.

At the height of her lustrous powers Diana appeared at a glittering charity event in New York filled with the cream of American society. Nine hundred of the wealthiest and most powerfully connected people on America's East Coast had paid £800 each for the privilege of dining with the world's acknowledged number-one celebrity. They were expecting a princess, but Diana arrived looking like a Hollywood superstar. She walked elegantly into the room, well over six foot tall in strappy high heels. Her bright blonde cropped hair acted like a beacon as she paced through the crowd. Her daringly revealing Jacques Azagury gown attracted appreciative eyes to her cleavage. Diamond and pearl drop earrings glittered at her ears. She was stunning. Henry Kissinger looked stunned. Hundreds of other Americans were entranced. Diana was there to receive the Outstanding Achievement Award at the United Cerebral Palsy charity dinner, a reward for her years of highly professional patronage to further the aims of the charity. She stood out in the starry company of New York society because she was tall, royal, beautiful and blonde. I somehow doubt if it would ever have happened had she still been mousy.

Diana was a universal icon, already convincingly deified in 1997 when she decided, a year after her divorce, to restyle her wardrobe. Christie's organised a celebrity sell-off at which seventy nine of her formal gowns were auctioned to eager collectors, raising $6 million for charity. Two years later, another universal blonde icon became the subject of a Christie's sale. This time it was Marilyn Monroe. Almost six hundred of her cultural cast-offs were sold, raising over $13 million for a handful of charities and for the widow of Lee Strasberg. A pair of red stilettos encrusted with rhinestones sold for $48,300. A hand-knitted brown cardigan sold for $52,900, and the sheath dress covered with tiny rhinestones she wore at John Kennedy's birthday tribute in 1962 went for over a million dollars. The bid smashed the previous world record for the sale of a dress: a blue velvet Victor Edelstein belonging to Princess Diana which had sold for £222,500. Monroe's driving licence went for $130,000, her make-up case fetched $240,000, and someone bought a strangely trashy little lot which included a plastic cup, a tissue-box cover and a piece of paper with the words 'he does not love me' written in pencil. The public's thirst for a soiled piece of celebrity was unquenchable. One year later, Christie's struck gold again when it auctioned off a sweaty item from the wardrobe of a third international celebrity blonde. This time it was Madonna. The black satin Jean-Paul Gaultier bra worn on her 'Blonde Ambition' tour sold for $20,000.

It is perhaps no coincidence that the twentieth century's three best-known blonde icons have literally sold themselves to the world, in photographs, on television and by distributing to the public the intimate contents of their wardrobes, to be fought over and then cherished as relics. Not one of them would have reached such heights of fame without an overbearing taste for public pawing. Like Monroe and Diana, Madonna was another dark-haired and ambitious narcissist with a streak of exhibitionism. Once she had tasted blondeness and fame, she couldn't get enough of the public's adoration. 'I've been provoking since I was a little girl. I'm very interested in being alluring,' she once confessed. Madonna's bare-faced pursuit of fame as a dancer, a singer and then as an actress and celebrity superstar was swift – it took her about five years – and as she rose through the ranks of stardom, she became hooked by and then utterly addicted to mass adulation. In the process of developing her brand of rebellious sexuality, she plundered the images of other iconic sex symbols including Mae West and Marilyn Monroe, plucking elements of their style – the winking suggestiveness of West, the voluptuous wet-lipped sexuality of Monroe – to lend character to her act. But the difference between Madonna and Monroe perhaps represents the social and sexual changes that have taken place since the '80s. While Monroe was a creation by and for men, Madonna has always considered women the dominant sex. She has always been her own boss, psychologically independent, driving herself with a business sang-froid, sharp image-management and a marketing savvy that has kept her on the top perch for years. To many she has revolutionised feminist politics. With her luxuriant sexuality, her powerful ambition and a personality which challenges rather than rejects or crumples before the male gaze, she has offered proof to millions of women that they can be strong and in control without losing their essential femininity. She has demonstrated that gender need be no barrier to achievement.

Part of her appeal lies in her embodiment of the American dream. Madonna started her public performances as a dark-haired Italian-American cheerleader in a Detroit suburb. Before long she had made her way to New York with $35 in her pocket and she ruthlessly set about pursuing her dreams. With her instinctive grasp of the pop aesthetic and of the evolving music business, she secured hundreds of millions of fans and, twenty years later she had become one of the richest women in the world, estimated to be worth between $300 and $600 million. Part of her success depends on being blonde. The colour-coding strategy began with her 1986 album *True Blue*, for which she appeared on the cover as a pure bleached-blonde for the first time, her head thrown back in erotic abandon. Sales ballooned to over 20 million copies worldwide. Her previous albums, for which she had been a brunette, had reached around 5 million. Madonna immediately recognised the commercial value of blonde hair and the pattern was set. For her next album, *Who's That Girl*, released a year later, she performed exuberant impersonations of Marilyn Monroe, highly voluptuous with bouffant blonde hair and revealing dresses. By now Madonna realised that she looked best when blonde. The camera picked up and highlighted the dramas of her mask-like face with its contrasting pale hair, kohl-ringed eyes, white skin and full red lips. As a brunette Madonna had been a sultry beauty, but as a blonde she was a goddess. And that meant more sales, more stardom and more power.

As a star who sees the marketing value of regular reinvention, Madonna has the hardest-working hair in showbusiness. Occasionally she has veered back to dark hair, often at times of emotional upheaval. She dyed her hair brown when having an affair with her bodyguard, Tony Ward, and then again when she had an affair with the basketball star Dennis Rodman. But whether her hair is straight, curly, long, short or spiky, it always in the end returns to blonde. 'Being blonde is definitely a different state of mind,' Madonna told *Rolling Stone* magazine. 'I can't really put my finger on it, but the artifice of being blonde has some incredible sort of sexual connotation.'

Madonna is perhaps our ultimate power-blonde. Sales of her albums have exceeded 500 million copies and she now commands the best songwriters, producers and choreographers in the business who will keep her on top for many years yet. She is a complex, ambitious, modern American woman, the fantasy role model of millions around the world.

America is a world–class maker of fantasies. It exports these fantasies, efficiently packaged on television, in the cinema and in magazines, to enamour billions all over the world. These billions watch the beautiful, slim, blonde and independent stars of *Sex in the City*, of *Friends*, and of countless other shows and movies. They become accustomed to a rich palette of blonde shades: Just Peachy, White-Minx, Honey Doux, Frivolous Fawn and hundreds more. They watch thousands of blonde anchorwomen on television. They follow the rise of blonde pop stars and blonde television personalities. They see blonde actresses scooping the prizes of success, fame and wealth in Hollywood. They gaze at the blonde covers of *Cosmopolitan* and other international glossy magazines. They see global advertising campaigns marketing blonde Western glamour in any language. And eventually they enter that white Western blonde world in their imaginations, regardless of how distant they are in ethnic or economic terms. These Western qualities seem to offer everything: success, sexuality and beauty. And millions of women, in Jakarta, in Lima, in Seattle or in Cardiff, in dyeing their hair blonde are buying some small sense of dignity and self-esteem along with the glamour. They are coming a tiny bit closer to the power of the American ideal.

Li'l Kim, Tina Turner and occasionally Naomi Campbell wear blonde wigs to grab attention with the unnatural contrast of blonde hair against dark skin. RuPaul, an African-American drag queen, explains the rationale: 'When I put on a blonde wig, I am not selling out my blackness. Wearing a blonde wig is not going to make me white. I'm not going to pass as white, and I am not trying to. The truth about the blonde wig is so simple. It really pops. I want to create outrageous sensation, and blonde hair against brown skin is a gorgeous outrageous combination.'

In Japan, thousands of young women now use special industrial-strength dyes to turn their strong black hair peroxide-blonde, as the *International Herald Tribune* recently reported on its front page. 'I want to look more American,' said one blonde Japanese 20-year-old whom I met in Tokyo recently. 'It's a form of rebellion, rejecting my Japaneseness in order to look more Western, to look better, maybe more like a film star.' Japanese fashion magazines, billboards and comics frequently feature blonde beauties who give the products they endorse some kind of magical Western superiority. The same holds for China. In Brazil, fashion magazines carry blondes on their covers, an anomaly which recently prompted the *New York Times* to comment that a stranger might 'mistake this racial rainbow of a country for a Nordic outpost . . . slender blondes smile from the covers and white faces dominate all but the sports glossies'. This in spite of the fact that only 40 per cent of Brazilians are white, albeit the richest and most powerful group in the country; and very few of them are naturally blonde.

Female beauty has become a standardised commodity, conspicuously white, Western, slim, young, wealthy and typically blonde. Its image is pumped out to all corners of the world by a global culture machine which is controlled by America. Yet why is America, a culture so publicly concerned with overcoming its problems of race, still so fixated on the blonde? Could it be Aphrodite? Are these cultural myths really so deeply embedded in our psyche? Is it to do with the obsession with youth in a country where breast implants and face lifts are now the norm for Hollywood actresses and no longer a rarity for housewives? Or is it something more sinister, subliminally embedded in our make-up? Are those who blonde themselves still subconsciously seeking to distinguish themselves from darker and less powerful ethnic groups? Are dark-haired women, equally, still blonding themselves in order to 'pass' as members of the white Anglo-Saxon power élite, and to rise in status as a result of their perceived attractiveness? There are no clear answers to these questions; but they provide us with some intriguing ideas as we observe the world's millions of lustrous blondes, flashing and scintillating, ravishing and seducing in the public eye, demonstrating their coolly bewitching, mesmeric powers.

AFTERWORD

Very little has been written specifically about blonde hair, in spite of its cultural interest and its sociological, psychological and biological significance. Academics, perhaps concerned about racial sensitivities, tend to ban it from intelligent debate. Several American women academics whom I approached refused to discuss it at all, and were indeed deeply affronted that I had thought that they might. Perhaps they were unable to shake off associations with the dumb blonde. And I was surprised to discover that the subject has been entirely neglected as an element of portraiture. While there has therefore been little to harvest on blonde hair itself, I owe a huge debt to many writers for their authoritative background material with which I have fleshed out my subject. Of particular help were works by Richard Corson, Christine Havelock, Susan Haskins, Pamela Norris, Georgina Masson, Helen Hackett, Marina Warner, Elisabeth Gitter, Ronald Pearsall, Eric Trudgill, Reginald Horsman, Mary Blume, Igor Golomstock, Piers Brendon, Barnaby Conrad, Thomas Doherty, Marlene Le Gates, Grant McCracken and Michael Renor.

ENDNOTES

1: APHRODITE RISING

12   'The girl with . . .' *Alcman: The Partheneion*, p. 45

14   'superior to any other statue . . .' *Natural History*, Pliny, p. 346

15   'embraced it intimately . . .' ibid., p. 346

17   'she appeared on . . .' *A History of Prostitution*, Sanger, p. 60

19   'the hetaira was . . .' *Sex Status and Survival*, Fantham, p. 51

2: THE EMPRESS AND THE WIG

25   'I told you . . .' *The Erotic Poems*, Ovid, p. 107

26   'Postumus, are you . . .' *The Sixteen Satires*, Juvenal, p. 128

27   'retiring exhausted . . .' ibid., p. 131

27   'It is hard to conceive . . .' *The Roman Empresses*, de Serviez, p. 192

29   'admired her beauty . . .' ibid., p. 353

29   'Foreseeing with . . .' ibid., p. 355

31   'Although, yourself at . . .' *Epigrams*, Martial, p. 97

3: THE DEVIL'S SOAP

4: IS SHE NOT PURE GOLD?

63 'Where did ever . . .' *Old German Love Songs*, Nicholson, p. 155

64 'Never will . . .' *Arthurian Romances*, Troyes, p. 288

65 'can hardly restrain . . .' ibid., p. 112

66 'hair as blonde . . .' *The Romance of the Rose*, Lorris and Meun, p. 37

67 'Her forehead white . . .' ibid., p. 42

67 'he who acquaints . . .' ibid., p. 73

5: THE CARDINAL AND THE BLONDE BORGIA

72 'Those tresses . . .' *Lyric Poems*, Petrarch, p. 100

72 'Amid the locks . . .' ibid., p. 136

72 'Never such a thief . . .' *Gli Asolani*, Bembo, p. 102

75 'She is of medium . . .' *Lucrezia Borgia in Ferrara*, Cagnolo, p. 39

75 'I rejoice . . .' *The Prettiest Love Letters*, Bembo, p. 65

75 'The glowing hair . . .' ibid., p. 53

79 'nobody believes . . .' Caterina Sforza to Ludovico Sforza, 24 September 1498, Archivio di Stato, Milano

6: FOUR BLOCKS OF CAVIARE AND A FEATHER BED

87 'Danae where one . . .' *Raccolta*, Vol. 2, p. 22

87 'the miraculous shrewdness . . .' *Raccolta*, Vol. 3, p. 259

88 'The painter's power . . .' 'Sonnets on female portraits', Rogers, p. 299

88 'not for the purpose . . .' 'Titian, Ovid and Sixteenth Century Codes', Ginzburg, p. 27

92 'Why nowadays . . .' *Dialogues*, Aretino, p. 165

92 'The actual identities . . .' 'Sex, Space and Social History', Goffen, p. 72

92 'For so infinite . . .' *Coryat's Crudities*, Coryate, p. 403

93 'Did you see . . .' *Courtesans of the Italian Renaissance*, Masson, p. 29

97 'could possibly . . .' ibid., p. 156

97 'So sweet and . . .' ibid., p. 157

98 'The houses . . .' *Habiti Antichi et Moderni*, Vecellio, p. 119

99 'All the women . . .' *Coryat's Crudities*, Coryate, p. 400

100 'The Women of . . .' *The Artificial Changeling*, Bulwer, p. 57

101 'Permit me to remind . . .' *Fashions in Hair*, Corson, p. 173

7: LIKE A VIRGIN

110 'Soe there are . . .' *Diary of John Manningham*, p. 152

111 'vile copies . . .' *Sculptura*, Evelyn, p. 25

113 'vij heads of haire . . .' *Queen Elizabeth's Wardrobe Unlock'd*, Arnold, p. 29

113 'She asked me . . .' *The Memoirs of Sir James Melville*, p. 38

113 'She entered to . . .' ibid., p. 38

114 'The face should be . . .' *The History of Vanity*, Woodforde, p. 49

114 'Her heare . . .' *English Women in Life and Letters*, Phillips and Tomkinson, p. 44

115 'yellow locks . . .' *The Faerie Queen*, Spenser, p. 193

116 'If there be any . . .' *The Anatomie of Abuses*, Stubbes, p. 67

116 'I would wish to . . .' *Cynthia's Revels*, Jonson, iv, i, 140

116 'If the haire . . .' *Alexander and Campaspe*, Lyly, iii, iv, 91

118 'Do you know . . .' *The Malcontent*, Marston, ii, iv, 35

8: SAINT-SEDUCING GOLD

126 'false locks . . .' *London Magazine*, Anon, 1768

128 'Alas, I'm sorry . . .' *Satirical Songs and Poems on Costume*, ed. Fairholt, p. 253

128 'Time was . . .' *The Lady's Magazine*, June 1775

128 'Machine: A very . . .' *Les Curiosités de la foire*, Landrin, i, vi

132 'Once upon a time . . .' Le Cabinet des fées, Lemirre, p. 261

134 'If you desire . . .' *The Complete Tales of the Brothers Grimm*, Zipes, p. 259

9: WRETCHED PICKLED VICTIMS

139 'turned her long . . .' *Middlemarch*, Eliot, p. 189

140 'old dreamland . . .' ibid., p. 628

140 'but when . . .' *Vanity Fair*, Thackeray, p. 813

140 'In describing . . .' ibid., p. 812

141 'I never gave away . . .' *The Letters*, Kintner, p. 288

141 'I was happy . . .' ibid., p. 300

142 'The soul's Rialto . . .' *Sonnets from the Portuguese*, Barrett Browning, p. 73

142 'These pieces of gold . . .' *The Works of John Ruskin*, Ruskin, p. 55

142 'You have much . . .' *Goblin Market*, Rossetti, p. 5

146 'tresses of golden . . .' *The Bram Stoker Bedside Companion*, ed. Osborne, p. 28

151 'my child-friends . . .' *Lewis Carroll Photographer*, Taylor, p. 94

152 'dwelt with intense . . .' *The Life and Letters of Lewis Carroll*, Collingwood, p. 362

153 'and in those . . .' *Sonnets of a Little Girl*, Dowson, p. 149

10: THE ARYAN AWAKES

156 'half of Europe . . .' *Introductory Lectures*, Arnold, p. 28

157 'the prejudices . . .' *Ivanhoe*, Scott, p. 544

157 'You come from . . .' *Coningsby*, Disraeli, p. 273

157 'it is an affair . . .' *Tancred*, Disraeli, p. 201

162 'I know not . . .' *German Colonisation*, Förster, p. 70

11: BODY POLITICS

170 'His head . . .' undated, untitled poem in British Library, Owen

170 'He didn't look . . .' *Memoirs of an Infantry Officer*, Sassoon, p. 89

177 'In this society . . .' *Nudism in Modern Life*, Parmelee, p. 235

180 'A head of . . .' *Cote d'Azur*, Blume, p. 107

12: THE MAN WHO WOULD BE GOD

186 'contamination of . . .' *Mein Kampf*, Hitler, p. 512

186 'Blondeness meant everything . . .' *Losing the Dead*, Appignanesi, p. 57

188 'Just as we breed . . .' *Master Race*, Clay and Leapman, p. 36

189 'Three SS men . . .' *Children of the SS*, Henry and Hillel, p. 239

199 'a healthy, lively . . .' *Produktsiia izo-iskusstv 6* (1933), p. 6

199 'wanted to present . . .' *Produktsiia izo-iskusstv 9* (1933), p. 7

13: BLONDE VENUS

209 'I always lit her . . .' *Oxford History of American Cinema*, vol. 5, Nowell–Smith, p. 97

218 'they live like rats . . .' *Hollywood's Wartime Women*, Renov, p. 22

219 'We believe that . . .' ibid., p. 22

14: DIRTY PILLOW SLIP

223 'She's Mae West . . .' 'Platinum Pain', Merkin, p. 76

226 'She knew it . . .' *Conversations with Billy Wilder*, Crowe, p. 165

227 'Every Saturday . . .' *Nostalgia Isn't What It Used To Be*, Signoret, p. 287

229 'Suspense is like . . .' *Films and Filming*, July 1959, p. 7

230 'Tear them down . . .' ibid., p. 400

230 'They had me down . . .' *The Making of The Birds*, Counts, p. 33

231 'blonde sorority . . .' *The Birds*, Paglia, p. 27

236 'It really meant . . .' *True Colours*, Gladwell, p. 74

15: OF PRINCESSES, PUNKS AND PRIME MINISTERS

242 'Move on . . .' *Making Waves*, Le Gates, p. 335

244 'There was one . . .' 'True colors', Gladwell, p. 77

246 'If you want . . .' *An Unfashionable Life*, Mulvagh, p. 72

256 'I've been provoking . . .' *Madonna*, Morton, p. 12

259 'When I put on . . .' *Lettin It All Hang Out*, RuPaul, p. 190

SELECT BIBLIOGRAPHY

Dates in brackets refer to original publication date.

INTRODUCTION

Etcoff, Nancy – *Survival of the Prettiest, The Science of Beauty*, London, 1999

Freedman, Rita – *Beauty Bound*, London, 1986

Ridley, Matt – *Sex and the Evolution of Human Nature*, London, 1993

1: APHRODITE RISING

Corson, Richard – *Fashions in Hair*, London, 1980

Fantham, Elaine – *Sex, Status and Survival in Hellenistic Athens*, Phoenix 29, 1975

Friedrich, Paul – *The Meaning of Aphrodite*, Chicago, 1978

Grigson, Geoffrey – *The Goddess of Love*, London, 1976

Havelock, Christine – *The Aphrodite of Knidos and Her Successors*, Ann Arbor, 1995

Homer – *The Odyssey*, (trns) R. Lattimore, New York, 1967

Page, Denys – *Alcman: The Partheneion*, London, 1951

Pliny the Elder – *Natural History*, (trns) John Healy, London, 1991

Sanger, William – *A History of Prostitution*, New York, 1859

2: THE EMPRESS AND THE WIG

Balsdon J.P.V.D. – *Roman Women, Their History and Habits*, London, 1962

Clement of Alexandria – *The Writings of Clement of Alexandria*, (trns) William Wilson, Edinburgh, 1867

Grigson, Geoffrey – *The Goddess of Love*, London, 1976

Juvenal – *The Sixteen Satires*, (trns) Peter Green, London, 1967

Martial – *Epigrams*, (trns) G.P. Goold, Cambridge Mass., 1990

Ovid – *The Erotic Poems*, (trns) Peter Green, London, 1982

Pliny the Elder – *Natural History*, (trns) John Healy, London, 1991

Pomeroy, Sarah B. – *Goddesses, Whores, Wives and Slaves*, London, 1976

Propertius – *Elegies*, (trns) G.P. Goold, Cambridge Mass., 1990

Serviez, Jacques Roergas de – *The Roman Empresses*, (trns) Bysse Molesworth, London, 1899 (1752)

Tertullian – *Disciplinary, Moral and Ascetical Works*, (trns) Rudolph Arbesmann, Washington, 1977

3: THE DEVIL'S SOAP

Bulwer, John – *The Artificial Changeling*, London, 1650

Duby, Georges – *Women of the 12th Century*, (trns) Jean Birrell, Cambridge, 1997

Fiero, Gloria (ed) – *Three Medieval Views of Women*, London, 1989

Haskins, Susan – *Mary Magdalen, Myth and Metaphor*, London, 1993

Howell, A. – *San Bernardino of Siena*, London, 1913

Norris, Pamela – *The Story of Eve*, London, 1998

Owst, G.R. – *Literature and Pulpit in Medieval England*, Oxford, 1961

4: IS SHE NOT PURE GOLD?

Cornell, Henrik – *The Iconography of the Nativity of Christ*, Uppsala, 1924

Eco, Umberto – *Art and Beauty in the Middle Ages*, (trns) Hugh Bredin, New Haven, 1986

Gabrieli, Francesco (trns) – *Arab Historians of the Crusades*, London, 1984

Hildegard of Bingen – *Physica*, (trns) Priscilla Throop, Rochester Vermont, 1998 (c.1158)

Jorgensen, Johannes – *Saint Bridget of Sweden*, (trns) Ingeborg Lund, London, 1954

Lorris, Guillaume de and Meun, Jean de – *The Romance of the Rose*, (trns) Charles Dahlberg, Princeton, 1971 (c. 1280)

Nicholson, Frank (trns) – *Old German Love Songs from the Minnesingers of the 12th to 14th Centuries*, London, 1907

Ribeiro Aileen – *Dress and Morality*, London, 1986

Saint Bridget – *The Revelations of Saint Birgitta*, (ed) William Cumming, Oxford, 1929

Silvas, Anna (trns) – *Jutta and Hildegard: The Biographical Sources*, Pennsylvania, 1998

Smythe, Barbara (trns) – *Troubadour Poets*, London, 1911

Troyes, Chretien de – *Arthurian Romances*, (trns) William Comfort, London, 1928

Warner, Marina – *Alone of All her Sex, The Myth and the Cult of the Virgin Mary*, London, 1976

Warner, Marina – *Monuments and Maidens*, London, 1985

5: THE CARDINAL AND THE
   BLONDE BORGIA

Bembo, Pietro – *Gli Asolani*, (trns) Rudolf Gottfried, London,
1505
Bembo, Pietro and Borgia, Lucrezia – *The Prettiest Love Letters
in the World*, (trns) Hugh Shankland, London, 1987
Cagnolo, Nicolo – *Lucrezia Borgia in Ferrara*, Ferrara, 1867
Clark, William – *Savonarola, His Life and Times*, Chicago, 1890
Fraser, Antonia – *Boadicea's Chariot*, London, 1988
Lightbown, Ronald – *Sandro Botticelli*, London, 1989
Petrarch – *Lyric Poems*, (trns) Robert Durling, Cambridge
Mass., 1976
Tinagli, Paola – *Women in Italian Renaissance Art*, Manchester,
1997

6: FOUR BLOCKS OF CAVIARE AND
   A FEATHER BED

Aretino, Pietro – *Dialogues*, (trns) Raymond Rosenthal,
Cambridge, 1972
Bloch, Konrad – *Blondes in Venetian Renaissance Paintings and
other Essays*, New Haven, 1994
Bulwer, John – *The Artificial Changeling*, London, 1650
Corson, Richard – *Fashions in Hair*, London, 1980
Coryate, Thomas – *Coryat's Crudities*, Glasgow, 1611
Cropper, Elizabeth – 'Rewriting the Renaissance', in *The
Discourses of Sexual Difference in Early Modern Europe*, (ed)
Margaret Ferguson, Chicago, 1986

Firenzuola Agnolo – *Dialogue of the Beauty of Women*, (trns) Clara Bell, 1892 (1548)

Freedberg, David – *The Power of Images*, Chicago, 1989

Ginzburg, Carlo – 'Titian, Ovid and Sixteenth Century Codes for Erotic Illustration', in *Titian's Venus of Urbino*, (ed) Rona Goffen, Cambridge, 1997

Goffen, Rona – 'Sex, Space and Social History', in *Titian's Venus of Urbino*, Cambridge, 1997

Goffen, Rona – *Titian's Women*, New Haven, 1997

Luigini, Federigo – *The Book of Fair Women*, (trns) Elsie M. Lang, London, 1907 (1554)

Masson, Georgina – *Courtesans of the Italian Renaissance*, London, 1975

Porta, Jean Baptista della Porta – *The Ninth Book of Natural Magick*, London, 1669

Raccolta di lettere sulla pittura, scultura ed architettura, Vols 2 and 3, Rome, 1757 and 1759

Rogers, Mary – 'The Decorum of Women's Beauty', in *Renaissance Studies*, Vol. 2, No. 1

Rogers, Mary – 'Sonnets on female portraits from Renaissance North Italy' in *Word & Image*, Vol 2, No 4, 1986

Vecellio, Cesare – *Habiti Antichi et Moderni*, Paris, 1860 (1598)

7: LIKE A VIRGIN

Arnold, Janet (ed) – *Queen Elizabeth's Wardrobe Unlock'd*, Leeds, 1988

Aske, James – *Elizabetha Triumphans*, London, 1588

Camden, Carroll – *The Elizabethan Woman*, London, 1952

Evelyn, J. – *Sculptura*, (ed) C.F. Bell, Oxford, 1906

Hackett, Helen – *Virgin Mother, Maiden Queen*, London, 1995

Manningham, John – *Diary of John Manningham*, (ed) J. Bruce, London, 1868 (1608)

Melville, James – *The Memoirs of Sir James Melville*, (ed) Gordon Donaldson, London, 1969 (1683)

Nichols, John – *The Progresses and Public Processions of Queen Elizabeth*, London, 1821

Phillips, Margaret and Tomkinson, William – *English Women in Life and Letters*, London, 1926

Pomeroy, Elizabeth – *Reading the Portraits of Queen Elizabeth I*, Hamden Conn., 1989

Spenser, Edmund – *The Faerie Queen*, (ed) Douglas Brooks-Davies, 1976 (1596)

Strong, Roy – *The Cult of Elizabeth*, London, 1977

Strong, Roy – *Gloriana, the Portraits of Queen Elizabeth I*, London, 1987

Stubbes, Phillip – *The Anatomie of Abuses*, (ed) F. Furnivall, London, 1877 (1583)

Wilson, Elkin – *England's Eliza*, Cambridge Mass., 1939

Woodforde, John – *The History of Vanity*, Stroud, 1992

8: SAINT-SEDUCING GOLD

Bassermann, Lujo – *The Oldest Profession*, (trns) James Cleugh, London, 1967

Bottigheimer, Ruth – *Grimms' Bad Girls and Bold Boys*, New Haven, 1987

Fairholt, Frederick (ed) – *Satirical Songs and Poems on Costume*, London, 1842

Friedländer, Walter – *Nicolas Poussin. A New Approach*, London, 1966

Landrin, – *Les curiosités de la foire*, 1775

Lemirre, Elisabeth (ed) – *Le Cabinet des fées*, Vol 2, Arles, 1988 (1735)

Warner, Marina – *From the Beast to the Blonde*, London, 1994

Zipes, Jack (trns) – *The Complete Tales of the Brothers Grimm*, New York, 1992

9: WRETCHED PICKLED VICTIMS

Anon. – *The Pretty Women of Paris*, Paris, 1883

Barrett Browning, Elizabeth – *Sonnets from the Portuguese*, (ed) Philip Duschnes, New York, 1950 (1897)

Browning, Robert – *The Poetical Works of Robert Browning*, London, 1906

Collingwood, Stuart – *The Life and Letters of Lewis Carroll*, London, 1912 (1898)

Dowson, Ernest – *The Poetical Works of Ernest Dowson*, (ed) Desmond Flower, London, 1967

Eliot, George – *Middlemarch*, (ed) W.J. Harvey, London, 1982 (1871)

Gitter, Elisabeth – 'The Power of Women's Hair in the Victorian Imagination', *PMLA* 99 October, 1984

Kintner, Elvan (ed) – *The Letters of Robert Browning and Elizabeth Barrett Browning: 1845–46*, Cambridge Mass., 1969

Pearsall, Ronald – *The Worm in the Bud*, London, 1969

Rossetti, Christina – *Goblin Market and Other Poems*, London, 1888

Rossetti, Dante Gabriel – *The Poetical Works of Dante Gabriel Rossetti*, (ed) William Rossetti, London, 1891

Ruskin, John – *The Works of John Ruskin*, (ed) E.T. Cook and Alexander Wedderburn, London, 1905

Stoker, Bram – *The Bram Stoker Bedside Companion*, (ed) Charles Osborne, London, 1973

Taylor, Roger and Wakeling, Edward (eds) – *Lewis Carroll; Photographer*, Princeton, 2002

Tennyson, Alfred – *The Poems of Tennyson in Three Volumes*, Vol 2, London, 1987

Thackeray, William – *Vanity Fair*, (ed) John Sutherland, Oxford, 1983 (1848)

Trudgill, Eric – *Madonnas and Magdalens*, London, 1976

Wullschlager, Jackie – *Inventing Wonderland*, London, 1995

10: THE ARYAN AWAKES

Arnold, Thomas – *Introductory Lectures on Modern History*, deliv. 1842, pub. 1874

Disraeli, Benjamin – *Coningsby*, London, 1983 (1844)

Disraeli, Benjamin – *Tancred*, London, 1905 (1847)

Förster, Bernhard – *German Colonisation in the Upper La Plata District with Particular Reference to Paraguay*, Naumberg, 1886

Galton, Francis – *Hereditary Genius*, London, 1869

Green, John R. – *A Short History of the English People*, London, 1915 (1874)

Horsman, Reginald – *Race and Manifest Destiny*, Cambridge Mass., 1981

Kemble, John – *The Saxons in England*, London, 1849

Macintyre, Ben – *Forgotten Fatherland*, New York, 1992

Mosse, George – *The Final Solution*, London, 1978

Ridley, Matt – *Genome: The autobiography of a species in 23 chapters*, London, 1999

Scott, Walter – *Ivanhoe*, (ed) A.N. Wilson, London, 1984 (1819)

Spotts, Frederic – *Bayreuth, A History of the Wagner Festival*, New Haven, 1994

White, Charles – *An Account of the Regular Gradation of Man*, London, 1799

11: BODY POLITICS

Berganzi, Bernard – *Heroes' Twilight*, London, 1965

Blume, Mary – *Cote d'Azur, Inventing the French Riviera*, London, 1992

Ellis, Havelock – *A Study of British Genius*, London, 1904

Ellis, Havelock – 'The Comparative Abilities of the Fair and the Dark', *The Monthly Review*, August 1901

Fleure, H. J. – 'The Nordic Myth', *Eugenics Review*, Vol XXII, No 2, July 1930

Fussell, Paul – *The Great War and Modern Memory*, London, 1975

Goodrick-Clark, Nicholas – *The Occult Roots of Nazism*, London, 1992

Mudge, G.P. – 'The Menace to the English Race', *Eugenics Review*, January 1920

Parmelee, Maurice – *Nudism in Modern Life*, London, 1933

Sassoon, Siegfried – *Memoirs of an Infantry Officer*, London, 1931

Suren, Hans – *Der Mensch und Die Sonne*, Stuttgart, 1924

Snodin Michael and Stavenow-Hidemark, Elisabet (eds) – *Carl and Karin Larsson, Creators of the Swedish Style*, London, 1997

12: THE MAN WHO WOULD BE GOD

Adam, Peter – *The Arts of the Third Reich*, London, 1992

Appignanesi, Lisa – *Losing the Dead*, London, 1999

Bonnell, Victoria E. – *Iconography of Power, Soviet Political Posters Under Lenin and Stalin*, Berkeley, 1997

Clay, Catrine and Leapman, Michael – *Master Race*, London, 1995

Fest, Joachim C. – *The Face of the Third Reich*, (trns) Michael Bullock, London, 1970

Fischer, Eugen and Gunther, Hans, (eds) – *Deutsche Köpfe Nordischer Rasse*, Munich, 1927

Glaser, Hermann – *The Cultural Roots of National Socialism*, London, 1978

Golomstock Igor – *Totalitarian Art in the Soviet Union, the Third Reich, Fascist Italy and the People's Republic of China*, London, 1990

Grunberger, Richard – *A Social History of the Third Reich*, London, 1971

Henry, Clarissa and Hillel, Marc – *Children of the SS*, London, 1977

Hitler, Adolf – *Mein Kampf*, (trns) Ralph Manheim, London, 1992

Martin, Terry and Suny, Ronald (eds) – *A State of Nations, Empire and Nation-Making in the Age of Lenin and Stalin*, Oxford, 2001

Taylor, Brandon and Van der Will, Wilfred – *The Nazification of Art; Art, Design, Music, Architecture and Film in the Third Reich*, Winchester, 1990

13: BLONDE VENUS

Becker, Lutz – 'Optimistic Realism, Soviet Cinema', in *Art and Power, Europe Under the Dictators 1930–45*, London, 1995

Brendon, Piers – *The Dark Valley*, London, 2000

Doherty, Thomas – *Pre-Code Hollywood; Sex, Immorality and Insurrection in American Cinema, 1930–1934*, New York, 1999

Eckert Charles – 'Shirley Temple and the House of Rockefeller' in Gledhill, Christine, ed – *Stardom; Industry of Desire*, London, 1991

May, Lary – *The Big Tomorrow – Hollywood and the Politics of the American Way*, Chicago, 2000

Nowell-Smith, Geoffrey, (ed) – *The Oxford History of World Cinema*, Oxford, 1996

Renov, Michael – *Hollywood's Wartime Women, Representation and Ideology*, Ann Arbor, 1988

14: DIRTY PILLOW SLIP

Conrad, Barnaby – *The Blonde, A Celebration of the Golden Era from Harlow to Monroe*, San Francisco, 1999

Counts, Kyle – *The Making of The Birds*, Cinefantastique, Vol 10, No 2, 1980

Crowe, Cameron – *Conversations with Billy Wilder*, London, 1999

Gladwell, Malcolm – 'True Colours, Hair dye and the hidden history of postwar America' in *The New Yorker*, 22 March 1999

Le Gates, Marlene – *Making Waves; A History of Feminism in Western Society*, Toronto, 1996

Macdonald Dwight – *On Movies*, Englewood Cliffs, NJ, 1969

Merkin, Daphne – 'Platinum Pain, The enduring hold of a depressed bombshell' in *The New Yorker*, 18 February 1999

Paglia, Camille – *The Birds*, London, 1998

Rosen, Marjorie – *Popcorn Venus; Women, Movies and the American Dream*, London, 1975

Signoret, Simone – *Nostalgia Isn't What It Used To Be*, New York, 1978

Spoto, Donald – *The Dark Side of Genius, The Life of Alfred Hitchcock*, New York, 1983

Swedland, Alan and Urla, Jacqueline – 'The Anthropometry of Barbie' in Terry Jennifer and Urla Jacqueline (eds) – *Deviant Bodies*, Bloomington Ind., 1995

15: OF PRINCESSES, PUNKS AND PRIME MINISTERS

Chapkis, Wendy – *Beauty Secrets, Women and the Politics of Appearance*, Boston Mass., 1986

Etcoff, Nancy – *Survival of the Prettiest, The Science of Beauty*, London, 1999

Gladwell, Malcolm – 'True Colors, Hair dye and the hidden history of postwar America' in *The New Yorker*, 22 March 1999

Le Gates, Marlene – *Making Waves: A History of Feminism in Western Society*, Toronto, 1996

Marowitz, Charles – 'The irresistible dumb blonde', *The Listener*, 6 January 1977

McCracken, Grant – *Big Hair; A Journey into the Transformation of Self*, London, 1997

Molloy, John – *Women: Dress for Success*, London, 1980

Morton, Andrew – *Madonna*, London, 2001

Mulvagh, Jane – *An Unfashionable Life*, London, 1998

RuPaul – *Lettin It All Hang Out*, New York, 1995

Sales, Nancy Jo – 'Hugh Hefner's Roaring Seventies', *Vanity Fair*, March 2001

INDEX

A NOTE ON THE AUTHOR

Joanna Pitman read Japanese at Cambridge University and was Tokyo correspondent for *The Times* from 1990 to 1994. She is now the photography critic for *The Times*. This is her first book. She lives in London with her family.

A NOTE ON THE TYPE

The text of this book is set in Bembo, the original types for which were cut by Francesco Griffo for the Venetian printer Aldus Manutius, and were first used in 1495 for Cardinal Bembo's *De Aetna*. Claude Garamond (1480–1561) used Bembo as a model, and so it became the frontrunner of standard European type for the following two centuries. Its modern form was designed, following the original, for Monotype in 1929 and is widely in use today.